Beckett's
Creatures

RELATED TITLES

Ten Ways of Thinking About Samuel Beckett: The Falsetto of Reason, Enoch Brater
978-1-4081-3722-2

The Plays of Samuel Beckett, Katherine Weiss
978-1-4081-4557-9

The Theatre of Martin Crimp, Aleks Sierz
978-1-4081-8441-7

The Theatre and Films of Martin McDonagh, Patrick Lonergan
978-1-4081-3611-9

Staging Samuel Beckett in Great Britain, edited by David Tucker and Trish McTighe
978-1-4742-4017-8

Staging Samuel Beckett in Ireland and Northern Ireland, edited by Trish McTighe and David Tucker
978-1-4742-4055-0

Beckett's Creatures

Art of Failure after the Holocaust

Joseph Anderton

Bloomsbury Methuen Drama
An imprint of Bloomsbury Publishing Plc

BLOOMSBURY
LONDON · OXFORD · NEW YORK · NEW DELHI · SYDNEY

Bloomsbury Methuen Drama

An imprint of Bloomsbury Publishing Plc

Imprint previously known as Methuen Drama

50 Bedford Square	1385 Broadway
London	New York
WC1B 3DP	NY 10018
UK	USA

www.bloomsbury.com

BLOOMSBURY, METHUEN DRAMA and the Diana logo are trademarks of Bloomsbury Publishing Plc

First published 2016
Paperback edition first published 2017

British Library Cataloguing-in-Publication Data
A catalogue record for this book is available from the British Library.

ISBN: HB: 978-1-4742-3453-5
PB: 978-1-3500-5443-1
ePDF: 978-1-4742-3453-5
ePub: 978-1-4742-3454-2

Library of Congress Cataloging-in-Publication Data
Names: Anderton, Joseph, author.
Title: Beckett's creatures : art of failure after the Holocaust / Joseph Anderton.
Description: London ; New York : Bloomsbury Methuen Drama, 2016. —
Includes bibliographical references and index.
Identifiers: LCCN 2015039999 — ISBN 97814742134535 (hardback)
Subjects: LCSH: Beckett, Samuel, 1906–1989 — Criticism and interpretation.
— Human behavior in literature. — BISAC: PERFORMING ARTS / History &
Criticism. — LITERARY CRITICISM / Drama. — LITERARY CRITICISM /
European / English, Irish, Scottish, Welsh.
Classification: LCC PR6003.E282 Z56324 2016 — DDC 848/.91409—dc23 LC
record available at http://lccn.loc.gov/2015039999

Typeset by RefineCatch Limited, Bungay, Suffolk

For Jackie and Emily

CONTENTS

ACKNOWLEDGEMENTS

I would like to thank James Moran, who has guided and informed this research from its inception and has been a wonderful mentor during all stages of the project. I am also thankful to Neal Alexander, for his invaluable advice and incisive reading at key times during the book's composition, and Mark Robson, for helping to shape the initial enquiries. Thanks are due to Mary Bryden for her feedback and encouragement; Stan Gontarski for his humane review of the proposal and thoughtful suggestions; Matthew Green for his constructive criticism; the staff at the Samuel Beckett Collection at the University of Reading for their warmth and help; and David Wheatley for introducing me to Beckett's work many moons ago.

I wish to express my gratitude to the Arts and Humanities Research Council for providing the necessary funding to undertake this research, and especially Lynda Pratt in the School of English at the University of Nottingham for her advocacy and hard work in securing this.

More than anyone, thanks and love to my wife, Emily Anderton, for her belief and patience, and my family for their support during this project, especially Harry and Lynda Penford, James Anderton and my brothers, Ryan, Steven and Richard.

Finally, thanks to the Estate of Samuel Beckett, Faber and Faber Press and Grove/Atlantic Press for permission to quote from Beckett's works:

ABBREVIATIONS

C   *Company / Ill Seen Ill Said / Worstward Ho / Stirrings Still* (London: Faber and Faber, 2009)

E   *Endgame* (London: Faber and Faber, 2006)

FN   *The Expelled / The Calmative / The End / First Love* (London: Faber and Faber, 2009)

HD   *Happy Days* (London: Faber and Faber, 2006)

HII   *How It Is* (London: Faber and Faber, 2009)

K   *Krapp's Last Tape and Other Shorter Plays* (London: Faber and Faber, 2009)

M   *Murphy* (London: Faber and Faber, 2009)

MC   *Mercier and Camier* (London: Faber and Faber, 2010)

T   *Trilogy – Molloy, Malone Dies, The Unnamable* (London: Calder, 1994)

TN   *Texts for Nothing and Other Shorter Prose, 1950–1976* (London: Faber and Faber, 2010)

W   *Watt* (London: Faber and Faber, 2009)

WFG   *Waiting for Godot* (London: Faber and Faber, 2006)

Introduction

In 1923, Virginia Woolf declared that 'On or about December 1910, human character changed. [. . .]. And when human relations change there is at the same time a change in religion, conduct, politics, and literature. Let us agree to place one of these changes about the year 1910' (1924: 4). In the same year that Woolf wrote this bold claim in her essay 'Mr Bennett and Mrs Brown', D.H. Lawrence heralded another of 'these changes' in *Kangaroo*: 'It was in 1915 the old world ended' (2002: 216). Ezra Pound pinpointed yet another specific moment in 1922 as the start of the new: the completion of James Joyce's *Ulysses*. He wrote to H.L. Mencken: 'The Christian Era ended at midnight on Oct. 29–30 of last year. You are now in the year 1 p.s.U. [post scriptum *Ulysses*]' (1971: 174). The inclination to specify transformative historical junctures continues through a Reich Ministry Report in which 1938 was marked as 'the fateful year' (Barkai 1991: 95), and, in a 1995 address to celebrate the fiftieth anniversary of the liberation of Auschwitz, the author and Holocaust survivor Elie Wiesel claimed that '[a]fter Auschwitz, the human condition is not the same, nothing will be the same' (Wiesel n.d.). As if finally, a new legally enshrined model of the human was drawn with the Universal Declaration of Human Rights in 1948. In less than fifty years, the human and its world had seemingly undergone a series of profound changes that amounted to an assault on the viability of an inalienable human essence.

If Samuel Beckett has made a comparably audacious pronouncement, it is in the 1946 piece 'The Capital of the Ruins' for a Radio Éireann broadcast about the post-Second World War rebuilding efforts at Saint-Lô in Normandy: '[S]ome of those who were in Saint-Lô will come home realizing that they got at least as good as they gave, that they got indeed what they could hardly give, a vision and a sense of a time-honoured conception of humanity in ruins' (Beckett 1986: 76). Beckett's phrase 'time-honoured conception of humanity in ruins' records the war's devastating impact on an established humanistic understanding of human character and relations. He does not name a particular date to convey the turning point as much as an emblematic place and its apocalyptic landscape. Where Beckett's assessment really differs from the previous pronouncements is in his apparently intuitive grasp of what is subdued or absent in the others: change is perceived as fundamental but the very possibility of change indicates it may be one among many. Beckett teases out the intricacies of the impermanent nature of things in his realization that 'Provisional is not the term it was in this universe become provisional' (1986: 75). In the words 'ruins' and 'become' from 'The Capital of the Ruins', Beckett indicates a transition, a movement from permanence to temporariness. They imply that the established understanding of humanity has suffered a catastrophic destabilization, which appears to initiate an intervening period. The first possible resolution to this interim is in the fact that 'ruins' maintains the chance of salvaging or resuming the former humanity. Beckett also supports a newly formed understanding of humanity as a second possibility through the use of 'conceptions' and 'provisional', which together signals a devised solution to the short-term provision. At the same time, in realizing the mutation of the word 'provisional' as 'not the term it was', Beckett implies a third meaning in which the human world is not only in an intervening period, waiting for a decisive return to or renewal of normative meanings that ground human culture, but also in the throes of constant flux. Going back to 'conceive' and 'provisional', then, these words also suggest the potential for change and, by extension, the on-going process of renewing, which leads Lois Gordon to claim that Beckett's radio address celebrates 'the dignity of survival in a contingent universe' (2013: 121). 'Survival' and 'contingent' capture the complex nexus that Beckett maintains between an enduring engagement with secure models of the human and the abandonment to a post-human condition that has witnessed the contingency of the human. After 1945, Beckett evokes a sense of openness to the human that was and the human that is always still to be.

Beckett's comments after the Second World War and the Holocaust recognize a significant time of change and are perceptive to the changeability of the human. The title of this book, *Beckett's*

Creatures: Art of Failure after the Holocaust, contains three related areas of inquiry that posit an altered mode of being and an innovative form of art in light of a historical watershed. However, mindful of the complexities in Beckett's phrases 'time-honoured conception of humanity in ruins' and 'universe become provisional', decisiveness is not characteristic of the imprecise word 'creature'. Neither is it endemic to Beckett's 'art of failure', which encloses both potency and impotence, nor claimed for 'after the Holocaust', which refers to the aftermath of a constellation of events, albeit seismic events in the reassessment of the human. As such, the following is meant only to converse with, not repeat, the conclusion that Terry Eagleton draws, in which Beckett 'maintains a compact with failure in the teeth of Nazi triumphalism, undoing its lethal absolutism with the weapons of ambiguity and indeterminacy' (2006: 67). Although this overview might strike one as an appropriation of equivocality, it nevertheless maintains the possibility of Beckett's work absorbing stable historical contexts and destabilizing ideological shifts, as 'ruins' and 'become' proffer, while also keeping alive its revisable dynamism, in the way Beckett's use of 'provisional' under erasure, as an inadequate yet necessary word, implies transition indefinitely. In contrast to the conception of Beckett's ambiguity as a direct challenge to absolutism, the point of departure for this book is in perceiving the aesthetic and political dimensions of the 'creaturely' suspension between human templates and post-human exposures, shorn from former normative significations and on the cusp of future indeterminacy, to broker the relevance of Beckett's art in the post-Holocaust context. Indeed, as Julia Lupton suggests, '*creatura* itself might be said to break into formed and formless segments, with *creat* indicating the ordered composition of humanity and the *-ura* signalling its risky capacities for increase and change, foison and fusion' (2000: 2). In a kind of Janus-faced looking back to embedded meaning and facing up to wild volatility, the creature is caught undecided amidst the dual forces of fixity and dynamism.

What is a Beckettian creature?

The creature is a concept that encompasses authorial tensions in the composition process as well as the antagonisms of power apparatuses and ideological systems. It is best understood as a

dynamic arising from creative and biopolitical *animations*, in which
the actions of authority and pressures of necessity impinge on the
very materiality or texture of the subject. In essence, the creature
describes a vulnerable post-human state that resides within the
human as a potential and is either actuated by other humans
or manifest as an anachronistic performance of the human. As
the human's constitutive properties and forms of meaning
become unviable, the creature's debased, melancholic life ensues.
One of the central claims I make is that Beckett's work is attentive
to the ways in which the creature embodies a suspended mode
of being resulting from the irresolvable tensions between
contradictory or interdependent forces. The Beckettian creature
marks the endurance of a crisis of the human that is sustained
by the idea, memory or hope of a liberating resolution. The
concept of the creature therefore acts as a versatile lens in this book
through which to view Beckett's mode of bearing witness, the
type of subject issuing from power struggles, the degradation of
the human in his humour and the ontological state of his surviving
protagonists.

Dictionary definitions of the word 'creature' reveal how its
creative resonance is interlaced with power tensions. In the most
general sense, it describes 'a created thing or being; a product of
creative action; a creation'.[1] This primary meaning of the creature
includes three interrelated types of creation: authorial, authoritative
and autocratic. The first *authorial* type refers to narratological acts
of creation, in the way Beckett or his author-narrators conjure
fictional beings and surrogate voices. The terms 'creature' and
'creatures' appear on twenty-nine occasions in the post-war trilogy
of novels *Molloy* (French 1951; English 1955), *Malone Dies* (1951;
1956) and *The Unnamable* (1953; 1958) often in this first sense,
referring to the created narrators and to the author-narrators' own
figments. For example: 'Yes, a little creature, I shall try and make a
little creature, to hold in my arms, a little creature in my image,
no matter what I say' (Beckett 1994, *T*, 226). The etymology
of 'creature', deriving from the Latin verb *creare*, meaning 'to
create', also suggests a fictitious or imaginary being, especially
an aberration or grotesque figure. These latter qualifiers establish
the second *authoritative* type of creation, in being a subject
answerable to another's control, 'a person who owes his or her
fortune and position, and remains subservient to, a patron; a

person who is ready to do another's bidding; a puppet, a cat's paw', which evokes a level of being that incites contempt or stirs up sympathy. Beckett often emphasizes the wretched side of this relationship: 'The essential is to go on squirming forever at the end of the line, as long as there are waters and banks and ravening in heaven a sporting God to plague his creature' (T, 341). The creature is defined in relation to a superior, in this case an absolute theological power, which lends the term the third *autocratic* type of creation, suggesting the omnipotent rule of divine creators over earthly creations.

The interrelations between authorial, authoritative and autocratic forms of creation are fundamental to the incarnation of Beckettian creatures and creaturely life. As much as these categories involve narratologically, politically and theologically formed creatures, the term 'creature' remains inextricable from the tenuous and yet tenacious borderlines between human and nonhuman animals. In the hunting image cited above, 'squirming forever at the end of the line', Beckett brings to mind a subordinate animal. Indeed, the creature denotes 'a living or animate being; an animal, often as distinct from a person', which is how the term appears in the book of Genesis: 'And out of the ground the LORD God formed every beast of the field, and every fowl of the air; and brought them unto Adam to see what he would call them: and whatsoever Adam called every living creature, that was the name thereof' (King James, Genesis 2.19). The theological connotation of the creature also suggests 'all created beings', which does implicate humankind and therefore encompasses both animals and humans, as in the phrase 'fellow creatures'. The creature is effectively a being that confuses the distinctions of human and nonhuman animals, which is a dynamic to which Beckett is attentive: 'my situation rather resembled that of an old broken-down cart- or bat-horse unable to receive the least information either from its instinct or from its observation as to whether it is moving towards the stable or away from it and not greatly caring either way. [. . .] I find myself wondering again if I was not in fact the creature revolving in the yard, as Mahood assured me' (T, 322). This resemblance to, deep kinship with and eventual replacement of, other creatures to the point of destabilizing and redrawing species' identities means creaturely life in Beckett's work underlines the contiguous and continuous nature of all living beings.

Although Beckett employs the term 'creature' in his earliest published work, including the critical essay *Proust* (1931) and the short story collection *More Pricks than Kicks* ([1934] 2010a), it is not until the post-war 'frenzy of writing' (Knowlson 1997: 356) that it takes on its fullest and most idiosyncratic expression of the creation types noted above. The creature in *Proust* is a victim of time, confronted with the overwhelming dimensions of the past and future, and managing memory, which 'completes the transformation of a creature of surface into a creature of depth' (1999: 50). In *More Pricks than Kicks*, the creature is versatile enough to apply to Belacqua as well as encompass admirable women and sexless animals. Evidently, Beckett employs 'creature' as an inclusive moniker in the early writing and, without the context of Beckett's art of failure after the Holocaust, the strongest indication of its prevailing resonance is in the general ideas of creation and subjection, whether at the hands of the author, phenomena or identity perception.

Much literary fiction exploits the associations with creation and subjection, notably Romantic literature, in which there is often a keen awareness of the author's role in original creation and a strong sense of affinity between the poet's personal voice and the protagonist. Indeed, 'the Romantics position the author as at the centre of the literary institution by insisting on the immediacy and spontaneity of poetic creation, on the work of art as the direct representation of the creative experience' (Bennett 2005: 62). In this regard, the creature also has an entrenched metafictional level that calls to mind the creative force, or, in Beckett, the 'deviser', which intimates the presence of an implied author while indicating the divine creator (2009a, C, 1). This relationship is alluded to in Gothic fiction, a genre that engendered one of the most familiar and enduring literary creatures, the 'monster' in Mary Shelley's *Frankenstein* (1818).[2] In this modern Promethean tale, the creature recognizes its created status and cruel abandonment: 'Remember that I am thy creature; I ought to be thy Adam, but I am rather the fallen angel, whom thou drivest from joy for no misdeed' (Shelley 2003: 103). Taking into account Beckett's metafictional leanings, 'creature' is an apt description for his characters in that it foregrounds their constructed nature while retaining the potential for an autonomous life. Like Frankenstein's monster, the creature maintains the impression of reliance on the creator in conjunction with a kind of recalcitrant or necessary individualism. Sophie Ratcliffe acknowledges a comparable duality in her book *On Sympathy* (2008). Referring to 'creature' as 'a term that critics lean upon when they are unsure as to how to refer to a fictional protagonist', she proposes that literary creatures are received as an artificial creation, associated with narratological functions, while simultaneously soliciting identification and recognition that attribute a discrete life to them (Ratcliffe 2008: 55, 57). 'Creature' is therefore a germane choice for emphasizing this concurrent attachment and delineation, and does not merely serve as a catch-all term for errant literary creations.

The focus on the creature in my own work underlines the significance of the on-going creative act for the existential status of the creations themselves, in order to identify a type of vitality that subsists despite the static, self-reflexive conditions of Beckett's work. The creature is effectively exposed to survival conditions, facing the task of acquiring meaning independent from the status offered by unfulfilling creative and ideological animations, which sees the creature anticipating a resolution while continuing nonetheless. As the author-narrators seek to extricate themselves from the mechanisms of creation, the ironic consequence is that they protract the creative process:

> The search for the means to put an end to things, an end to speech, is what enables the discourse to continue. No, I must not try to think, simply utter. Method or no method I shall have to banish them in the end – the beings, things, shapes, sounds and lights with which my haste to speak has encumbered this place (Beckett 1994, *T*, 301–2).

The creature endures in the act of creation as it is occupied by other creaturely figments. It lives on with the imperative to pursue the expression, identity and meaning that will offer completion, but it is effectively penned in the void. In the most general sense, the creature is the subjectivity in flux driven by various 'creative' impetuses and consigned to the creaturely life of negotiating the remnants of established values. The creature therefore stands out as a particularly applicable concept in terms of investigating Beckett's art of failure and his dehumanized characters alongside the contemporaneous crises in expression and humanity.

The last human and becoming-animal

As Beckett studies commenced in earnest in the 1960s, Martin Esslin's and Theodor Adorno's influential analyses of Beckett's plays alluded to the idea of the immediate post-war works engaging with the aftermath of Western religious and philosophical traditions, and subsequently an exposure to an ideological vacancy. For these critics, Beckett's post-war texts seemingly figure as a kind of wake and awakening. They are a wake to the loss of normative meaning, accentuated in the grim post-1945 context of destabilization and disillusionment where 'the certitudes and unshakable basic assumptions of former ages have been swept away' (Esslin 2001: 23). It is also an awakening to the provisional identity of the human, whereby '[h]umankind, whose general species fits badly into Beckett's linguistic landscape, is only that which humanity has become' (Adorno 1982: 126).

Esslin's *The Theatre of the Absurd* (1961) situated Beckett amongst other contemporary dramatists, and, in the process, popularized Beckett's vision of the human condition and the profound formal impact of 'absurd' drama. Esslin associates Beckett's aesthetic with a transhistorical value, displaying the emptiness and senselessness intrinsic to human existence. However, although Esslin's introduction is cited as 'undoubtedly the most influential fifteen pages in the history of Beckett criticism in English' (Murphy 1994: 17), his initial reading holds less weight for the generations of criticism that follow, partly owing to Beckett's own assessment of 'absurdity'. When asked whether artistic enterprise is impossible without rigorous ethical standards, Beckett replied:

> [M]oral values are not accessible and not open to definition. To define them, you would have to make value judgements, and you can't do that. That's why I have never agreed with the idea of the theatre of the absurd. Because that implies making value judgements. You can't even talk about truth. That is part of the general distress (Juliet 1995: 148–9).

Esslin's value judgement reveals his use of a humanistic paradigm; he promotes a rational and decorous vision of a bygone humanity that acts as a frame of reference to the absurdity on stage. The devaluation of human ideals and purpose cannot be acknowledged without addressing its implicit counterpoint, and the theatre audience observes this discord, aware of the fact that one is unable to evaluate without firm criteria of what constitutes value.

In Esslin's usage, the theatre of the absurd denotes the 'sense of the senselessness of life, of the inevitable devaluation of ideals, purity, and purpose' through the 'unity between its basic assumptions and the form in which these are expressed' (2001: 24). Although this book does not revisit Esslin's notion of the absurd specifically, the way in which Esslin is keen to stress the historical foundation of this essential vision remains relevant. He explains how the dramatic techniques of the theatre of the absurd were 'elements that arose from the zeitgeist, the atmosphere of the time, rather than deliberate theoretical considerations' (2001: 12). Each playwright is included under Esslin's umbrella term by virtue of an intuitive experimentation with form and a shared perspicacity on the expressive requirements of the post-war period. Therefore, the theatre of the absurd refers to an existential condition, but Beckett's insight into life develops supposedly from ideological shifts occurring at a distinct historical juncture.

The value of existential and essentialist readings declined by the 1980s when Beckett studies followed mainstream literary theory into a poststructural interrogation of language and meaning. Curiously, Esslin's contemporary Theodor Adorno, whose essay 'Versuch, das *Endspiel* zu verstehen' ('Trying to understand *Endgame*') was published in the same year as Esslin's book, returned to prominence during this decade, profiting from a 1982 translation into English by Michael T. Jones for an edition of *New German Critique*. According to David Weisberg, Adorno's essay 'might still be the best piece of criticism on a single work by Beckett' (2006: 6), precisely because it manages to propose the cultural significance of Beckett's play while doing justice to its resistant nature. Adorno famously asserts that Beckett's *Endgame* (E [1957] 2006a) 'cannot chase the chimera of expressing its meaning with the help of philosophical mediation. Understanding it can mean nothing other than understanding its incomprehensibility' (Adorno 1982: 120). According to Adorno, Beckett's play educes the malfunctioning structures of conventional thought and value, which elevates *Endgame* to a new level of commentary suitable for critiquing contemporary society and culture. The 'truth content' (Adorno 1982: 120) of Beckett's work is implicitly connected to its aesthetic formation, specifically the dramatic and linguistic material that organizes its emptiness. As David Cunningham notes, 'the "meaninglessness" of the work is determinately "enunciated", via its realization in "the aesthetic material", thus becoming a kind of *aesthetic meaning*' (2002: 133). The artistic merit and social significance of *Endgame* is achieved in the workings of the play as a whole, developing a negative revelation through the dramatic embodiment of meaninglessness. In other words, the meaning of Beckett's text is its meaninglessness.

Yet, besides the dominant message of Adorno's seminal essay, peripheral details regarding his motivation and approach are also significant to the current study. Adorno's essay is, in part, a defence of Beckett's work against Georg Lukács' denunciation in *The Meaning of Contemporary Realism* (1957). Lukács rejects the static form and asocial detachment of modernism in general, arguing that Beckett's solipsistic psychopathology and primitivism in particular celebrates insularity and exalts abnormality. He writes that Beckett 'presents us with an image of utmost human degradation – an idiot's vegetative existence' (Lukács 1963: 31). In response, Adorno contests Lukács' objections to Beckett's reduction of humans to 'animality', pointing out the irony in 'a kind of artistic behaviour denounced as inhuman by those whose humanity has already become an advertisement for inhumanity' (1982: 125, 126). For Adorno, the simple relegation of the human to the nonhuman other is itself a cursory reduction of Beckett's characterization. Beckettian Man is not animal per se, but rather the 'image of the last human' (1982: 123); he is the end product of previously esteemed philosophy and education. The orderliness and selectivity of 'perspective' that Lukács lauds in realism is left in tatters in *Endgame* for Adorno precisely due to Beckett's fidelity to prior epistemological foundations: 'thoughts are dragged along and distorted like the day's left-overs' (1982: 121). Hence, the animal state of Beckett's figures is apparent in a vision of what humanity has become as a result of human properties. Adorno sees this degradation in Beckett as the culmination of humanity's trajectory; it is the nemesis to humanistic hubris.

However, in Adorno's own reading he employs animal analogies to describe Beckett's characters. They are 'flies that twitch after the swatter has half smashed them' and 'not a self but rather the aping imitation of something non-existent', while the audience are like 'people who, when visiting the zoo, wait attentively for the next move of the hippopotamus or the chimpanzee' (1982: 128, 143, 140). Adorno's recourse to the animal suggests that animality is bound up with the last human, that modernity's 'progression' bears the hallmarks of a regression in the ontogenetic process. Therefore, for Adorno, it is not that Beckett's figures are 'ahistorical', as Lukács implies, but that 'only the result of history appears – as decline' (1982: 125). Adorno's dialogue with Lukács, in effect, points out a humanist teleology in which catastrophe is viewed as a backward step, contrary to advancement. In contrast, Adorno's position is closer to the concomitance of progression and retrogression. He is more open to the idea of a paradoxical progress that is itself a mode of decline, which suggests that the Beckettian last human conveys a process of ruination. This explains Adorno's assertion that 'Endgame is true gerontology' (1982: 142). The means of enlightenment have aged, suggesting that sage cognition and judgement have matured and become senile. In its depiction of decrepit and unsound old age – the stage when enriching life experiences, knowledge and wisdom are typically extensive – Beckett's play actually evokes earlier stages of both human life and pre-human organic evolution. The final image of the human encloses an atavistic vestige of humanity's origins.

Adorno's reference to the last human's primitivism as it appears in Beckett's work comes into contact with the related but crucially different concept of 'becoming-animal' that Giles Deleuze articulated in *A Thousand Plateaus* (1980), co-authored with Félix Guatarri, and his book a year later on Francis Bacon, *The Logic of Sensation*. Whereas Adorno's view of the last human concertinas a progressive view of evolutionary history from brute animal to civilized human to bring separated poles together, Deleuze and Guattari challenge the validity of such clearly defined and discernible identities. On the relationship between human and nonhuman animals, they argue that '[i]t is no longer a question of graduating resemblances, ultimately arriving at an identification between Man and Animal at the heart of a mystical participation. It is a question of ordering differences to arrive at a correspondence of relations' (Deleuze and Guattari 1988: 236). The basis of this identification looks past similar characteristics to recognize different but equivalent dynamics in the lives of creatures. Hence Deleuze can explain that 'A man can never say: "I am a bull, a wolf . . ." But he can say: "I am to a

woman what the bull is to a cow, I am to another man what the
wolf is to the sheep"' (1988: 237). The initial aspect of becoming-
animal is not to imply the animality of the human, but to accept the
affinity of relations that disturbs the neatness of the categories.

Although Beckett's figures of dehumanization and animalization
are not always conversant with Deleuze's concept, the term creature
itself does imply a type of indistinct equivocality related to
becoming-animal. Beckett scholars such as Shane Weller point out
that Beckett's representation of 'animalization' can largely be
understood on the level of resemblance or 'similitude (comme)'
(2013: 21), as Beckett's creatures appear and act in ways broadly
comparable to animals. Yet, as Weller also acknowledges, 'becoming
animal is a means of liberation from signification' (2013: 22), in
which the definitions of human and nonhuman animals appear
superficial. It is this release from human and humanist determinants,
and likewise pure animality, that enters Beckett's protagonists into
a creaturely tension, analogous to becoming-animal, not merely
through resemblances to animals, but owing to an exposure to the
collapse of discernibility as either per se. For Deleuze, it is this non-
identity that generates the genuinely kindred relationship: 'it is a
deep identity, a zone of indiscernibility more profound than any
sentimental identification' (2003: 25). In becoming-animal, then,
the human is animal, the animal is human, and both are neither; all
distinctions are porous to the point of lacking utility, which situates
living creatures in a mutual, anti-hierarchical relation. This idea is
particularly radical because it does not merely degrade the human
into an animal state nor reveal the animal base of the human, but
suggests that both categories flow into one another.

Becoming-animal does not exactly compare distinctly human
and nonhuman animals because it does honour the meanings on
which such identities would depend. In an essay on the animal turn
in the humanities, Kari Weil affirms that 'Deleuze and Guattari
want to free humans and animals from meaning altogether and thus
undo the very identities that confirm a distinction between human
and animal' (2010: 12). Beckett's treatment of the relationship
between human and nonhuman animals does appeal to the surface
identities that allow for a network of resemblances between species,
while at the same time leaving space for the indistinctiveness of
becoming-animal. Dislocated from the security of binary significations, human and nonhuman animals slip into a 'rhizomatic'

relation, which Deleuze and Guattari describe as a more lateral, fluid alternative to an 'arboreal' hierarchical root structure. Beyond genealogy, similarity and alterity, '[t]here is neither imitation nor resemblance, only an exploding of two heterogeneous series on the line of flight composed by a common rhizome that can no longer be attributed to or subjugated by anything signifying' (Deleuze and Guattari 1988: 10). As Weller argues in an earlier essay, this is not always the case in Beckett, who maintains as well as collapses human and nonhuman animal distinctions. Weller writes that the 'distinction is radically expanded, to the point at which it becomes absolute' and yet it is also 'collapsed, such that the very essence of the human is resituated in the animal' (2008: 219). This double movement is therefore evocative of the creaturely dynamic that describes a shifting tension between human identity, animal proximity and the anonymity of 'becoming'. Surface identity is crossed, confused and retraced in Beckett's work, not wiped out altogether. It is important that this liminality is appreciated as the effect of an ambiguous form of writing too, since Deleuze and Guattari articulate becoming-animal forcefully in relation to an alienating literary style, namely Franz Kafka's, as Weil affirms: 'It should come as no surprise that the author Deleuze and Guattari most associate with "becoming animal" is Kafka. They describe Kafka's writing itself as a form of becoming where words are wrenched or uprooted from their meanings and turned into "deterritorialized sounds"' (2010: 11). The liberation from signification is foremost in the undoing of semiotic, linguistic and narrative meaning. Although not always quite as neutral as suggested here with Kafka, this aesthetic registering of an ontological blurring is a prevalent creaturely component of Beckett's art of failure in his post-war work.

In conjunction, then, Esslin's elucidation of the zeitgeist's window on the absurd human condition, Adorno's reckoning on the image of animality attending the last human, and Deleuze and Guattari's destabilization of discrete human and nonhuman animal identities, intersect with Beckett's own creaturely dynamics without naming the creature. They identify related areas of historical crisis, humanistic reassessment and aesthetic enactment to form a constellation of inquiries navigated in Beckett's art. The current study is equally concerned with temporal upheavals of the essential, challenges to anthropocentric identifications and their manifestation in artistic forms, all of which indicate Beckett's oblique, elliptical historical relevance. The creature and its attendant meanings, which have yet to be applied to Beckett's work thoroughly, open up parallels between artistic and socio-political issues to relate Beckett's work to his contemporary milieu, which was dominated by a sense of disenchantment, particularly towards a humanist model of meaning and purpose, after the devastation of the mid-twentieth century. The Second World War and the Holocaust transformed, or rather revealed, the idea of the human as people had witnessed its creaturely potential.

Concepts of the creature and creaturely life

The creature is an especially ambiguous and polyvalent concept, and it is therefore necessary to outline its theorized form in order to understand what it might signify for Beckett. Julia Lupton's 2000 essay 'Creature Caliban' on Shakespeare's figure of servitude and monstrosity marks the inchoate stage of conceiving creatureliness. Lupton begins with the notion that '*creatura* is a thing always in the process of undergoing creation: the creature is actively passive or, better, passionate, perpetually becoming created, subject to transformations at the behest of the arbitrary commands of an Other' (2000: 1). Lupton's emphasis rests on the process of creating the creature and its endless potential, focusing on the perpetual act of manipulating an inferior other, which serves to differentiate the superior maker. As an identity in action, the creature is an indeterminate figure, defined as much by the forces inflicted upon it as the results of the subjugating process.

In terms of Caliban as a subject of political theology, or autocratic creation, he was a creature prior to the appearance of his master Prospero, and Lupton therefore describes him as resistant to both universal and particular conditions: 'He subsists within an unredeemed Creation not yet divided into nations, forming the forgotten ground of a heterogeneous universalism irreducible to either the economies of a normative humanity or the semiotic coherence of individual culture' (2000: 3–4). Despite the creature Caliban's antecedence to anthropological and cultural borderlines, his blank statelessness means he is readily reflective of the arriving oppressive systems that give creatureliness relevance for 'smaller world' definitions (Lupton 2000: 3), such as gender, race, colonial and postcolonial studies.[3] As Lupton notes, the term creature 'can even come to characterize the difference between male and female or between majority and minority' (2000: 1–2). This expansiveness raises the possibility of applying creaturely dynamics to Beckett's representation of women, for example, or his work in relation to the contexts of Ireland. Without insisting on an either/or logic between the ways in which Beckett can be read or discrete applications of creatureliness, it is fair to say that the authorial, narratological creatures present in Beckett's work are more compelling in dialogue with the subjects of authoritative creation and the intense crises in epistemology, expression and identity that the Second World War and the Holocaust triggered. This is primarily because of the biopolitically constituted limit figures of these events, in which a 'time-honoured conception of humanity' is left in ruins through the actions of authoritative power that is increasingly autocratic in its exertions on the materiality of life and fundamental judgement on human identity.

The philosopher Roberto Esposito defines 'biopolitics' as 'the increasingly intense and direct involvement established between political dynamics and human life (understood in its strictly biological sense), beginning with a phase that we can call second modernity' (2012: 69). These political interventions have a way of conflating the particular and the universal, exercising power to promulgate a way of life to the extent of making it indistinct from life itself. The creature is thus created as an exception to this particularly expansive cultural sphere of signification that assumes the capacity for deciding upon normative human meaning. As an excluded alterity figure, the creature is exposed to the basic homogeneity of all beings in 'the infinity of life that burgeons around the human at its limit point' (Lupton 2000: 3). This no man's land on the edge of humanity is particularly noticeable in Beckett's post-war work, in which his creatures are largely akin to others biologically speaking and yet exist on the frontier of a socially, culturally and politically endorsed human life.

Beckett briefly recognizes an analogue to this type of uncanny being, both familiar and alien, as early as his first published novel *Murphy* (M [1938] 2009b). The title character is described as not 'rightly human' by the 'chandlers' eldest waste product' (*M*, 50). 'Not rightly human' comes close to the creature's predicament; it suggests a being that remains human, but fails to correlate with humanity's vision of the human. Coincidentally, the fact that a character metaphorically reduced to excrement can justifiably cast such a judgement on Murphy shows how the hierarchy system of creation and subjection works, in which each individual jostles for the higher, more human, rank. While Beckett's 'not rightly human' is still human, it is an aberration of the approved anthropological template, which means its identity is necessarily measured in accordance with a stable human ideal. Marco Bernini uses the term 'creaturely level' to examine a similar relation to the completely developed, proper human, describing a stratum 'occupied by undeveloped human cognisers as opposed to (and sometimes rancorously opposing) fully fledged Humans or, as Beckett writes in a letter to George Duthuit in 1948, "the illusion of the human and the fully realized"' (2015: 86). This 'fully realized human' comes to haunt Beckett's creatures who are stuck as 'illusions of the human'. They are similarly erroneous, thrown into relief against the correct human, 'negatively defined as a being that is "neither . . . nor" and that is incapacitated or disempowered with respect to motion and speech' (Weller 2013: 23). And yet, the potential to be impoverished and attenuated, to be an amorphous and ambiguous being, to be cast out as inhuman, is endemic to the human. The creature is therefore both foreign and indigenous to the human. It can appear through a negation of the human to reveal its other, or through eliciting the alter ego that was latent in the human already. Ironically, to apprehend the human fully, or 'Human' in the uppercase, as Bernini has it, is to remain cognizant of the illusion of the human that resides within the Human as potential.

The real significance of creaturely life for Eric Santner is that it marks a political threshold. In his book *On Creaturely Life* (2006), Santner suggests that the political constitutes the human's passage into creaturely life and yet it is the political that distinguishes humanity from the creature: 'human beings are not just creatures among other creatures but are in some sense *more creaturely* than other creatures by virtue of an excess that is produced in the space of the political and that, paradoxically, accounts for their "humanity"' (2006: 26). This contradictory state, in which the political appears simultaneously to make and take humanity, is misleading if creaturely life is perceived in isolation from human life. On the contrary, creaturely life forms a dimension of human life, it is 'the threshold where life becomes a matter of politics and politics comes to inform the very matter and materiality of life' (Santner 2006: 12). According to Santner, the creature's political being correlates with biopolitics and evokes the essential vitality known as 'bare life' that Michel Foucault, and subsequently Giorgio Agamben, expounds. Foucault proposes that politics permeates the raw substance of being and makes a decision on what constitutes a life worth living: 'For millennia, man remained what he was for Aristotle: a living animal with the additional capacity for a political existence; modern man is an animal whose politics places his existence as a living being in question' (1990: 143). As Foucault intimates here, the political sphere of human life was once an ancillary property that confirmed humanity's place at the summit of the Aristotelian *scala naturae*. When the political supplement is divested, as it virtually is for Beckett's creatures as marginalized aberrations, the resulting being is proximal with bare life and effectively beyond the human 'frame', which, according to Cary Wolfe, 'decides what we recognize and what we don't, what counts and what doesn't' (2013: 6). It is not clear whether this removal includes a newfound autonomy, as Aristotle's assessment of stateless peoples implies: 'The man who is isolated – who is unable to share in the benefits of political association, or has no need because he is already self-sufficient – is no part of the *polis*, and must therefore be either a beast or a god' (2009: 5). However, according to Foucault, political being is conflated with being itself in the modern age, which realizes the transition from the contingency of politics, or its place as a human privilege, into creaturely terrain and the matter of the human. In Foucault's initial conception at least, biopolitics appears to narrow the margins between anthropological and ethnological perspectives by reducing 'man the animal with politics' to 'man the animal of politics'. Political meaning is not an extra capacity above and beyond the human's corporal, natural life. It is complicit in shaping the material quality of being.

The bare life dissociated from structures of human life, or what Lupton calls 'pure vitality denuded of symbolic significance and political capacity' (2000: 2), results in a perilous example of a politically constituted state of being; the condemnation to political irrelevance produces biopolitical subjects. This lack of signification is not dissimilar to the concept of becoming-animal, and the ensuing accentuation of physical vulnerability, or what Aristotle optimistically calls 'self-sufficiency', is a defining aspect of Anat Pick's understanding of creaturely life. In her book *Creaturely Poetics* (2011), Pick draws heavily on French philosopher Simone Weil (who coincidentally wrote a meditation called *Attente de Dieu* (1950) on the love of God, neighbours and friends) to expound literary and filmic sensibilities attentive to the shared bodily conditions of living creatures. Pick argues that '[a]nimals have traditionally been perceived as pure necessity, material bodies pitted against human mindfulness and soulfulness' (2011: 4). The separation is a mistake for Pick, who emphasizes the pressing physicality of human life too, which forges an ineluctable point of relation, encompassed by the term 'creaturely'. She asserts: 'The creature, then, is first and foremost a living body – material, temporal, and vulnerable' (Pick 2011: 5). Contrary to the characteristically modernist gravitation towards interiority, Pick goes on to examine art forms that convey the immediacy and exposure of flesh and blood materiality, including William Golding's *The Inheritors* (1955). It is precisely this bodily reality that Chris Counsell identifies in Beckett's drama, namely *Waiting for Godot* (*WFG* [French 1953; English 1955] 2006b), as it discloses 'existence as a purely creatural affair, one which cannot "transcend" the material for it consists of the material' (1996: 117). Furthermore, in relation to Beckett's prosaic art of failure, creaturely poetics means 'being open to the physical realities that challenge or confound thought' (Pick 2011: 8), which is evident in Beckett's treatment of the strained cognitive and discursive faculties of his author-narrators as they encounter empirical and phenomenological data. Subsequently, as Beckett's creatures deviate from tenuous norms, experience the loss of symbolic meaning and navigate the margins of socio-political spheres, they are consigned to the intensified biological and ontological vulnerability associated with bare life, which throws into doubt their acknowledgement as human. The Beckettian creature effectively ends up close to Hannah Arendt's description of the human without reciprocity: 'a man who is nothing but a man has lost the very qualities which make it possible for other people to treat him like a man' (1973: 300). The segregated life of the merely human is not seen as veritably Human; it is a creaturely realm, in closer proximity with the nonhuman animal.

For Santner, however, the creature emerges as the new subject of political interventions that pervade the core of human existence specifically. Creaturely life is removed from politics that govern a particular way of life and is exposed to the biopolitics that regulate life itself, altering the meaning of 'state politics' to suggest an authority that grants the very state of human being. Santner makes it clear that creaturely life is a human component that 'pertains not primarily to a sense of shared animality or a shared animal suffering but to a biopolitical *animation* that distinguishes man from animal' (2006: 39). This 'biopolitical animation' occurs most obviously for Santner in a judicial prorogation, which draws heavily on Agamben's readings of the German political theorist Carl Schmitt. Santner asserts that 'creaturely life is just life abandoned to the state of exception/emergency, that paradoxical domain in which law has been suspended in the name of preserving law' (2006: 22). The state of exception rejects valued principles in order to safeguard them, which undermines the sanctity of the rule and underlines its provisional status. As such, the state of exception indicates an alternative jurisdiction: a default set of rudimentary actions invoked when the ideal order fails or no longer suffices. Agamben argues that concentration and extermination camps are the paradigmatic sites of biopolitical activity under a sustained state of exception. They represent 'an extreme and monstrous attempt to decide between the human and the inhuman, which has ended up dragging the very possibility of the distinction to its ruin' (Agamben 2003: 22). As facilities introduced to solve an excess population that was labelled the *Ballastexistenzen* in Nazi Germany, or lives that were encumbrances and a 'waste of space' (Rees 2005: 54), concentration and extermination camps prevent unworthy life from becoming unmanageable. It appears that when the exception becomes the rule, the unexceptional, there is a kind of devolution in the name of revolution, whereby a primitive intervention invoked by rationalized prerogatives or 'necessity' supersedes the former ideological structure. Hence, creatures abandoned to the state of exception are subjects of an order at once enlightened and barbaric.[4]

Although Santner rejects 'shared animality' as a determining part of the creature, his recourse to the state of exception at least suggests a more atavistic human jurisdiction founded on the basic components of power relations. Indeed, when Adolf Hitler invoked the 'Decree for the Protection of the People and the State' and pursued the Nazi regime's *Gleichschaltung* that marked a twelve-year long state of exception, he inaugurated a biopolitical domain that reintroduced the primacy of sovereign power, identity and alterity, and survival, which effectively sanctioned a kind of wild, unruly will to power disguised as self-preservation. Anat Pick makes two salient claims on this front, writing that 'if the Holocaust proved anything at all, it is that Jewish (and other) bodies are animal bodies' and that 'the notion of "crimes against humanity" in fact obscures the Holocaust's fundamental unravelling of the human' (2011: 51). As the brutish reassessment of meaningful living beings and reassignment of basic categories takes places, it is clear that biopolitical power assumes an autocratic creative role in shaping the definitions and conditions of life forms. The human category is rendered a guise in the process, which, once denuded, reveals the persistent anatomy and mental spirit of life, akin to what J. M. Coetzee's avatar Elizabeth Costello calls the shared 'substrate of life' in *The Lives of Animals* (1999: 35). This biopolitical craftwork intersects with Beckett's creaturely narrative dimensions to suggest a biopolitical and literary axis, as both are concerned with making their subjects. When Beckett employs the *poioumenon* (a literary genre in which the work is about its own making) for example, as he does in his post-war trilogy of novels, his work reflects on the power dynamics involved in the mutual ordering and structuring of worlds in art and reality. As H. Porter Abbott contends, 'tyranny is rooted in the imagination. The creating of art, like the making of worlds, is a matter of cramming, jamming, wedging, bending, poking. Nothing is sacred in this process' (1996: 141). Beckett's art of failure is similarly preoccupied with the endless process of creation, and yet it undermines authority through self-reflection to uncover the obvious corruptions and contrivances it entails. He does not circumscribe, dominate and naturalize meaning, as with the biopolitical state of exception, but rather is attentive to the revisable potential of meaning. Beckett effectively 'bears witness to a potentiality, to a subject that is capable of becoming the subject of its own desubjectification: a subject that resists and evades biopolitical control' (Lund 2009: 76). His aesthetic survives on the ability to unravel systems that supposedly determine signification and inadvertently betray value as contingent. Beckett's attentiveness to the making of meaning in his writing therefore evokes the elemental or biotic material that biopolitical animations manipulate, drawing together authorial, authoritative and autocratic forms of creation as a result. As such, it is possible to discern how Beckett's subtle contextual relevance also pertains to a larger ontological scale, as Adorno expresses in his notes on *Endgame*: 'B[eckett]'s genius is that he has captured this semblance of the non-historical, of the *condition humaine*, in historical images, and thus transfixed it' (2010: 162). Beckett's evocation of the human as a floating, malleable and provisory category recalls the repercussions of biopolitical interventions felt after the Holocaust and, in doing so, conveys the essential paradox of the human condition: to be human is to be provisional, in flux, and potentially inhuman. In this way, the historical moment discloses the precarious condition of the human.

The essential captured in a temporal image is pivotal to Santner's notion of the creature. Apropos of Walter Benjamin, he suggests that inapprehensible fragments of history reify the abstruseness of nature to reveal the natural historical distance between the human world and its human meaning. Santner's explanation is worth quoting at length:

> The opacity and recalcitrance that we associate with the materiality of nature – the mute 'thingness' of nature – is, paradoxically, most palpable where we encounter it as a piece of human history that has become an enigmatic ruin beyond our capacity to endow it with meaning, to integrate it into our symbolic universe. Where a piece of human world presents itself as a surplus that both demands and resists symbolization, that is both inside and outside the 'symbolic order' [. . .] that is where we find ourselves in the midst of 'natural history'. What I am calling creaturely life is a dimension of human existence called into being at such natural historical fissures or caesuras in the space of meaning (2006: xv).

Santner's Benjaminian 'natural historical fissures or caesuras' are intimately related to the idea of 'the open', considered in different ways by Rainer Maria Rilke and Martin Heidegger. In contrast to Heidegger's view of the animal as *weltarm*, or 'poor in world', belonging to its environment without conscious reflection, Rilke suggests that the human ability to form the world, what Heidegger calls *weltbildend*, aligns man with the poor in world. According to

Rilke's eighth duino elegy, consciousness distances man from the
'pure space' of the world, the open, whereas animals are united
with their environment (1963: 77). Man therefore borders on the
animalistic poor in world, not because he is incognizant and merely
exists, reacting to the things he encounters around him, but because
he is unable to apprehend the world in an immediate sense. The
human world is impoverished as a result of a self-constructed and
mediating worldview, complete with lexical signs and conceptual
values.

It is the remote position in relation to the open – accentuated by
historical moments that expose the hiatus in world meaning – that
forms the creaturely dimension. The decisive event here is the
human's dislocation from the construction, as it enacts the 'traumatic
disruption' of creaturely life, which is shown to be not quite animal
but not exactly human (Santner 2006: 10). For Santner, the natural
historical status of artefacts beyond the 'symbolic universe' leads to
a state akin to Benjamin's 'petrified unrest', or *undeadness*, the
space between real and symbolic death', which Santner takes to be
the ultimate domain of creaturely life (2006: xx). This definitive
space of the creature between types of death resonates profoundly
in the purgatorial images of Beckett's work and conjures the
Muselmann's death-in-life. When the ability to effect the world-
forming mediation is redundant, the human withdraws from human
life, endures a symbolic death and is thrown into a creaturely realm
between the open and the construction. Santner writes that
'[c]reatureliness is thus a dimension not so much of biological as of
ontological vulnerability, a vulnerability that permeates human
being as that being whose essence it is to exist in forms of life
that are, in turn, contingent, susceptible to breakdown' (2011: 6).
By all accounts, the creature is a figure of trauma that beholds
the lost idea of the human as a melancholic reminder, but moves
into the future as the post-human, bearing the remnants of the
human with it.

Santner's conception of creaturely life is the most thorough
attempt to articulate this mode of being and the chapters that follow
both apply and expand upon his key notions relevant to Beckett's
work. However, my understanding of creaturely life, as shaped by
Beckett's evocations, departs from and develops Santner's model in
several respects. While this study also makes use of Walter Benjamin's
work for an insight into creaturely life, one of the concepts derived

from his comments is left unsaid in Santner. As discussed in Chapters 1 and 2, Beckett's art of failure suggests a conception of the sovereign and creature in which positions of power slide into weakness and contrariwise. Although Benjamin's few references to the creature offer ample opportunity for interpretation and are by no means prescriptive, this is clearly a dynamic of the creature that is present in Benjamin's work and yet Santner does not dwell upon it. This is perhaps because the simultaneously potent and impotent Beckettian author-narrator makes such a creaturely dynamic more apparent. The term '(in)sovereignty' is introduced as a result to describe this shifting of power, which is key to the dichotomous nature of Beckett's creatures as creators and creations.

Whereas Santner's creaturely life centres on the human who experiences a process of destitution to become something other than human 'between real and symbolic death' (2006: xx), the analysis here is also intermittently directed towards the close proximity with animalistic and, to a lesser extent, the mechanical elements that the fall from humanity suggests. Santner writes that creatureliness is 'a specifically human way of finding oneself caught in the midst of the antagonisms in and of the political field' (2006: xix). Pieter Vermeulen follows Santner's lead in an essay on creaturely life in J.M. Coetzee's *Slow Man* and the unravelling of the novel as a literary form that gave shape to human life. He insists that this is 'a creaturely, and not an animal, form of suffering: not just the physical pains of biological life, but also a sense of vulnerability and precariousness that comes from the tenuousness of the forms that used to provide human life with meaning' (2013: 665). Even so, there is a greater interpenetration between human and nonhuman animals as the human subject is drawn into the matter of bare life. Admittedly, the loss of symbolic meaning must be felt as creaturely, yet the dearth unveils human animality, or simply 'being', in as much as 'animality' or 'being' express the immediate, sentient and senescent dimension shared between the human and the nonhuman. Beckett communicates this irreducible physical reality concisely in *The End* (FN [1954] 2009c), in which the narrator dwells with rats and is made aware of his raw materiality: 'living flesh, in spite of everything I was still living flesh' (FN, 53). The creature's intimacy with the animal is therefore retained in this conception of Beckett's creatures, which involves working through the notions of the 'open' and 'construction' in order to think about broken human forms of making meaning, the use of the animal status in power relations and identity structures, the realization of human captivation in bodily conditions through humour, and vulnerability as a contact point in human and nonhuman animal types of survival. If creaturely life is a mode of being between the human and bare life, my understanding of the creature pays attention to the 'foul brood, neither man nor beast' that Beckett describes in *Molloy* (*T*, 19) but still considers the extent to which a denuded human might have an affinity with nonhuman animals.

The intersection between Beckett's creatures and the biopolitical nature of the Holocaust as an example of creaturely life is also a prevalent component of this analysis, which means expanding on aspects of the creature that are underdeveloped in Santner. The Nazis' denationalization and dehumanization of the Jews marks a remarkable state intervention in the classification of life granted political value and deemed unworthy of living. This signals a strong case for a contextually grounded creaturely life. However, Santner offers only a passing reference to the *Muselmann* in a footnote in his book *On Creaturely Life*, which is quoted in Chapter 4, whereas the contention here is that the creaturely life in Beckett occurs through an awareness of the precarious and provisional condition of the idea of the human during this era. In relation to 'the constructedness of the category of the human', critics such as Richard Carter Smith argue that 'Beckett's fiction treats its perfect emptiness as a generative principle for art rather than a political ill to be rectified' (2012: 221). The emptiness of the human is indeed a prompt for creation, allowing Beckett's author-narrators to subsist on the open-ended flux of subjectivity and self-expression without the limits of a fixed meaning. But the vacancy of the human does not promote autonomous self-definition alone, as it simultaneously alludes to the condition of emptiness as a political consequence and the potential for others to exercise control. The authorial, narratological creation that Carter Smith identifies is redolent of an analogue authoritative creation, particularly biopolitical decisions on life, which diverts attentions away from politics as the management of significations to an active hand in making and taking meaning. Therefore, this book considers how Beckett's creatures resemble the *Muselmann* as a biopolitical figure that conveys the inhuman potential that resides within the human, as

Dominick La Capra has also noted: 'One might also see Samuel Beckett as having had the daring to stage, in an incredible series of radically disempowered beings, the – or at least something close to the – *Muselmann*'s experience of disempowerment and living death' (2004: 187). The parity between the *Muselmann* and the Beckettian creature is made apparent here through reference to the *Muselmann* as a witness in relation to Beckett's art of failure, the identity anxieties that give rise to the Jew as creature in relation to Beckett's master–servant relationships and the Nazis' orchestration of torturous survival conditions that bear comparison to the purgatorial lives of Beckett's characters.

Beckett after 1945

Beckett experienced Nazi ideology and propaganda in pre-war Germany; fled to Roussillon and the Vichy 'free zone' in southern France during the Nazi occupation of Paris; served with the French Resistance group Gloria SMH, mediating information for the Allies; grieved the death of his close friend Alfred Péron who was imprisoned at Mauthausen; and helped rebuild the hospital at Saint-Lô. That Beckett was involved in and had first-hand knowledge of the impact of the Second World War and was a secondary-witness to the Holocaust is not disputed. In fact, as Lois Gordon asserts: 'The war may have synthesised everything he had seen and studied so far in his life and allowed him to retreat to "the room" in order to engage the world of his imagination' (2013: 122). As much as the events of the war might influence Beckett, the fact remains that he does not or cannot explicitly address these events in his prose and drama.

Besides a few rare exceptions, Beckett scholars tend to avoid extracting coded references to the concentration and death camps from Beckett's texts, and quite prudently. Antoinette Weber-Caflisch's French-language analysis of *The Lost Ones*, *Chacun son dépeupleur* (1994), for example, details the striking likeness that Beckett's searching figures have to the malnourished and demoralized prisoners in the Nazi camps. In a reference to Weber-Caflisch's book, Jean-Michel Rabaté describes how she 'shows that "*si c'est un homme*" used twice in the last section of the text quotes directly Primo Levi's book *Si c'est un homme* (*Se quest'un uomo*). The

questers, called here the "vanquished," do resemble those
concentration camp inmates who had abandoned all hope and who,
as Levi narrates, were "Muslims"' (2010: 113). Weber-Caflisch's
study clearly leans towards a representation of the camps as a site
and specific experience whereas the extent of Beckett's engagement
with the Holocaust is invariably more indirect and diffuse, attentive
to certain testimonial problems, power struggles and survival
conditions as they filter into everyday life.

However, several Beckett scholars have attempted to gauge the
extent of the relationship between the Holocaust and literary
responses to mass trauma. In 'What Remains of Beckett: Evasion
and History', Daniel Katz refers initially to the violence of the
'image ban' that Adorno points out, and maintains that the absence
of the atrocities of the Holocaust in Beckett's work is appropriate,
not owing to ethical sensitivity or even artistic inadequacy, but by
virtue of the severe and forceful manner of its interdiction. For
instance, in light of Knowlson's observation that Estragon in
Waiting for Godot was originally named 'Levy', Katz suggests that
Beckett removes the Jewish name to impose an uncompromising
image ban (2009: 153). In pursuit of further elisions, Katz turns to
Agamben in order to explore the common ground with Beckett
oriented around the idea that 'one speaks by proxy precisely when
most speaking for oneself' (2009: 149). He also queries and refines
several of the arguments that Agamben sets out in *Remnants of
Auschwitz* (1999). Katz suggests that *Muselmann* does not designate
the 'non-human created by the camps', but demonstrates a kind of
Freudian *witz*, or 'rhetoric of survival' by adopting a pseudonym to
shift the emphasis of degradation away from the denomination
'Jew' (2009: 152). Since he refrains from further comment, Katz's
allusion to Jewish perseverance and Freud's study of jokes invites a
sustained analysis of humour as a defence or anaesthetic in times of
extreme adversity, which forms a part of my study of Beckett's
humour in Chapter 3. He also takes issue with Agamben's
philosophical appropriation of 'the ineluctable link to one's own
singularity' in the Levinasian concept of shame. According to Katz,
Agamben is insensitive to the individuality of Holocaust accounts,
and therefore lacks subjective and historical specificity in his focus
on the enunciation of testimony. In effect, the thrust of Katz's essay
foregrounds the tension between the ethical obligation and
implications in exacting, denoting and naming the catastrophe, or

approximating, connoting and 'not-naming'. In other words, Katz addresses the differences between articulating and evoking the narrative of Auschwitz, which are issues that charge Beckett's elision with ethical relevance. Beckett's strict silence on the Holocaust is a significant response to the event that shows how art can bear witness while respecting the idea that the horror is beyond artistic representation.

Jackie Blackman's 'Beckett's Theatre "After Auschwitz"' also explores the 'unsayability' of catastrophe, noting that Adorno tempers his famous assertion '[t]o write poetry after Auschwitz is barbaric' to admit that '[p]erennial suffering has as much right to expression as a tortured man has to scream' (Adorno quoted in Blackman 2010: 71, 79). The latter formulation stresses entitlement, not efficacy, and is therefore in close proximity with Agamben's analysis of the ethical obligation to bear witness to the inability to bear witness or, as Beckett implies in Watt (W [written in English in 1943; published in English in 1953] 2009d), eff the ineffable (W, 52–3). From this expressive duty, Blackman extends a more biographical reading in response to Michel Foucault's question: 'How can one define a work amid the millions of traces left by someone after his death?' (Foucault 1999: 207 quoted in Blackman 2010: 74). She suggests that, short of a textual signature, biographical 'traces' remain in the artwork that indicate contextual information and aesthetic decisions, which, in turn, disclose the expressive dilemma that compels one to express what cannot be expressed. Thus, it is 'possible to read Beckett's early plays as a very personal and unique creative response to the unsayability and unplayability of Holocaust narrative – a story impossible to represent, yet, a story which must be repeatedly told and somehow understood' (Blackman 2010: 82).

In two other valuable essays, Blackman expands upon Beckett's unperformed play Eleutheria, written in 1947, and the Jewish presence in Beckett's post-war work. Blackman accepts Alain Badiou's perception of Beckett as a 'Resistant Philosopher' whose commitment to silence, or rather, a kind of spoken voicelessness, is a 'radical and intimate, violent and reserved, necessary and exceptional action' (Badiou 2005: 5 quoted in Blackman 2007: 326). However, Blackman again finds historical and socio-political 'traces' in Beckett's work that remain despite, and as a result of, the general erasure of specifics. In fact, in contrast to Katz's insistence

on the particularity of each trauma, the most striking reflection of
the Jewish situation that Blackman points out is in the complete
negation of distinction. For Jacques Derrida, this contradictory
identity of non-identity is inherently Jewish, or at least a humorous
Jewish self-image: 'the more one dislocates one's self identity, the
more one says "my own identity consists in not being identical to
myself, in being a foreigner, the non-coinciding with the self," etc.
the more Jewish one is!' (Cixous 2004: 83 quoted in Blackman
2007: 334). Blackman mobilizes the idea that biographical 'traces'
do not define the text's scope, but are further evidence of the feeling
and incompetence that make up Beckett's artistic toolset after the
war. These tools are incapable of representing an extra-literary
reality but can perforate the materials of production to reveal the
reality of producing.

For James McNaughton, the inability to convey a past that
deserves recognition is also a portal into Beckett's historical
predicament. Crucially, McNaughton arrives at this conclusion by
way of Beckett's German diaries, which meticulously record
Beckett's trip through Germany in the years prior to the annexation
of Austria in 1938. As McNaughton notes, it is 'more antiquarian in
its documentation than reflective' (2005: 108). Moreover, the critic
develops his historical perspective on Beckett in spite of the author's
supposed lack of 'historical sense' and 'disgust of sweeping historical
narratives' (McNaughton, 2005: 102). Against the aesthetic protest
of modernist art, which experiments with form to frustrate the
rationalization of oppressive regimes, Beckett's diaries take the first
steps towards a view of logical structure and precise detail as absurd
and meaningless. Thus, in his diaries, Beckett's fidelity to an
intrinsically flawed method divulges its own weaknesses.
McNaughton clearly sums up the crux of the duty to remember and
elusiveness of veracity: 'Far from making him an ahistorical writer,
as Beckett's critical reputation often has him, this paradox reveals
Beckett caught between the fear of forgetting the past and greater
fear of rationally misshaping it' (2005: 111). The historical event
itself is at risk of oblivion if not treated or if wrongly treated. The
difficulty, then, is how to attend to the historic event without
reducing it to an inadequate historical narrative.

A handful of other critical texts elucidate themes that are central
to *Beckett's Creatures*. Peter Boxall's *Since Beckett: Contemporary
Writing in the Wake of Modernism* (2009), for instance, includes

sections on what he calls 'a Beckettian mode of remembrance' (2009: 86), which is close to the kind of agitated, performative form of creaturely testimony explicated in Chapter 1. Boxall describes how Beckett, along with Austrian author Thomas Bernhard, develops 'a form with which to express the uncanny presence of the past, but for both writers this presence, this continuity between present and past is achieved only through a kind of radical discontinuity, through the erection of a boundary between present and past' (Boxall 2009: 92). This kind of separation from the past but traversal of the schism between past and present filters into Beckett's writing style. For Boxall, 'the experience of literary correction and disintegration' seen in Beckett (Boxall 2009: 109), whereby the very substance of the text involves its deconstruction, appropriately conveys this simultaneous proximity and distance; the past is on the edge of the tongue but always in the process of being revised or erased. For the most part, however, Boxall's text either concentrates on Beckett's literary legacy and his parity with later writers, such as Bernhard and Sebald, or is interested in the texture of temporality and testimony in Beckett. The present work extends the relationship between Beckett and the Holocaust to identity thinking in power struggles, humour as a reaction to suffering and the prevalence of survival.

Alysia Garrison's essay '"Faintly struggling things": Trauma, Testimony, and Inscrutable Life' (2009) focuses on Beckett's relationship with trauma theory and how both transhistorical trauma and the historical trauma related to the Holocaust are evident in the last text of Beckett's trilogy. She argues that '*The Unnamable* formalises wounded forms of life by an aesthetic of diminishment' (Garrison 2009: 92). In terms of transhistorical trauma, this diminishment occurs as Beckett's subjects fade or are fragmented physically to become more spectral and through the inability to account for this collapsing subjectivity. Nevertheless, this increasingly bare life demands to be heard and seen, giving rise to 'the luminous trace that endures' as 'memory gasps' (Garrison 2009: 97, 98). In the second half of the essay, Garrison explains how more precise images and terms such as 'tears' and 'ash' act as 'placeholders for specified loss' (2009: 99). Although a secondary or distant witness, Beckett still uses his experience or knowledge of the events according to Garrison and his texts are therefore inevitably marked by these memories. One of Garrison's key claims, then, is that the transhistorical and historical registers of trauma entwine so that nonspecific visions of trauma are always suggestive of specific traumatic events and vice versa. The notion that Beckett's novel 'can be read as an *effect* or *symptom* of the atrocities' resonates with my own approach to Beckett and the Holocaust, whereby the modes of creaturely life evident in Beckett serve to illuminate 'life's distorted alterity under contingent biopolitical duress' and 'the annihilation of expression and the return of ghostly remains, a testimonial form appropriate, perhaps, to witness what remains of the human in the inhuman in the aftermath of traumatic limit events' (Garrison 2009: 93, 101). Although Garrison only touches on these areas, the biopolitical dimension and the human/inhuman divide offer potential for further development in the attempt to associate Beckett's work with the political dimensions of the Holocaust and post-Holocaust views of the human.

Recent criticism shows that historical and socio-political considerations are a burden for Beckett that cannot be lifted with representational tools. Rather, the manifestation of the war and Holocaust in Beckett is bound with his preoccupation with narrative, language and representation – with the failure of art. It is not my intention to suggest that Beckett attempts to represent the experience of enduring the camps or speaks on behalf of real victims or survivors, but more that his post-war work bears the products of the period. Beckett was subject to the broad cultural impact of this era, an impact that dominates postmodern thinkers who 'insisted that the Holocaust marks a break in the trajectory of the West, one which provokes us to rethink the implications of the project of modernity' (Milchman and Rosenberg 1998: 2). He is at the epicentre of this shift in thinking about art and the human condition, and his art of failure shows his sensitivity to two key elements that pertain to the Holocaust as a traumatic experience and exercise in dehumanization, and yet lead to more diffuse responses to the perceived rupture in value systems and structures of meaning in the post-Holocaust cultural watershed in the West: evocations of the unspeakable and the idea that the human has entered a survival mode or post-human phase, both of which are made clearer through the concept of the creature. This context is evident in Beckett's work not only through traces that permeate his writing, but in creaturely modes of expression (testimony, humour) and being (power, survival) that constitute the texture of his work and go beyond the idea that 'Beckett's skeletal characters and desolate landscape are haunted by the ghosts of Auschwitz' (McDonald 2002: 142). What might be considered direct references or allusions to the historical context in Beckett, then, are generally eschewed in favour of these pertinent conditions or states made apparent by the catastrophe while having repercussions for the status of art and the human 'after the Holocaust'.

Overview of *Beckett's Creatures*

It remains to offer some prefatory notes on the focus of each chapter. Chapter 1 examines Beckett's alternative type of testimony to the crisis facing the act of bearing witness after Auschwitz. It expounds the voice of incapacity in Beckett's trilogy, which is unable to attest positively to past experiences or retrospectively account for oneself. However, with reference to Benjamin's notion of the 'sovereign as creature', I employ the term '(in)sovereignty' to describe how Beckett's author-narrators illustrate the convergence of impotence and potency as they articulate their failures and salvage a level of testimonial value in confronting the unspeakable. This insight acts as a gateway to the necessary and continual processes of testimony that generate a creaturely subjectivity. As organic, progressive and unified versions of testimony collapse, Beckett conveys subjects exposed to mechanical rigidity, incessant enunciation and ruinous ambivalence. The final point is that fiction itself figures as a mode of testimony, deferring the subject's complete identification but allowing Beckett's author-narrators to recognize the identity dilemma that constitutes the partial subjectivity of the creature.

The second chapter studies more explicit assertions of power between Beckett's 'pseudo-couples' to explicate processes of identification through alterity. I underline how the influence of an absent master provides a sense of objectivity for the creatures in *Watt* and *Waiting for Godot*, which preserves the possibility of meaning and identity, and grants a means of avoiding the subjectivity invested in failure, but ultimately give rise to a related creaturely subjectivity immersed in melancholy. One of the dominant claims of this chapter is that the necessary others in Beckett have a contextual equivalent in the Nazis' persecution of the Jews, and that the biopolitical power that enforces these identity positions reveals the unsettling proximity with the nonhuman animal. In the governance of space and care, sovereign masters decide who is human and what is inhuman, and this is reflected as Beckett's subaltern creatures are subjugated and take the place of animals. The dynamics of master–servant relationships, however, mean that the two roles are contracted to one another and this traces a creaturely tension between others. The attempt to impose a vulnerable, subhuman status invariably backfires on the master to expose them as equally dependent on the servant.

Chapter 3 revisits Beckett's art of failure to examine how humour and laughter act as emergency measures at the limits of language to respond to and recommence the possibility of speaking the impossible. I contend that Beckett's humour degrades the elevated sphere of human language and reason to the level of the body. In this way, his prose works evoke amusing textual performances and equally his physical humour on stage depends on words. In *Endgame* this convergence of language and the body enacts a tension that contributes to the creatures' suspended conditions, as the dialogue sustains their physical incarceration. This is a tragicomic predicament that extends to readers and spectators as Beckett's metanarrative techniques embroil the implied audience in the characters' static dynamics. More than this, Beckett's dark humour recognizes the comedy of this captivation so that laughter essentially reflects on and contributes to the enduring tragicomic complexion.

The fourth chapter on survival is concerned with an underlying spirit that drives Beckett's corpus and produces the insistent but onerous tone of his writing. Beckett negotiates diminishing creative opportunities to develop an aesthetic of survival that echoes the debased life that persists in a post-human world. With recourse to Santner's concept of creaturely 'undeadness', which describes an excess of life granted by the subject's investment in a repetition compulsion, I argue that Beckett's *Waiting for Godot* and *Endgame* exploit the vitality in iterability to evoke a 'still life' that simultaneously encompasses the stasis of sameness and the activity of difference. Finally, this focus on repetition applies to the spiral narrative structures of *Molloy* to illustrate that Beckett's creatures are essentially caught in a psychological performance of the past that sees them adhering to dead structures of meaning in the hope of reviving them.

1

Testimony:

Bearing witness to the event and self

In 1956, in a rare insight into his writing's relationship with the zeitgeist, Beckett said: 'My people seem to be falling to bits. [. . .] I think anyone nowadays who pays the slightest attention to his own experience finds it the experience of a non-knower, of a non-can-er' (quoted in Shenker 1979: 162). The act of bearing witness in Beckett's post-war work must negotiate the remnants of context and identity left in the wake of this ignorance and impotence. The contemporaneous conditions of testimony after the catastrophes of the Second World War and the Holocaust, 'nowadays' as Beckett puts it, are suffused with similar deficiencies in knowledge and ability. The traumas of these events destabilize the credible witness and subvert language's capacity to relate the experience adequately. The witness must therefore contend with absence and negation over detail and fact to bear witness to the tribulations of attesting without reliable information and lacking sound means of expression. Parallel to these testimonial obstacles, Beckett's writing contests the idea that a verbal or written account can apprehend historical and biographical events in a decisive way. He begins the task of imparting the obscured accounts of struggling narrators and, in doing so, confronts the challenge of giving voice to the voids that follow what cannot be repeated verbatim.

However, to complicate matters in Beckett, the kind of lucid statement in which Beckett acknowledges ignorance ('non-knower') and impotence ('non-can-er') as the conditions of experience does exercise the ability to point out inability. The recognition that witnesses cannot fully know or relate their own experiences at least grants the possibility of a disappointing but incontrovertible fact from the effort to bear witness to oneself, thus giving the witness a kind of perceptivity towards their deficiencies. Of course, the extreme implication of this devaluation of testimony is the disturbing suspicion that the witness was not there or a denial of the event itself. As such, testimony cannot rest on this inability to capture the experience. It must act out its ignorance and impotence, rather than simply absorb incapacity as knowledge. The complete absence of testimony, while indicating the fact that the event exceeds transmission, would allow the significance of that fact to fade away. It is the obligation to keep trying that underlines the catastrophe's capacity to elude testimony and, paradoxically, bears witness to the magnitude of the event.

An echo of this engagement with the unspeakable occurs in Beckett's post-war writing in which he 'pays attention' to the experience of impossibility, concentrating on an art of failure that marks a significant re-direction in his writing practice after 1945. In his oft-quoted dialogues with art historian Georges Duthuit, first published in 1949, Beckett claimed that the Dutch artist Bram van Velde was remarkably open to failure, that this artist wanted 'to make of this submission, this admission, this fidelity to failure, a new occasion, a new term of relation, and of the act which, unable to act, obliged to act, he makes, an expressive act, even if only of itself, of its impossibility, of its obligation' (Beckett 1983: 145). Beckett identifies a combination of inadequacy and continuation, hopelessness and responsibility that describes art as an interminable bind. The repetition of the word 'act', for instance, indicates an imperative to perform that must be honoured. These observations on failure resound in the fallible author-narrators of Beckett's subsequent work and serve to intimate the testimonial value of his art in the post-Holocaust context.

In committing to the onerous fidelity to failure, Beckett not only adumbrates the impossibility of bearing witness but also generates a distinctive type of subjectivity. Beckett was accustomed to the wretchedness of expressive acts as he composed and reworked his material. In a letter to Pamela Mitchell, Beckett wrote: 'I am absurdly and stupidly the creature of my books and *L'Innommable* is more responsible for my current plight than all the other good reasons put together' (2011: 27). Beckett evokes a creaturely subjectivity through the martyrdom in the writing of failure. He is a kind of suffering figure produced by the conditions of obligation. In his reflections on the creative process, referring specifically to his 1953 French text *L'Innommable*, Beckett shows that the travails of testimony and elusiveness of the traumatic event also apply to authorial and autobiographical terrain. As with his people 'falling to bits', Beckett includes himself in a creaturely category of being that is worn down by insistent acts. But whereas Beckett's creatures are doomed to failure owing to their deficiencies as author-narrators, Beckett's own creatureliness is connected to the intention to produce impotence, to 'fail better' as he puts it in the 1983 minimalist text *Worstward Ho* (C, 81). The characteristics of this creaturely dynamic, including the tension between making and being made by something, the urgency and flux of dehumanizing imperatives, and the transgression of typical notions of artistic competence, are the foundations of Beckettian testimony.

This chapter examines the expressive difficulties that Beckett embraces through the author-narrators in his trilogy of novels *Molloy*, *Malone Dies* and *The Unnamable* to unearth a historically significant engagement with the challenges facing acts of witnessing and bearing witness. Following an exposition of Beckett's increasing subjection to the artistic deadlock between need and failure after 1945, the first section draws parallels between the crisis of communication inflicted by the Holocaust, frequently expressed by the metonym 'Auschwitz', and Beckett's artistic engagement with ignorance and impotence. With recourse to Walter Benjamin's notion of the 'sovereign as creature', I argue that an alternative brand of '(in)sovereign' testimony emerges in Beckett's work. This authenticity without authority vouches for a degree of ineffability within experience that is not unique to the psychosomatic trauma of disaster, but rather exists within the necessary fracture between the event and act of relation that constitutes testimony.

Since the ability to apprehend and depict events is largely wanting for Beckett's author-narrators, the principle of continuation becomes paramount. The ensuing inorganic forms and mechanical methods of storytelling not only question the agency and humanity of Beckett's narrators, they also contribute to the contingent, creaturely aspect of narrative practice itself. Beckett subverts the view that narration is a particularly human mode of meaning and indicative of humanistic enlightenment through reason, through the very rigidity of logical processes, particularly when conducted under the duress of obligation. The broken image of the human leads into the concept of 'ruin', or an identity in disorder, which signals a simultaneous possession and dispossession of self that parallels the division between a founding voice and its figments in Beckett's prose. Consequently, the concluding section concentrates on the fiction of testimony, which also implies the testimony of fiction, to discern the extent to which Beckett's narrators produce valuable accounts due to, rather than despite, their difficulties with epistemology and communication.

'Impossibility of expressing': Art of failure and lacuna of testimony

Although Beckett's post-war writing never directly refers to the events of recent history in an effort to represent them artistically, it is impossible that his own experiences and the general conditions of the day had no bearing on his work after 1945. Knowlson's biography pays testament to the profound influence of the wartime period on Beckett, asserting that 'It is difficult to imagine him writing the stories, novels and plays that he produced in the creative maelstrom of the immediate post-war period without the experiences of those five years' (1997: 351). Beckett himself specified a moment in the wake of the war, only months after Victory in Europe Day, as a point of personal enlightenment that changed his thoughts on writing or, to use Beckett's words, either a 'revelation' (quoted in Shainberg 1987: 106) or 'the turning-point, at last' (quoted in Lake 1984: 48). Yet Knowlson is quick to remind readers that understanding the post-war change as 'THE revelation' is in danger of obscuring the ground that was prepared by other important episodes previously in Beckett's life (Knowlson 1997: 353). Indeed, the decisiveness of this post-war watershed is somewhat muddled as Beckett was already articulating a 'literature of the non-word' as early as 1937 in the 'German' letter to Axel Kaun (2009e: 520). The fact remains, however, that his immediate post-war writing is markedly different from the handful of texts written before 1938 and it would be misleading to perceive the anomalous war years as a regular concentric ring of growth in the cross-section of Beckett's personal and artistic history. In short, Beckett could not have responded to the catastrophes in his inimitable style without the many influential relationships and life experiences prior, but the war years are certainly an outstanding period of his life that coincides with an artistic development that burgeoned after the Holocaust.

Beckett's earlier comments to Kaun in 1937 foresee a literary approach that would betray the inadequacy of representational art and take advantage of the weakness of words, '[t]o drill one hole after another into it until that which lurks behind it, be it something or nothing, starts seeping through' (2009e: 518). Beckett wants to impugn and assault language to discover the real substance or void behind, and as several Beckett scholars have explicated, chiefly Matthew Feldman, it is likely that a synthesis of Arthur Schopenhauer's and Fritz Mauthner's writings provided Beckett with some of the fillip needed to practise these sentiments in his creative writing.[1] Although Beckett's sustained engagement with related ideas comes to fruition much later, we know from his letters that he studied Schopenhauer's philosophy in 1930 and would have encountered the German philosopher's treatise on representation as a subjective illusion that conceals the objectivity of 'will' (Beckett 2009e: 33). Borrowing from the ancient Hindu Upanishads, Schopenhauer describes representation in *The World as Will and Representation* as 'Maya, the veil of deception, which covers the eyes of mortals' (1969: 8). Beckett conveys a comparable occluded separation in his letter, although he concentrates on language as the predominant obstacle to either the noumena or oblivion hidden behind, particularly the 'terrifyingly arbitrary materiality of the word surface' (2009e: 518). He therefore converses with Mauthner's *Critique of Language* and the supposition that 'he must try to redeem the world from the tyranny of language' (Mauthner quoted in Ben-Zvi 1980: 187). For both, language offers a pale imitation of reality and is unfit for faithful communication yet it dominates human cognition and memory. Beckett shares Mauthner's disdain for language and hazards an approach to its negation: 'At first it can only be a matter of somehow inventing a method of verbally demonstrating this scornful attitude vis-à-vis the word. In this dissonance of instrument and usage perhaps one will already be able to sense a whispering of the end-music or of the silence underlying all' (2009e: 519). Beckett postulates a way of using language to abuse language, which is the first inkling of his future art of failure.

Crucially, there is no specificity to the proposed whisper of objectivity 'underlying all'. Through the 'mask' of language lies the nondescript, non-representational echelon that is impersonal and ahistorical. However, Beckett's use of *darzustellen* (represent) and *höhnische* (scornful) in the German letter retains the impression of an authorial application of words that conflicts with the impartiality behind words. The translation of *wörtlich darzustellen* as 'verbal demonstration' in the published volume of letters is more sympathetic to Beckett's later performativity, whereas the 'representation literally' of this mocking perspective towards language would surely preclude the perforation or dissolution of language to an extent, so that one would not see through it as much as reterritorialize language with the ability to deride. Without reaching for the Joycean 'apotheosis of the word' as such, it seems Beckett keeps faith in literature as the forum where language can implode and therefore inscribes a further level of subjective intention into the proposed 'literature of the non-word'. Since Beckett's early formation of this aesthetic sensibility leans on the literary agency to manipulate words in order to disclose the non-word, it seems language attacks itself in a schizophrenic, self-abasing fashion, and can therefore imply a literary meta-intention in which the perverted alter ego of language bores through the limits of its orthodox self.

Beckett was evidently contemplating literature's need for a new direction before the Second World War and the Holocaust. Before he could put it into practice, world affairs ensured a hiatus in his writing. In the aftermath of the war, the damage done to epistemological and expressive models not only vindicated the speculative germs of Beckett's 'literature of the non-word', it also galvanized his instigation of an 'art of failure' that emerged fully after his 'revelation', when Beckett became more attuned to the active, verbal quality of inadequacy. Still, it is notable that in his division of 'instruments' and 'usage' in the German letter, Beckett already identifies the lack of harmony between the means and the ends that is fundamental to a negative form of testimony accentuated massively after the Holocaust, namely the act of bearing witness that can only generate the emptiness of language through the schism between the witness's voice and the event. Owing to the effort to adequately represent events and experiences through words, it can be inferred that testimony normally assumes a positive approach to language compared with the Beckettian impetus to undo. Nevertheless, what can be described as two forms of truth through deposition – testimony's *how it was* through language and Beckett's *how it is* behind the untruth of language – amount to the same thing, as the German letter shows that attempts to deconstruct language must also fall back on attempts to employ language, so to speak, if only to interrogate itself. Beckett gains clarity on this dynamic after the war and properly enlists the inevitable attempt to use language when he shifts to first person author-narrators, thereby transferring the primary struggles with language to storytelling creatures who consider the 'the kind of light that should be brought to bear and the most effective means of doing so' (*T*, 86). With recourse to his creatures' virtually inexhaustible obedience to language despite their resignation to its limitations, Beckett can mitigate the scornful intent behind literary forms that use language to abuse it. It is through Beckett's creatures and the disappointment inherent to their tenacious pattern of attempt and failure that Beckett can expose the inevitable fault lines of testimony and generate the silence that accompanies language.

After the rebuilding effort at Saint-Lô, Beckett went back to Foxrock for a short period and experienced a revelatory change in his mindset. He later recalled the moment in conversation with Charles Juliet:

> Up to that point, I had thought I could rely on knowledge. That I had to equip myself intellectually. That day, it all collapsed. [. . .] Yes, up to 1946 I tried to learn as much as possible in order to try and have some degree of power over things. Then I realised that I was following the wrong path. But perhaps all paths are wrong. Still, you have to find the wrong path that suits you best (Juliet 2009: 25, 31–2).

The exact wording of Beckett's response lacks authority since Juliet reconstructed the conversations from recollection. Nonetheless, Juliet's perception of Beckett's sentiments is insightful, as it appears that Beckett now frames his discussion of literature as a personal enterprise, expressed in negative terms and with shades of its

interminability. Beckett is apparently aware of his previous errors
and the ubiquity of unsuitable ways altogether, moving from an
incisive negation of the mask of language to the inexhaustible
continuity of an endeavour condemned to failure. As with Beckett's
use of 'provisional' under erasure in 'The Capital of the Ruins',
'wrong' is not entirely the word it was when Beckett may only have
wrong paths available to him. Even so, in order for something to be
amiss there must be at least the idea of the correct and successful,
and Beckett leaves open an unattainable 'right' path in the typically
Beckettian word 'perhaps', in the implied opposite of 'wrong' and in
the avatar 'suitable wrong path'. The gist of Beckett's comment
therefore includes a sense of temporary dissatisfaction that is
curiously persistent through a cycle of attempt and inevitable
failure, regardless of whether in pursuit of the right way or the right
kind of wrong way. This subtle but significant adjustment in
Beckett's approach indicates that language is unable to finally
impart the non-word, as its deconstruction must be performative in
nature; the silence must be continually said, not ultimately received.
If Beckett's 1937 letter was largely intent upon cutting through
language caustically to access the 'end-music or silence' beyond the
specificity of representation, the post-war revelation reaffirms that
vestiges of canonical models and linguistic efficacy may drive a
protracted engagement with ignorance and impotence.

Beckett is alive to the liminality of his artistic enterprise as he
continues to articulate this new direction in his correspondence
with Georges Duthuit between August 1948 and April 1951. In this
exchange, Beckett reveals the ambition for an absolutely inexpressive
art that Duthuit finds incredulous. The abstract style of Bram van
Velde's paintings encourages Beckett in this respect, as it purportedly
borders on what Beckett labels 'non-relation': art discrete from all
connections and relationships between the 'artist and the outside
world', the 'I and non-I', subject and object, and the inner plurality
of the self (2011: 138, 139, 140). Indeed, Beckett feels an affinity
with the manner in which the painter exhibits 'the same stuckness'
on the edge of this dissociation from personal, social and historical
material (2011: 129). However, as much as van Velde comes close
to painting the absence of relation, Beckett also finds the Dutchman
resuming 'the beauty of attempt and failure', rather than the
painterly equivalent of the 'calm language of the no' that besets
Beckett (2011: 130, 98). The extremity of this latter dissenting

approach is not lost on Beckett and he clearly still shares in Duthuit's appreciation of van Velde's work when he writes: 'I can hear you say that these are highly successful failures' (2011: 130). It is notable too that Beckett is not appraising van Velde with received terms when he refers to failure, which is imbued with the idiosyncratic sense of being too successful by conventional standards and thereby failing to completely fail. On the contrary, Beckett is keen to praise the extent to which artists turn away from pursuing the old achievements of expression and representation, in a gesture he calls the 'grand refusal': 'it is the *gran rifiuto* that interests me, not the heroic wrigglings' (2011: 140). Rather than recoil from the vanguard after tradition and be drawn back into the compromises of relational art, the 'great adventure' for Beckett involves a complete disregard of the outside of art and an unflinching openness to failure, without past successes.

In instances where Beckett articulates his grand refusal, however, the presence of imperatives, worth and utility creeps back into the schema, like leftovers from the forms he is rejecting. For instance, when Beckett reflects on Duthuit's *Les Fauves* (the wild beasts) (1949) and the Frenchman's objection to Italian art, he articulates the unedited version of his well-known 'nothing to express' statement included in 'Three Dialogues'. Beckett addresses formalism's maximum of possibility and realism's maximum of truth, after declaring an interest in 'what lies behind the two attitudes'. On one side, Beckett writes, is 'the passion of the achievable, in which the noblest researches are vitiated by the need to extend its limits' and on the other is 'respect for the impossible that we are, impossible living creatures', unable to capture time or space (2011: 156). Far from siding with either the invention of formalism or the engagement of realism though, Beckett wants to access the condition of failure inherent to them both, which effectively penetrates and conflates the two attitudes. Behind each is 'painting quite simply a destiny, which is to paint, where there is nothing to paint, nothing to paint with, and without knowing how to paint, and without wanting to paint, and all this in a way that something comes out of it' (Beckett 2011: 156). Beckett's avowal of disinterest discloses the contradiction of his grand refusal. He injects an imperative tone through 'quite simply a destiny', before voicing a constrained artistic dilemma that combines a sense of impossibility, in the artist's pointless, ill-equipped and apathetic predicament, with the necessity of possibility, in the image of a product ('something') from the process. Although Beckett declines to chase the maximums of expression, representation and aestheticism, he nevertheless inherits traces of their productive agendas, in the strange success and efficacy of neutrality and inability: 'Not to have to express oneself, nor get involved with whatever kind of maximum, in one's numberless, valueless, achievementless world; that is a game worth trying, all the same, a necessity worth trying, and one which will never work, if that works' (2011: 103). The paradox of Beckett's new direction emerges in conceiving of necessary actions and valuable functions in relation to an indifference to the expression of self, representation of the world or compositional significations alone.

Beckett's concurrent strategies of refusal and imperative attest to a transitional tension. The artist simultaneously negotiates the residue of accepted conventions, autonomy and engagement included, and the 'stuckness' of an obligation to create without the means or inclination to create, which 'expresses the impossibility of expressing anything' (2011: 170). Since Beckett's anti-heroic twitchings towards failure cannot decisively shake off the memory of 'forms that do not easily let go', he, like van Velde, remains in something of an intermediate position, not only racked by his own feelings of imperative and inability, but also encumbered with the 'wrong' forms (2011: 129). As with life's gradual journey into death, Beckett's artistic endeavour 'will be boundary work, passage work, in which as a result the old rubbish can still be of some use, while the dying is going on' (2011: 132). The 'old rubbish' of the past that Beckett initially derided in a scornful attitude now lingers on the margins of his own borderline art, locked in the dialectic of past convention and future creativity. Therefore, he will not be exempt from at least eliciting the 'passion of the achievable' or getting 'caught up somewhere' in the 'unutterable' time and space of 'impossible living creatures', without determinedly partaking exactly in what he deems a futile investment in dying forms: 'What all that amounts to is the wish to save a form of expression which is not viable. To want it to be, to work at making it be, to give it the appearance of being, is to fall back into the same old plethora, the same old play-acting' (Beckett 2011: 156, 98, 166). As Beckett frequently reiterates the urge to avoid outmoded forms of expression in his letters to Duthuit, he also demonstrates the conditions of a process, in which a pervasive debt to the 'same old' attends each steps towards his goal. When he distances even his own notions and lexicon of failure, for example, he cannot help continuing to employ them. Beckett claims 'I feel myself moving away from ideas of poverty and bareness' because '[t]hey are still superlatives' (2011: 195). He clearly wishes to escape this framework of deficiency, perhaps because it situates his work overtly in opposition to richness, fullness and success, which cultivates an unwanted lineage. All the same, 'collapse', 'weariness', 'weakness', 'poverty' and 'impotence' litter his subsequent letters (2011: 195), as if the most recent past has become habitual too.

Beckett's conflicted relationship with old successes and new failures, and with relation and non-relation, means he is not only a 'creature of habit'. He is also another type of 'impossible creature' because the constrictive condition of being created by the past while dreaming of autonomous acts of creation causes him to encounter the perpetually enacted irreconcilability of truth, possibility and failure. In an attempt to surpass relation, for example, Beckett embarks upon a negative strategy that cannot be entirely extricated from the value systems and contexts it negates. Anthony Uhlmann explains that 'rather than being divorced from context, Beckett developed an aesthetic strategy that worked through deliberate negation. [. . .] Beckett's works evoke the power of the contexts from which they emerge by outlining their absence' (2013: 2). Hence, Lois Gordon can describe *Waiting for Godot* vaguely as 'a product of the war' and Beckett's 'response to the complexity of human goodness and evil' (2013: 110). This strategy of outlining the absence of context to reveal the salient conditions of production is conducive to a reading of testimony, particularly after recent philosophy and critical theory on Holocaust testimony and the manner in which contexts exceed representation to leave a fundamental gap in deposition, or 'lacuna' as Giorgio Agamben theorizes in *Remnants of Auschwitz* (2002: 33). Rendering relational forms incomplete through the burdensome peddling of them is key to the contextual significance and creaturely dimension of Beckett's form. It is therefore productive to think of the absence of extra-literary referents not as an imperious erasure but as a necessary result of representation and expression in ruins, as the work of the ignorant and impotent creature that tries and fails. In effect, Beckett's sliver of non-relation is included as part of his creatures' stories, but only through their inability to positively capture what exceeds language, which is itself continually traced through the author-narrators' repeated attempts within Beckett's immediate post-war texts to relate meaningful accounts.

When representational and expressive writing is called to the stand to account for the events of the Holocaust, the demonstration of a form of narration that can only muster its inadequacy has confirmed importance. In his reading of Holocaust testimonies, Agamben extrapolates the impossibility of bearing witness from Primo Levi's accounts of his incarceration at Auschwitz. He discusses the limitations of the living speaking for the dead and questions how a survivor can testify for the ultimate experience of an extermination camp. The notion of a hiatus or lapse in the act of bearing witness emerges in his work, as testimony lacks the crucial experience and is formed *in absentia* of the true witness. Echoing Levi, Agamben affirms that '[t]he survivors speak in their stead, by proxy, as pseudo-witnesses' (2002: 34). Having endured the Holocaust, the *salvati*, the saved, stand beside the lacuna that the *sommersi*, the drowned, are submerged in, speaking on their behalf as the nearest representative, offering a contiguous but necessarily distant account. It follows that the death camps present an ineluctable problem for testimony since they throw the qualified witness into a state without reflection; the experience is not retainable because death is never part of the victim's knowledge. Agamben observes that 'here the value of testimony lies essentially in what it lacks, at its center it contains something that cannot be borne witness to and that discharges the survivors of authority' (2002: 34). Despite the risk of undermining the survivors' stories, Agamben proposes that the point at which the witnesses' accounts subside marks the threshold where the complete experience begins. This means the survivors can only testify to their alienation and give voice to their silence. As Laurence Simmons notes, the survivor is 'the witness who bears witness to the impossibility of bearing witness' (2007: 28).

Agamben does not advocate the impossibility of speaking, though, which would mean that the gaps in testimony are simply unexpressed, but rather that the missing experience of the camps remains through speaking. Fatalistic prisoners known as *Muselmänner* hold particular significance for Agamben as figures enduring a state of being bordering on human life and entering a mesmerized existence. The irony of the *Muselmann*'s experience as a being resigned to death is that while being subjected to the extreme destructive power of Auschwitz, the person is also stripped of the awareness required to testify to that human experience. In a cruel muting of testimony, not dissimilar to how the deceased's stories are silenced, the *Muselmänner* are reduced to what Levi describes as 'faceless presences', figures 'too empty to really suffer', 'too tired to understand' and 'on whose face and whose eyes not a trace of thought is to be seen' (1979: 96). These anonymous, vacuous shells are dispossessed of their individual stories, numb to their own conditions and unable to account for their on-going existence on death row. Agamben is drawn to the fact that the *Muselmann* is wholly constituted by its own nescience, which means the *Muselmann* lives through what the survivors objectify in the aftermath: the impossibility of bearing witness due to not really being there.

However, in several first-hand accounts, the *Muselmänner* do reflect on and attest to their descent in a kind of double impossibility – living through the impossibility of bearing witness and then bearing witness to the impossibility of bearing witness. In David Matzner's Holocaust account entitled *The Muselmann* (1994), the author articulates his return from imminent death. Matzner writes 'I became a *Muselmann* – camp slang for someone whose days, because of deteriorating physical or mental condition, were known to be numbered' (1994: 56). As opposed to the given meaning, as a state without self-consciousness and thus a condition to be diagnosed only by an onlooker, Matzner's usage suggests an interim on the fringe of life and death that can be resolved either way and reflected upon. In such cases, Agamben takes the claim 'I was a *Muselmann*' as an aphorism for the paradox in testimony: 'I, who speak, was a *Muselmann*, that is, the one who cannot in any sense speak' (2002: 165). This kind of impossible account of a shrouded experience and its severance with the self in the present is intriguing to Beckett after the war, given that, in 1948, he points out the cry common to those in purgatory in Dante's epic poetry: 'Io fui' (I was) (2011: 92). In a reversal of the testifying *Muselmann*, like Matzner, who accounts for a period when he was not altogether present and therefore bespeaks the loss of himself, the aporetic phrase 'I was' means the subject in the present pours over its own absence. The point is that their testimonies amount to an avowal of incapacity, which, as Daniel Katz affirms of the deictic 'I' in Beckett's trilogy, 'troubles the already uncertain status of subjective assertions, hovering between constatation and performative' (1999: 21). For figures not present at their own experience but attempting to tell the tale regardless, the performance of testimony envelops a necessary futility that, in its persistent failure, accounts for the one who cannot speak and that which cannot be spoken.

It is this performance of unspeakability that gives Beckett's obligation to failure testimonial significance. The 'unintelligible, unchallengeable need' (Beckett 2011: 141) to speak despite the inability to communicate positively is the transferrable element and historical parallel between Beckett's writing and Holocaust testimony. Furthermore, in terms of the dislocation from event and self, an obscure ontological status and a curious claim to testimony, Agamben's theorization of the *Muselmann* bears comparison with Beckett's creatures. Beckett presents figures that also drift into detached mental spaces and become oblivious to the external world, yet they do return to their physical conditions intermittently to recognize their plight. In effect, Beckett's creatures vacillate between the absent *Muselmann* that Levi describes and the self-reflective *Muselmann* that Matzner describes. They are withdrawn, etiolated creatures that also recognize the lack of objectivism or self-presence that would positively vouch for their experience.

As with the paradoxical testimony of the *Muselmann*, Beckett's creatures negotiate a fundamental absence that causes the concomitant inability to speak and imperative to speak. Beckett's *The End* (1954) is the first of four *nouvelles* written in the mid-1940s. It follows an itinerant protagonist as he tramps from the city to a seaside cave to a dilapidated rural cabin. In a fugue state he gravitates towards the periphery of society, as though intuitively searching for a rightful home. Towards the end of the story, the narrator offers this assessment of his presence in the world: 'Normally I didn't see a great deal. I didn't hear a great deal either. I didn't pay attention. Strictly speaking I wasn't there. Strictly speaking I wasn't anywhere' (*FN*, 51). The narrator's sensory faculties are disengaged, leaving him virtually blind and deaf to his surroundings. This detachment from the external setting means he is absent, and though the narrator at least recognizes that a 'there' exists, at this point he is merely a reflection on his emptiness. Shortly after this insight, a political speaker in the street labels the narrator a 'living corpse' (*FN*, 52). Although the context for Beckett's tale is very different, this depiction of a zombie-like creature is clearly reminiscent of the *Muselmann*'s automatic, desensitized existence. Both are physically present, yet their empirical consciousness has failed so that they are effectively removed from the environment. At the same time, Beckett's narrator remains aware of his radical lack of presence, thereby articulating the inability to speak as a conscious witness.

The paradoxical articulation of absence recurs in Beckett's play *Endgame* (*E* [1957] 2006a). The two protagonists, the blind master Hamm and lame servant Clov, are bunkered in a bare grey room where they pass time with jaundiced prattle. In the background, Hamm's parents Nagg and Nell peer out of trashcans, beg for food and reminisce about better times. These figures appear to inhabit a post-apocalyptic world, with Hamm declaring, 'Outside of here it's death' (*E*, 9). When Clov goes to survey the crepuscular view from the window, Hamm reflects on his absence from the former world and ignorance of the implied catastrophe:

Hamm   Do you know what it is?

Clov   (*as before*) Mmm.

Hamm   I was never there. (*Pause.*) Clov!

Clov   (*turning towards Hamm, exasperated*) What is it?

Hamm   I was never there.

Clov   Lucky for you.

He looks out of window.

Hamm   Absent, always. It all happened without me. I don't know what's happened (*E*, 44).

Hamm says 'I was never there', that he was not strictly present in the world at the time. He has no knowledge of the event since the ambiguous 'happening' transpired without his conscious attendance. After this exchange, Hamm goes on to ask Clov what has happened, but the servant is also nonplussed, repeating the Beckettian refrain 'I don't know.' As with Agamben's vision of the *Muselmann*, the nature of the experience appears to have rendered the witnesses ignorant. Therefore, the implied catastrophe resides in the ellipsis; it is sustained in the inability to relate exactly what has occurred. In an echo of the rhetorical technique 'occultatio', in which the speaker draws attention to what he will not explicitly discuss, the incipient event of *Endgame* casts a shadow over the entire play. Although the characters' unawareness enforces an interdiction on the catastrophe, its absence is felt through the circumlocution that Hamm and Clov must necessarily conduct.

Absence and deficient memory also destroy the accuracy of relayed experiences in Beckett's later play *Footfalls* (*K* [1976] 2009f). This play centres on the character May pacing a corridor as she converses with a disembodied female voice. Their conversation makes it known that May nursed her mother during ill health, before the disembodied voice begins to commentate on May's movements. In the 'sequel' (*K*, 112), May relates a discussion between the mother Mrs Winter and daughter Amy, in which the former is shown to confuse the events of the past. The elderly lady is adamant that Amy was at Evensong, but the daughter denies it, claiming 'I observed nothing of any kind, strange or otherwise. I saw nothing, heard nothing, of any kind. I was not there' (*K*, 113). When addressing this part of the play, it is common to refer to the phrase 'not properly born' that Beckett derived from his attendance at a Karl Jung lecture in London in the 1920s (Juliet 2009: 13). In this emphasis on an existence over a real life, Beckett implies the creature of authorial creation, a constructed figment rather than an organically born being. Yet Beckett's comment to the actress Billie Whitelaw, 'Let's just say you're not all there' (Beckett quoted in Kalb 1989: 235), also suggests a mentally and physically diaphanous subject, especially in the idiomatic sense of mental incompetence, which lends the play significance in the context of obstacles to testimony. Despite Mrs Winter insisting that 'I heard you distinctly' (*K*, 113), the impression is that the elderly lady is suffering from delusions and that her point of view is no longer reliable. As with several of Beckett's characters, Mrs Winter's deterioration into misremembering causes the act of bearing witness to be tantamount to invention since she is without the stable psychological foundation to trust her experiences and commit sound impressions to memory. The play is doubly equivocal in that the entire account comes from May, the 'anagrammatical other' of Amy (Ackerley and Gontarski 2004: 202), which suggests that these stories implicate the main character but are projected as discrete events.

When read literally, these three absences in Beckett's work insist that there is no person at the event; people were not physically in attendance. It is a prevalent point in the relationship between Beckett's work and the historical context of testimony in that it foregrounds the difference between actual absence and psychological detachment. Beckett himself was not a Holocaust survivor, but a secondary witness on the periphery of the event, and therefore absent in a real way. In contrast to this distinction, the absence in 'I was not there' can mean that Beckett's creatures experience a fundamental gap in their memories due to the inability to apprehend or digest events. Peter Boxall argues that this frail type of memory in Beckett's work befits a post-Holocaust world:

> It is as if the modernist forms of recovery, the Proustian Madeleine, the Joycean epiphany, are not adequate to the kinds of witnessing that are demanded by the Holocaust. It is in Beckett's writing, in Beckett's adaptation of the modernist forms that he inherited from Joyce and from Proust as well as from (a protomodernist) Kleist, that he develops a form that can simultaneously remember and forget, that can at once preserve and annihilate (2009: 127).

Beckett's narrator-authors are denied the essence, revelation or transcendence that Proust, Joyce and Kleist afford. There is no release from doubt or moment of clarity to grasp the crux of past experiences. In terms of the Holocaust's demands on testimony and forms of recovery, however, the Beckettian memory suggests a form of remembrance in which the declared truth is less valid than the on-going process of remembering and failing to remember. The psychological states of Beckett's creatures means they are constantly outlining the lacuna of testimony that is central to Agamben's subsequent model of bearing witness.

The extent of the absence from event and self that paradoxically preserves and undermines testimony in Beckett is such that 'his work has become, or is becoming, a cipher for unspeakability *within the field of Holocaust studies itself*' (italics in original) (Jones 2011: 3). It is true that, as an author associated with meaninglessness, Beckett's work has been appropriated to figure as the voice of testimony in the specific context of the Holocaust. As David Jones' *Samuel Beckett and Testimony* demonstrates, current scholarly discourse is wary of attributing the mechanics of unspeakability solely to the Holocaust context, preferring instead to present the lack of historical or biographical foundations as a constitutive point of Beckett's testimony. My own work accepts the fact that testimony in Beckett is not concerned with explicitly representing historical contexts, but that fact does not make the contexts for Beckett's testimony irrelevant. The peculiarity of theory on Holocaust testimony means that blindness, deafness and muteness to the event are valuable forms of bearing witness. It is – self-evidently – not the case that every contemporaneous literary text that is not ostensibly about the Holocaust is, by virtue of its silence, related to Holocaust testimony. Beckett, however, is clearly compelled to perform the highest fidelity to failure, and it is his outstanding commitment to such a restrictive project that coincides with post-Holocaust unspeakability more concretely, making his work historically significant though not contextually bound. While the 'shearing-off of enunciation from context' (Jones 2011: 20) gives us an insight into Beckett's engagement with lacunae as the fundamental components of testimony in general, it is the extremity of this severance that actually parallels the violent dislocation of account from event that Holocaust testimony magnifies. Despite the difficulties in attesting to the Holocaust, then, Beckett is unable to avoid his work's affinity with testimony after Auschwitz.

The accounts that Beckett's narrators proffer engage with the aporia of Holocaust testimony in the way that, in Agamben's reading, the Holocaust survivors are fundamentally compelled to 'pronounce the unpronounceable' or the manner in which the *Muselmann* vouches for the 'unexperienced experience' of death (Blanchot 1986: 7, 72). Both scenarios comprise an inherent absence that denies the witnesses the ability to attest for themselves finally, and compels them to expose the spaces between object and subject that occur in testimony. The narrators in Beckett's work cannot document articles as proof or retain impressions beyond doubt since they are open to the possibility that their story, their communicable existence, could consist in the interminable struggle to stamp their authority on events that essentially elude them. That is, they are condemned to an autobiographical mission that is beyond them experientially at first and then expressively.

Fallibility and dissociation

The inability to account for oneself through reasoned discourse encloses dehumanizing elements, both in the way it devalues esteemed human properties and renders the substance of human life immediate as epistemic truth evaporates from representation. In turn, these dynamics make us aware of two inhuman components of testimony: how lived life is estranged and escapes attempts to account for it, and how testimony as a form is divested of humanistic prestige as a consequence. It is possible to join Kari Weil at this point in aligning trauma and animal studies in the way '[b]oth raise questions about how one can give testimony to an experience that cannot be spoken or that may be distorted by speaking it' (2010: 9). Admittedly, Beckett is not primarily concerned with detailing specific traumas or the lives of animals, but the ineffable nature of traumatic and animal experiences comes into contact with the necessity and inefficacy of bearing witness in Beckett's work. Indeed, the creaturely substrate of life, manifesting from destabilized human and nonhuman animal distinctions, is noticeable in the serfdom to a fragile language that cannot capture experience and the resulting precariousness of the human status in Beckett, where the species identity is 'that of the tight-rope over which we sprawl' (Beckett 2011: 117) in the wake of normative models of knowledge and expression. A shared point of creatureliness for testimony and the subject, then, is the contingent and on-going nature of their significations, or what the German-Jewish philosopher Franz Rosenzweig labels the 'everlastingly creature' as a 'continuously subjected subjectivity', which helps to explain the lack of a secure presence in the phrase 'I was not there' (1971: 120). This dynamism forms a backdrop to the ways Beckett's narrators evoke the obstacles to testimony and effectively bear witness to the impossibility of bearing witness, which applies to realities more ranging than human being alone. They are unable to offer a positive testimony because they are subject to ruptures immanent to the nature of experience and transmission of knowledge. In their sustained efforts to bear witness to themselves through a 'farrago of silence and words' (Beckett 2010b, *TN*, 27) Beckett's creatures must essentially trace the impassable aperture of their life stories to offer an alternative form of testimony that gives voice to the unspeakable.

Raul Hilberg uses the phrase 'I was not there' as the title of his 1987 paper on the ways in which, for survivors, secondary and postmemory witnesses alike, the catastrophe renders language naive. He highlights the inadequacy of literary and plastic arts, announcing 'the Holocaust has caught us unprepared. Its unprecedentedness and, above all, unexpectedness, necessitates the use of words or materials that were never designed for depictions of what happened here' (Hilberg 1988: 21). Hilberg asserts the shocking nature of the event has exposed weaknesses in the articles of representation. Majorie Perloff finds a similar inadequacy in words in her essay on Beckett's engagement with the wartime context. She writes: 'To use words like *war*, *Vichy*, *Resistance*, *Auschwitz*, *atom bomb* would inevitably be to short-circuit the complexity of the experiences in question' (2005: 99). Hilberg and Perloff suggest that language is too crude to do justice to the singularity of experience. Words malfunction under the strain of honouring intricacies that exceed their capacity.

Despite the inappropriateness of language, Hilberg notes that there are still 'rules' that failing writers must heed, one of which is 'silence'. The paradox of the Holocaust, he avers, is that it plunges both the deceased and surviving victims into reticence, and yet testimony must break this silence in order to recognize it. Hilberg remarks 'there cannot be silence without speech. Silence can only be introduced between words, some times with words' (1988: 23). The acts of speaking and writing are therefore crucial in disclosing the fact that, although this is an event that language cannot communicate, only the effort to testify will reveal the silencing effect of the Holocaust. It is necessary to explore the protracted struggle to bear witness in order to underline how the event can exceed testimony and, at the same time, reveal itself in the all-important spaces and silences of failure.

With the legacy of flawed empirical encounters and epistemological uncertainty, Beckett's narrators find it difficult to settle on an accurate reconstruction of the event as it happened or offer a commentary of life as it is presently unfolding. The trilogy of novels that Beckett produced during a prolific four-year spell after the war is his principal foray into a mode of narration deprived of the authority to assert the truth. In *Molloy* and *Malone Dies*, the title characters are storytellers but, whereas Molloy undertakes an autobiographical project that stipulates he apprehend and reproduce the chain of events he experienced, Malone attempts to shirk this responsibility in favour of devising narratives that act as a supposed distraction from self-reflection. The two texts offer differing responses to the authorial role and autobiography, but essentially display similar faults that serve to obscure their narratives and subvert the author as a consolidating agent.

In part one of *Molloy*, the narrator writes in his mother's room about the journey he takes to find her. Without saying as much, Molloy is a paid writer, selling his stories to a man who comes to collect the pages. He says, 'Yes, I work now, a little like I used to, except that I don't know how to work any more' (*T*, 7). Molloy reveals that he is returning to a previous vocation, apparently after a hiatus, and that he is unable to carry out his duties as before. Molloy's inability to work shows in the resulting interior monologue, with its tenebrous view and digressive texture. For example, Molloy witnesses the moon through a window, but his attempt to describe its movement only leads to convoluted hypotheses:

> Two bars divided it in three segments, of which the middle remained constant, while little by little the right gained what the left lost. For the moon was moving from left to right, or the room was moving from right to left, or both together perhaps, or both were moving from left to right, but the room not so fast as the moon, or from right to left, but the moon not so fast as the room. But can one speak of right and left in such circumstances? That movements of an extreme complexity were taking place seemed certain, and yet what a simple thing it seemed [. . .]. How difficult it is to speak of the moon and not lose one's head, the witless moon (*T*, 39).

The opening sentence of the passage offers a rather lucid account of the shifting triptych that the window frame and the moon create. After the first use of the conjunction 'or', however, Molloy introduces a series of further alternatives that turn his attempt at accuracy into an unwieldy language game. Molloy repeats and inverts the words 'left' and 'right' to produce a semantic satiation effect in which the words appear to lose their function in plotting the imagined space. The simple slant rhyme 'moon-room' also draws attention to the aural patterns in the passage to distract from the movements discussed. The 'simple thing' thus spirals into a complicated list of possibilities owing to Molloy's determination to understand his situation. When the 'complexity' of the scene first appears to dawn on him, even this concession includes the contradictory phrase 'seemed certain' to undermine its resolution. It is evident that Molloy is compelled to talk about things that elude him in both comprehension and expression.

Molloy's unreliability is compounded when he realizes that he witnessed a crescent moon the night before. His answer to this anomaly stretches the suspension of disbelief to breaking point: 'here I had to do with two moons, as far from the new as from the full and so alike in outline that the naked eye could hardly tell between them, and that whatever was at variance with these hypotheses was so much smoke and delusion' (T, 42). Molloy privileges the more radical solution of two moons in order to dispel other possibilities as mere fallacy. The consequence is that the reader must accept that Molloy resides in an unearthly world or, more likely, that he confuses the time period of these sightings. Molloy's inability to assign memories to particular days is detrimental to the veracity of his story and reduces it to conjecture.

Beckett's focus on fallible perspectives also impacts the narration in the following text of the trilogy, *Malone Dies*. Malone is a bed-stricken figure planning to use stories as a game to occupy his dying days. He intends to describe the present state; tell tales about a man and a woman, an animal, and a stone; and finally draw up an inventory. The story that Malone produces follows a 'precocious' boy named Sapo, his love of nature, his 'poor and sickly' parents as they deliberate their son's future and his encounter with a farming family called the Lamberts (T, 187). Malone chooses to refer to the adult Sapo as Macmann and relates how his character ends up in an asylum, has a relationship with an elderly nurse called Moll and is then under the charge of Lemuel. Malone's narration begins to blur his present situation with the fictional tale, but in a more obvious passage of self-reflection, he wishes to understand the relationship between reality and fiction:

All I want now is to make a last effort to understand, to begin to understand, how such creatures are possible. No, it is not a question of understanding. Of what then? I don't know. Here I go none the less, mistakenly. Night, storm and sorrow, and the catalepsies of the soul, this time I shall see that they are good. The last word is not yet said between me and – yes, the last word is said. Perhaps I simply want to hear it said again. Just once again. No, I want nothing (T, 199).

Malone embarks on a confabulation with himself, contradicting statements with two abrupt negatives and an affirmation. His attempts at assertion lead to denials, meaning that Malone's initial intent to express what he wants results in the disappointing 'I want nothing.' As he tries to decipher his desires, he must make do with ignorance, continuing with mistaken premises so that he conducts a rather nugatory activity. Hence, Malone appears to demonstrate the catalepsies of the soul as his narrative mode descends into an entrancing vacillation. He is increasingly unresponsive to external stimuli the more he is embedded in the workings of his own broken storytelling and the fictional lives of his characters.

It is noticeable that although Beckett's author-narrators struggle with incompetence in their efforts to bear witness to the past, there is no obvious catastrophe that prevents them from relating their stories. Beckett's trilogy does not fixate on a single traumatic experience that escapes his creatures, but on problematic autobiographical projects that, for Molloy, Moran and Malone at least, carry on in ordinary, if strangely inapprehensible, circumstances. Their depositions seem to take place at a point in time when any incipient event has vanished, but its lingering impact has also destabilized acts of bearing witness to the unexceptional, leaving figures racked with problems comparable to the crisis of enunciation in post-Holocaust attempts to testify. In this way, the author-narrators' accounts extend beyond the task of recovering one lost event and yet are still burdened with the difficulties inherent to attesting for oneself in the distant or near past.

Although Agamben concentrates specifically on the impact of Auschwitz, he also traces several problematic dynamics that apply to bearing witness in general. Bearing witness, as opposed to witnessing only, is an attempt to articulate observed situations without the essence going missing or being distorted in the process between seeing and saying. For Agamben, '[t]he aporia of Auschwitz is, indeed, the very aporia of historical knowledge: a non-coincidence between facts and truth, between verification and comprehension' (2002: 12). This introduces the wordplay on 'baring' witness, which evokes the struggle to uncover knowledge faithfully, or lay bare unbearable personal experiences, considering the added task of reconciling the looking eye in the past with the speaking 'I' in the present. Agamben draws on the disparity between initial event and subsequent statement, the experience and the gathered account. As with Molloy's confusion with the moon, the 'non-coincidence' of testimony sees the shift from a fidelity to the truth to an explanation of how the event now appears. The witness retrospectively incorporates himself and his posterior thoughts into the remembered event, thereby contaminating the experience with extraneous material. The act of testimony therefore updates the witnessed experience and betrays the space in between the witness at the event and the clinical 'I' bearing witness but not strictly there. The witness is unable to repeat the experience exactly and can only resort to an admixture of the past and present.

This retrospective disjunction is an element of testimony that Jacques Derrida prefigures in his *Memoirs of the Blind* (1993). Derrida's text focuses on the practice of self-representation in the painterly arts to offer an acute insight into the interaction between eye and object. But whereas Agamben identifies the aporia between actual experience and reconstituted facts, Derrida emphasizes the fracture in each moment of witnessing. He asserts that 'a witness, as such, is always blind. Witnessing substitutes narrative for perception. The witness cannot see, show, and speak at the same time, and the interest of the attestation, like that of the testament, stems from this dissociation' (Derrida 1993: 104). The discrepancy between observation, demonstration and enunciation, that inevitable fissure in the passage from spontaneous moment to meditated account, is where the taciturnity of testimony emerges. In Derrida's later essay 'Poetics and Politics of Witnessing' (2005a), predominantly on Paul Celan's 1948 poem 'Todesfuge' (Death Fugue) and the possibility of perjury that is inherent to testimony, he reaffirms his view that 'speech can be dissociated from what it is witness to: for the witness is not *present* either, presently present, to what he recalls' (2005a: 76). Derrida lights on the problem of remembering and presenting the memory at once, rapidly shifting from past to present, thinking of then but speaking now. As with Agamben's 'non-coincidence', the words betray the thought gap that occurs in the transition from recollection to articulation.

Beckett's work is a precursor to the momentary non-coincidences and dissociations that Agamben and Derrida dissect. In the second part of *Molloy*, for example, Gaber's role as a messenger evokes the difficult transposition of reliable information that constitutes testimony. In an attempt to bypass the erasing effect of delay, Gaber adopts an instantaneous method of reflection:

Gaber understood nothing about the messages he carried. Reflecting on them he arrived at the most extravagantly false conclusions. Yes, it was not enough for him to understand nothing about them, he had also to believe he understood everything about them. This was not all. His memory was so bad that his messages had no existence in his head, but only in his notebook. He had only to close his notebook to become, a moment later, perfectly innocent as to its content. And when I say that he reflected on his messages and drew conclusions from them, it was not as we would have reflected on them, you and I, the book closed and probably the eyes too, but little by little as he read. And when he raised his head and indulged in his commentaries, it was without losing a second, for if he had lost a second he would have forgotten everything, both text and gloss. I have often wondered if the messengers were not compelled to undergo a surgical operation, to induce in them such a degree of amnesia (*T*, 107).

For Gaber, memory is not a resource. He must resort to the spontaneity of thought and speech, almost concurrently, with the least interference from recollection or reason. Gaber's reflection is bent back on what he considers only to the slightest degree, meaning he performs his ideas with the minimum of cognition, attempting instead to hit intuitively upon the import of his notes. Such forgetfulness aligns Gaber with the Nietzschean celebration of the animal's amnesia, without consideration of the past but rather 'fettered to the moment' (Nietzsche 1997: 57). In this way, Gaber deposes the idea of the messenger as mediator, who typically passes on what is known. He is a passive conduit, in contradistinction to the 'you and I' mentioned in the passage above, who are presumably adept at data collection and retrospective comprehension. In their complicity, the 'you and I' implies the relationship between a masterful author complete with transmissible idea and the reader as a reflective receiver. Gaber, on the other hand, is a vacuous witness, oblivious to the secret information he carries and literally performing his duty.

Gaber's instinctive commentary, his inclination to gabber, is an example of the expressive dilemma that finds its fullest expression in the third text of Beckett's post-war trilogy, *The Unnamable*. The anonymous, asexual narrative voice in this notoriously difficult monologue acts as a rendezvous point for many of Beckett's past characters, including Molloy and Malone.² The text also vaguely relates the stories of two new figments, Mahood and Worm. It is a fragmented, self-reflexive musing on the nature of existence, which grows increasingly anxious the more the uttered words appear to form the sole condition of being. Beckett takes the belatedness of enunciation a step further in *The Unnamable*, problematizing the acute levels of mediation between thought and words that expand the distance between event and account, memory and language. The narrative voice wonders 'how can you think and speak at the same time, how can you think about what you have said, may say, are saying, and at the same time go on with the last-mentioned' (*T*, 377). Beckett points out that there is no means of simultaneously speaking and reflecting. The narrative voice is either occupied with speech or dwelling on the spoken, meaning the subject is not truly present to what it delivers or contemplates.

Beckett's magnification of latency in *The Unnamable* shows that dissociation is not only a problem of vague retrospection, but also a difficulty in occupying a present space and being in the moment. Time appears to be running away immediately, each instant colliding with the living being, and every second burying the last: 'they arrive, bang, bang, they bang into you' (*T*, 399). In the aftermath, the mental and linguistic tools of reflection are overdue so that memory cannot lay claim to the essence of experience. Yet, in the present, the cognitive powers to process experience become inundated by the ensuing action. The present is always slipping into the past, and thus always distorted. As David Jones notes, '[t]estimony is doubly belated: not only is the listener receiving a post-hoc account, but that account originates in an experience from which the witness is effectively absent' (2011: 6). In Beckett's work, this discrepancy between received, stored and transmitted data, each of which have their own inherent obstacles to overcome, is intrinsic to the testimony of his creatures who lack the vantage from which to master their experiences.

(In)sovereign author-narrators

As we have seen, the dissociation between witnessing and bearing witness in Beckett's trilogy fills attestation with cognitive and creative material foreign to the original event. For Derrida, the distance between seeing and saying calls into question the sovereignty of the subject. The word 'sovereign' is typically associated with the supreme power of a monarch, pontiff or autocratic political figure. In terms of literary or testimonial authority, sovereignty is used to take the idea of absolute rule and apply it to spaces of meaning. In his distinctive fashion of harrying words, Derrida introduces a variation on sovereignty, in closer proximity with the beast, from the French words *savoir* and *faire*. He describes how knowledge involves a certain know-how [*savoir-faire*] to be made known [*faire savoir*], which can remove the resulting understanding from the original point of knowing (Derrida 2009: 34–38). In fact, making known can mean 'making like' knowledge, which implies 'fabulous' elements that breathe life into the account, and therefore borders on the 'rogue' status also associated with the beast (Derrida 2009: 35, 19). Derrida exploits this impression of knowledge elsewhere in relation to testimony, noting '[f]or it to be guaranteed as testimony, it cannot, it must not, be absolutely certain, absolutely sure and certain in the order of knowing as such' (2005: 68). More than this, he claims that an assured avowal is the *sine qua non* of falsification: 'That is the essence of lie, fable, or simulacrum, namely to present itself as truth or veracity, to swear that one is faithful, which will always be the condition of infidelity' (2009a: 91). In Derrida's reading, testimony presupposes a personal belief that appeals to others, which can be rejected as a false impression or a feigned pledge. Testimony therefore encloses a degree of uncertainty as opposed to absolute fact.

Beckett and his author-narrators show that the act of bearing witness to one's experience does not always involve a claim to the authority associated with sovereignty. As a writer closely affiliated with the experience of a non-knower, it is clear that Beckett is not interested in depicting reality as a verifiable experience. On the contrary, Beckett's focus on ignorance modifies the idea of *savoir-faire* to accentuate an expertise in making known what is unknown, in the sense that he reveals asininity as opposed to dispelling myths. In an interview with Israel Shenker, Beckett explains this orientation towards ignorance:

I'm not master of my material. The more Joyce knew the more he could. He's tending toward omniscience and omnipotence as an artist. I'm working with impotence, ignorance. I don't think impotence has been exploited in the past. There seems to be an esthetic axiom that expression is achievement – must be an achievement. My little exploration is that whole zone of being that has always been set aside by artists as something unusable – as something by definition incompatible with art (1979: 162).

Beckett embraces the struggle to express, and inability to create, that the sovereign author subjugates. The traditional vision of the author conceives a figure who gives a complete and efficient form to an object. For Jean-Paul Sartre, the author assumes the responsibility of 'introducing order where there was none, by imposing the unity of mind on the diversity of things' (1950: 27), while Michel Foucault recognizes the concept of the author as synonymous with 'a principle of a certain unity of writing' (1999: 215). Given that the received author is the single agent who negotiates and consolidates all of the many constituent elements required to make up the work of art, the 'unity' that both Sartre and Foucault identify is closely related to the 'omni' that Beckett mentions and, by his own concession, is without.

However, as Beckett suggests, he is 'using' and 'exploiting' the material set aside in the past. Through his focus on failure, or 'my dream of an art unresentful of its insuperable indigence and too proud for the farce of giving and receiving' as he described it to Duthuit (Beckett 1983: 141), Beckett himself is tasked with succeeding in crafting an art of failure. He must make decisions on the appropriate way to depict his author-narrators as impotent figures, which retains an impression of the artistic achievement that he associates with his compatriot Joyce. Beckett's trilogy is a *tour de force* with regard to its ability to give form to deficiency and make ignorance known, which, contradictorily, brings sovereign power into contact with impotence to produce a creaturely tension. As noted earlier, when Beckett writes 'I am absurdly and stupidly the creature of my work', he underlines the sense of obligation he has to an insistent task. But as the creature of his work, Beckett also embodies a peculiar aspect of the creature, namely its association with creativity. Beckett is both the author and subject of his writing, acting at once as potent source of the work and subservient minion to its design.[3] This is a creaturely junction between producer and product, related to the idea of a divine maker who moulds creatures 'in his own image' (Genesis 1.27), but is simultaneously a subject under the control of another. Beckett effectively exemplifies the dichotomous composition of the creature, implicated in both strength and weakness, and this is a status that extends to his author-narrators.

Beckett's focus on impotence in his work yields authorial and narrative positions that are incongruous to a conventional understanding of sovereignty as absolute rule. It is patent that both Beckett and his narrating creatures are exposed to the thraldom of creative tasks. Yet, he does evoke the 'sovereign as creature' that Walter Benjamin describes in his 1925 doctoral dissertation entitled *The Origin of German Tragic Drama*.[4] In this text, Benjamin initially presents an image of sovereignty analogous to the unifying power of the traditional author. He writes that '[l]iterature ought to be called *ars inveniendi*. The notion of the man of genius, the master of *ars inveniendi*, is that of a man who could manipulate models with sovereign skill' (Benjamin 1977: 179). Benjamin refers to literature as the art of invention to promote the creative talents and adept control of a writer, but he goes on to derive a contrasting view of sovereignty from seventeenth-century baroque drama:

> The antithesis between the power of the ruler and his capacity to rule led to a feature peculiar to the *Trauerspiel* which is, however, only apparently a generic feature and which can be illuminated only against the background of the theory of sovereignty. This is the indecisiveness of the tyrant. The prince, who is responsible for making the decision to proclaim the state of emergency, reveals at the first opportunity, that he is almost incapable of making a decision (1977: 71).

Benjamin aligns an artistic genre with a political theory in this passage to outline the power dynamics in the creative process. He refers to the sovereign duty to make decisions, which is equally inherent to efficient forms of narration, as Beckett notes in *Molloy*: 'you cannot mention everything in its proper place, you must choose, between the things not worth mentioning and those even less so' (*T*, 41). The problem is that the individual who can make a decision can also make another to counter his original order. There is no necessity for the sovereign to commit to his decrees or develop an effective means of governing his material. Instead of making known, the sovereign's authority makes it difficult to stand by any single view; everything he announces can be renounced. In

Benjamin's view, the sovereign power to choose alternatives makes the sovereign incapable of living by an order other than the constant flux of decision making.

The power to override decisions that amounts to indecisiveness also undermines the narrative efficacy of Beckett's author-narrators. Molloy, for example, is continually at a loose end: 'my resolutions were remarkable in this, that they were no sooner formed than something always happened to prevent their executions' (*T*, 32). The complication to which Molloy refers is that he changes his mind or, more accurately, his mind is never fully made. While his general orientation towards the mother persists, the satellite thoughts and actions that surround his quest are far from refractory. Molloy's resolutions are always provisional, threatening to swerve at any point: 'How agreeable it is to be confirmed, after a more or less long period of vacillation, in one's first impressions. Perhaps that is what tempers the pangs of death. Not that I was so conclusively, I mean confirmed, in my first impressions with regard to – wait – C' (*T*, 15). The extent to which Molloy is 'confirmed' here is clearly questionable as the passage is rife with uncertainty in 'more or less', 'impressions', 'perhaps', inconclusiveness and the moment of hesitation at the end. The very instant a decision is formed, Molloy is aware of other possibilities or problems, which can send him back to square one.

Similarly, Malone's attempts to establish an order are confounded in *Malone Dies*. In an aside during his account of Macmann's stay at the House of Saint John of God, Malone considers the ambivalence of his narrative as he moves from precision to distortion. He remarks, 'A thousand little things to report, very strange, in view of my situation, if I interpret them correctly. But my notes have a curious tendency, as I realize at last, to annihilate all they purport to record' (*T*, 260–1). The inability to proceed with an idea causes the application of power to be capricious, ready to reverse itself as opposed to reassert. Malone claims to realize this problem finally, but he actually produces a liar paradox so that the very claim to annihilate is itself open to annihilation. It is impossible to accept Malone's realization of this curious tendency as true without the same logic undermining itself. Beckett's author-narrators can exercise the power of inconstancy in that they can nullify every statement they make, but it is that sovereign privilege that casts them as creatures.

In Molloy's provisionality and Malone's impuissance, Beckett works with a combination of changeability and ineffectuality that evokes sovereign power but places emphasis on what I label the '(in)sovereign'. In an effort to distance conventional notions of authority, this term suggests that from *within* a position of power, in sovereignty, comes a dearth of practical power, *in*sovereignty. In other words, the sovereign creature is theoretically potent but pragmatically incapable. The term '(in)sovereign' therefore avoids simply negating the ability to decide in order to retain a sense of the sovereign power that slides into creaturely asininity. The proximity between these two states is evident in Beckett's art of failure itself, which invests the author's creative skills into an exhibition of indigence. This hybridity manifests itself within the work in the form of author-narrators who conduct their own stories and develop fictional constructs, but are ultimately unable to reign over a determined meaning. In their extended conflicts with decisions that are not fixed, they demonstrate the instability of creaturely '(in) sovereignty'. Beckett's creatures cannot command thought and expression with the unquestioned supremacy of a deity, only the uncertainty of the lowly creature.

The creaturely junction between potency and impotence is most arresting in Beckett's treatment of reason, that instrument of knowledge and wisdom that gives Homo sapiens a name. His author-narrators frequently appeal to rational analysis as they try to understand and articulate the situations they encounter. Despite this, their reasoning is often inefficient, distending the processes of logic as opposed to making sense. For example, after stealing several silver items from Lousse, Molloy rigorously describes a knife rest because he is unaware of the name and function of the object. Such scrutiny of the knife rest proliferates thought rather than dispels Molloy's ignorance: 'there was no doubt in my mind that it was not an object of virtue, but that it had a most specific function always to be hidden from me. I could therefore puzzle over it endlessly without the least risk' (*T*, 64). Molloy is adamant that the knife rest is useful and not merely an aesthetic article, but because its function is inscrutable, he can contemplate the object knowing that such examination is in vain. In this case, it is the opportunity to indulge in reflection that drives Molloy's reasoning, not the possibility of knowledge. While rationality does not have active power, in the sense that it fails to settle on explanations, causes or meaning, its template continues to serve as a pastime and actually sustains the enigma game for Molloy.

The perpetuation of thought through the empty rhetoric of reason is intrinsic to the style of narration in Beckett's trilogy. Adorno, for one, finds this kind of engagement with reason at the centre of narration, asserting that 'communicative language postulates – already in its syntactic form, through logic, the nature of conclusions, and stable concepts – the principle of sufficient reason' (1982: 139). The ordering of language into sentences itself suggests a rational being organizing thoughts. However, it follows that, without a stable foundation to apply language, such as an empirical experience, a reliable memory or a conceived idea – that is, a known point of causality – language is forced to revolve infinite possibilities. Beckett's author-narrators apply this level of reason to evoke a spectrum of thinking that ranges from fruitless bouts of rationalization to the paralysing aporia in which every remark is negated.

Molloy's inclination towards sincerity, for instance, frequently neutralizes much of the conviction in his narrative undertaking, which results in a strange admixture of unreliability and honesty. As he grows familiar with his ignorance, Molloy can explicitly identify his predicament: 'notions like mine, all spasm, sweat and trembling, without an atom of common sense or lucidity' (*T*, 68). Molloy is able to articulate his own lack of clarity, but the narrative project grows stagnant when this is the only lucid judgement. Consequently, Molloy must entertain the reasonable exploration of obscurities in an attempt to further his narrative, if only to return to his tendency towards inaccuracy, which is a point he highlights early on when he says 'The truth is I don't know much' (*T*, 7). Molloy does not fabricate his account purposely to deceive since he has no reliable truth to conceal. Even so, he knows a more truthful account does exist and that his version is always parallel to reality, throwing an unattainable truth into relief. Again, this is a fact that he expresses distinctly: 'I am merely complying with the convention that demands you either lie or hold your peace. For what really happened was quite different' (*T*, 87–8). It is evident that Molloy's lack of awareness is a condition he realizes; he is not blissfully ignorant. Molloy must therefore direct reason towards his lack of sovereignty as a substitute for reason's inability to work through his epistemological shortcomings.

For Adorno, the unavailing reasoning in Beckett means that '[t]he sovereign *ego cogitans* is transformed by the *dubitatio* into its opposite' (2010: 173). Adorno argues that the logical mind inflicts its own undoing, which echoes Beckett's own view that '[t]here is at least this to be said of the mind, that it can dispel mind' (Beckett quoted in Begam 1996: 39). The power of reason, in this respect, is to reveal its own weakness and reflect on its failure. This mental faculty is incapable of apprehending reality but does manage to illuminate its own inadequacy, recognize unproductive cycles of logic and realize the holes in testimony that captivate the creature. As such, the power of Beckett's creatures rapidly shifts from the original position of sovereignty, to the servitude to reasoning processes, to a re-evaluation of the decline into indecision. The point is that Beckett's (in)sovereign creatures accept the conventional forms of testimony, expose the drawbacks of communicative language and reasoned judgements, but salvage testimonial value in bearing witness to the crisis of positive testimony.

Beckett develops this blurred division between sovereign and creature more distinctly in *Malone Dies*. Malone shares Molloy's type of reasoning without result, and it eventually contributes to the apathetic disposition that Malone courts, which would bypass the temptation to resolve any inconsistencies in his account. First, Malone says 'I will not weigh upon the balance any more, one way or another. I shall be neutral and inert. No difficulty there' (*T*, 179). Malone goes on to express his intention not to be mired in an approach that neurotically catalogues details: 'My desire henceforth is to be clear, without being finical' (*T*, 181). He effectively renounces his position as sovereign author by refusing to make authorial decisions on conflicting ideas and choosing to be equivocal rather than selectively organize the text. He wants to concede a lack of ability and dismiss his influence upon the account. Indeed, he would rather defer his responsibility in favour of an arbitrary process: 'If I had a penny I would let it make up my mind' (*T*, 252). Malone's hope of relinquishing his authorial voice is aimed at vanquishing his identity from the forefront of the text, to dissolve the author in the writing and surrender to the spontaneity of creation.

However, Beckett highlights the contradiction in Malone's decision not to decide, which is a conflict that makes it difficult to determine the author-narrator's level of efficacy in the text. Malone's intentions continue to interfere with his absences so that he appears to fail on two fronts. First, the decision to be ambiguous suggests Malone can retain sovereign power, albeit through a paradoxically resolute irresolution. Even when he does manage to recede into Macmann's story, the fulfilment of his original intention is still detectable, which reinserts Malone into his supposed absence from the narrative process. Second, Malone's original decision to be detached is frequently undermined, as he is not completely neutral but intermittently self-aware: 'I must simply be on my guard, reflecting on what I have said before I go on and stopping, each time disaster threatens, to look at myself as I am. That is just what I wanted to avoid' (*T*, 189). In this way, Malone's decision to be passive is not possible, which shows him powerless in one sense, but more distinctly the author in another; his decision is undone but, consequently, he is revealed as the figure behind the narrative. The paradox is that when Malone decides to be less present, he is ineffective in that he re-emerges in the author-narrator position, but at the same time he is also indulged in that his decision to be less present is not carried out, therefore effectuating his desire to be less potent. Ironically, Beckett accentuates the convergence of potency and impotence in (in)sovereignty when Malone insists that his sovereign presence is attenuated.

The concomitance of failure and success continues in the final text of the trilogy, *The Unnamable*. This stunted text is made up almost entirely of aporetic revolutions around narrative incompetence, but it also conveys the great significance of reflecting on inability. In the opening pages of the text, the narrative voice develops an accurate description of his position albeit through a fractured narrative style:

> The fact would seem to be, if in my situation one may speak of facts, not only that I shall have to speak of things of which I cannot speak, but also, which is even more interesting, but also that I, which is if possible even more interesting, that I shall have to, I forget, no matter. And at the same time I am obliged to speak. I shall never be silent. Never (*T*, 294).

The narrator of *The Unnamable* illustrates the fact that the crux of the matter is beyond his expressive capabilities. Although a 'fact' is clearly understood, it is delivered in such an interrupted way that the narrator loses his train of thought altogether. In repeatedly trying to elaborate on his inability to speak through the phrases 'not only' and 'but also', the narrator shows he is unable to develop an idea. Beckett presents a narrative voice that cannot speak but continues nevertheless, and it is only through this fidelity to failure that the genuine aphonia, or voiceless quality, of Beckett's creatures is heard.

Shortly after his attempt at facts, the narrator of *The Unnamable* continues: 'I shall remark without further delay, in order to be sure of doing so, that I am relying on these lights, as indeed on all other similar sources of credible perplexity, to help me continue and perhaps even conclude. I resume, having no alternative' (*T*, 296). The narrator's testimony lies precisely in the 'credible perplexity' that pervades his endeavour. He can honestly pronounce his confusion, although that same confusion both invalidates the understanding of his own incomprehensible situation and prevents him from accepting his ignorance unconditionally. Hence, *The Unnamable* does not merely pinpoint incertitude. It is the regenerative process of trying to speak, failing to speak and addressing that failure that entails a performative element that guarantees the credibility of the perplexity. When the narrator later says, 'But what is the right manner, I don't know' (*T*, 338), it is clear that there is authenticity in impotence here, as the narrator concedes that the right manner is elusive but that ignorance is also oddly the right manner. Whereas the ability to decide results in indecision, the narrator's investment in indecision returns to a kind of decisive act. Thus, Beckett's author-narrators convey the experience of the 'non-knower' and 'non-can-er', thereby dethroning the imperious human by divulging frailties within the formerly sovereign human mind, but they also reveal a vestigial authority in their ability to diagnose this unspeakability. In effect, Beckett's creatures acknowledge that their errant accounts are beside the point and yet necessary if they are to outline the gaps that attest to the impossibility of bearing witness.

Obligation to testify: Mechanics, enunciation, ruin

The (in)sovereign position of Beckett's author-narrators in the post-war trilogy shows that although sovereign indecision undermines their testimonies, they regain some credibility in the protracted and honest nature of their expressive dilemmas. The narrative voice in *The Unnamable* utters the words 'I cannot speak' and 'I shall never be silent' (*T*, 294) in an echo of Beckett's widely cited point of view on art from his dialogues with Duthuit: 'there is nothing to express, nothing with which to express, nothing from which to express, no power to express, no desire to express, together with the obligation to express' (1983: 139). The obligation to speak despite the inability to speak presents a strained condition for Beckett's creatures apparent not only in their testimonies but also in their understanding of themselves as subjects. The on-going urge to do what cannot be successfully done produces precarious identities occupied with mechanical processes, composed of speaking acts and reflecting on the loss of self.

A self-sustaining and transformative pressure to speak drives Beckett's trilogy, which, according to Lawrence Miller, 'asks the reader to accept the intention for the deed, and to be satisfied with the pains taken rather than any product' (1992: 98–9). A similar focus on process features heavily in psychotherapy, as in the way Shoshana Felman and Dori Laub frequently refer to the imperative to speak in their psychoanalytical and literary study of testimony. They focus on a number of examples in which articulation fails and it becomes doubly imperative to speak in order to convey the elliptical space underlying the act itself. Laub writes:

> This imperative to tell and to be heard can become itself an all-consuming life task. Yet no amount of telling seems ever to do justice to this inner compulsion. There are never enough words or the right words, there is never enough time or the right time, and never enough listening or the right listening to articulate the story that cannot be fully captured in *thought, memory* and *speech* (Felman and Laub 1992: 78).

The mind's incapacity to apprehend the traumatic event belies the fact that the act of speaking itself can, on the one hand, be understood as a cathartic process, a purging of everything that can be said without hitting on the crux, thereby exhausting language's power to relate the event. In conjunction with a playful reference to stupidity, Molloy alludes to this therapeutic quality: 'sorrow does more harm when dumb, to my mind' (*T*, 110). On the other hand, testimony can be the all-important act of not expelling. In this sense, the act of bearing witness is a cyclical inculcation in order to learn by rote the burden of inscribing the experience. It is this deed that discloses the survivor's inheritance from the trauma, namely the duty to speak the unspeakable.

Felman relates an anecdote about a cohort of students that assimilated the trauma they studied in her university module on testimony. She points out the students' impulse to both expel and retain the information, which, in this case, resolves itself in a faltering discourse. One student writes: 'Caught by two contradictory wishes at once, to speak or not to speak, I can only stammer' (Felman and Laub 1992: 56). There is evidently a need to tell and a simultaneous compulsion not to relive, which results in a verbal non-fluency. This defective language emerges as a kind of hesitancy from these conflicting urges. However, the student's stammer is a reaction in the true sense of the word: an action provoked by and therefore congruent with the initial event. The problem is that reaction indicates an automatic consequence of an instruction and consequently lacks the personality of a wilful response. As a programmed testimony, reaction obliterates human agency in the act of bearing witness.

The continual act of speaking is crucial in order to invoke negative or coincidental testimony. If Beckett's narrators are to demonstrate the non-experience of ignorance and non-story of impotence, they must employ methods of continuation that oblige failure. However, this mode of testimony would appear to actuate automatic, insubstantial and disintegrated forms of existence. The nature of speaking the unspeakable means there is no final success, which places emphasis on the act itself and, in turn, reduces the human element of narration to mechanical rigidity, incessant enunciation and ruinous ambivalence. The obligation to testify therefore impacts upon the subjective status of the witness, divesting him or her of an organic, progressive and unified way of attesting to oneself. When the inability to relate life and account for oneself meets the necessity to try, testimony discloses a suspended, creaturely subjectivity.

Paul Sheehan argues that an increased focus on the inhuman occurs as part of the development of a modernist narrative form. In *Modernism, Narrative and Humanism* (2002), Sheehan expounds the notion that modernist literature subverts the humanistic values of narrative, explaining that, 'implicit in humanism is the idea of autonomy, the belief that man is measure of all things and maker of all meanings; and mastery, that he has dominion over himself and his world' (2002: 6). This empirical and epistemological proficiency correlates with the classic image of the author, which allows Sheehan to affirm that narration 'is human-shaped. It is a uniquely human way of making order and meaning out of the raw material of existence' (2002: 9). The ability to narrate suggests a distinctively human mode of comprehension and assessment of being in the world. Beckett, however, plays a particularly disruptive role in the move from the humanistic order of realism to the inhuman flux of modernity. The creaturely state of (in)sovereignty in Beckett's trilogy means the author-narrators negotiate the convergence of impotence and potency that lacks dominance over positive meaning while producing a valuable testimony of unspeakability. Appropriately, then, Sheehan uses Beckett as an example of the narrative process going awry: 'Narrativised subjectivity is wrenched out of its human-shaped literary vessel and transplanted to something inhuman' (2002: 161). Despite this, Sheehan understates the human catalyst in the transition to the inhuman. He perceives the inhumanity of the narrative form as a consequence of the absence of human ways of making meaning. Conversely, Beckett's narratives appear to be benighted as a result of a misguided reliance on the properties that set the human apart as a species. The creaturely hybridity of Beckett's narrators is compounded by the mental faculties, such as reasoned reflection, that Malone accredits to humanity's ascent: 'I suppose the wisest thing now is to live it over again, meditate upon it and be edified. It is thus that man distinguishes himself from the ape and rises, from discovery to discovery, ever higher towards the light' (T, 255). Given that Beckett's creatures pursue the wisest course of action and further enlightenment, their uncertain narration is actually born out of an attempt to step up to the author role. Sheehan does acknowledge this irony, noting that 'it is the pursuit of certainty that actuates the flights of rigorous logic, the mathematical gymnastics of permutation and enumeration, and the unstoppable flux of recall' (2002: 155). Beckett's author-narrators take on the rational, unifying perspective but, as it transpires, their brand of reason is an inadequate tool for their investigations and often results in the discord of an inhuman narrative form. Beckett's inhuman narration is therefore a product of the inefficacy of human narrative forms.

Having no alternative, Beckett's author-narrators persist with language and logic even as these faculties appear outmoded, resulting in the unproductive motions of uncanny narrative processes. This narrative form includes a mechanical aspect in its repetitive, incessant activity, but it is different from the humanistic mechanisms that Sheehan describes. The sovereign author who is able to render meaning explicit through a structured narrative is shown to be a mechanical figure in Sheehan's study, efficiently processing relevant material and fabricating a final product, whereas modernism is composed of the inconstancy of 'voice'. As Sheehan writes: 'Machine, in short, is one of the prior conditions for making narrative comprehensible, whereas voice offers the chance for difference, variation and irregularity, pulling against narrative's machinelike precision' (2002: 11). For Sheehan, it is usually voice that fragments a text and machine that makes writing coherent, but Beckett's author-narrators show that they are subject to patterns of thought and habitual behaviours that do not yield results. Since the mechanisms of narration rotate without a satisfactory product, the Beckettian creature is condemned to a mundane and desolate process.

Beckett's *The Unnamable* is a prime example of narration that goes through the motions of storytelling, grinds out discursive husks and gets snagged reflecting on its own unavailing mechanism. In a typically autologic passage, the narrator says: 'The only problem for me was how to continue, since I could not do otherwise, to the best of my declining powers, in the motion which had been imparted to me. This obligation, and the quasi-impossibility of fulfilling it, engrossed me in a purely mechanical way, excluding notably the free play of the intelligence and sensibility' (*T*, 322). The emphasis here is on continuation, as the narrator recognizes a mechanical compulsion to keep speaking despite his 'declining powers'. These declining powers signal the diminishing possibility of sating the obligation, although the chance of success clearly persists, which in turn perpetuates the duty to speak. The narrator therefore faces the contradiction of being locked into allotted motions, such as the contrivances of storytelling. Malone, for one, 'appears and disappears with the punctuality of clockwork, always at the same remove, the same velocity, in the same direction, the same attitude' (*T*, 296). The narrator of *The Unnamable* is at the centre of a mechanism that encircles him with familiar imperatives, figures and tropes.

Yet, anticipating Derrida's use of 'free play' to describe the 'disruption of presence' (Derrida 1978: 292), the narrative voice in *The Unnamable* refers to the 'free play of the intelligence and sensibility', which respond to other stimulants besides the central structure of his obligation. These suggestible cognitive and sensory faculties can distract the narrator from his established motions. As such, while the narrator recognizes that 'It's a circuit, a long circuit' (*T*, 414), the possibility of difference is maintained: 'the play of lights is truly unpredictable. [. . .] They are perhaps unwavering and fixed and my fitful perceiving the cause of their inconstancy' (*T*, 296). Without achieving the full comprehension or appreciation suggested in intelligibility and sensibility, the stability of the system is susceptible to misprision and encourages the narrator to reengage with the 'same old irresistible baloney' raised in the obligation to speak (*T*, 380).

By accounting for a sense of system and free play in the obligation, Beckett problematizes the categories of voice and machine, making them virtually indistinct. Sheehan argues that *The Unnamable* integrates both voice and machine, labelling it 'a performative example of voice *as* machine' (2002: 174). He suggests that a mechanical compulsion underwrites the mercurial nature of voice in Beckett's text, thereby positing the regular patterns and repetitive cycles associated with the machine as the source of the flux. The text is based on a 'mechanical impetus that the voice cannot cast off' (Sheehan 2002: 175). Beckett traces the voice's vacillation with such stamina in *The Unnamable* that, without quite exhausting voice, its capricious ways become more familiar and less organic. The structure of the obligation tempers the voice's ability to diverge so that the narrator surmises: 'What prevents the miracle is the spirit of method to which I have perhaps been a little too addicted' (*T*, 305). The point to emphasize is that the machine, which Sheehan's study connects to humanistic narration but typically suggests something inhuman, is conflated with voice, which Sheehan appears to associate with the modernist shift away from the human. Since the possibilities of voice become part of a process in *The Unnamable*, the categories of machine and voice, human and inhuman, overlap to such an extent that the boundaries are obscured. The upshot is a creaturely composite, in which human and inhuman are in close proximity, or rather, the inhuman is actually what the human can become.

The admixture of machine and voice, human and inhuman, is one way of thinking through the creaturely subjectivity endemic to a process of testifying for oneself through means that obstruct positive testimony. An undertaking that fixes on the imperative to speak as much as what is spoken engenders dehumanized witnesses, consumed by the effort to give voice to human experience. Taking the language and logical mechanics of human narrative structures to their extremes shows that an inhuman being is the potential of the human. The imperative to speak in Beckett reveals the human in a broken form and this presents problems for a conventional understanding of testimony that aspires to correlate event and self. Whereas testimony typically attempts to marry tale and teller in order to assert that an individual was present at an event, Beckettian testimony questions the degree to which a human subject is present in an account.

In a variety of ways, Derrida and Agamben also illustrate how attempts to coincide identity and incident repeatedly fail, and that a juridical model of testimony is commonly unfulfilled. Nevertheless, it is through the continuous act of bearing witness to failure that the interplay between potency and impotence, machine and voice, human and inhuman, generates the outline of the human subject, even if that outline is the residue of human properties that develops through or alongside an inhuman image. Derrida, one of the most influential figures in decentring the subject, notes that 'a fable is always and before all else speech' (2009: 34). To tell a story is to speak, regardless of the accuracy of the tale and, subsequently, invention will always convey an oratorical activity, which in turn intimates a speaking subject. It appears that a being is present within the act of enunciation, but as Agamben explicates, this ephemeral type of subjectivity is contrary to the idea of a complete identification with a stable foundation of self. In *Remnants of Auschwitz*, Agamben expands upon Michel Foucault's argument that 'enunciation is not a thing determined by real, definite properties; it is, rather, pure existence, the fact that a certain being – language – takes place' (Foucault quoted in Agamben 2002: 139). This use of language at the moment it is employed emphasizes the tongue of a speaker prior to its attendant semantic value and thus evidences a state of being or, rather, a simultaneous coming into being for both language and subject. Agamben goes on to relate the particular role that the pseudo-witness performs within this event: '*The authority of the witness consists in his capacity to speak solely in the name of an incapacity to speak – that is, in his or her being a subject'* (italics in original) (2002: 158). This paradoxical condition marks the witness as the pure existence achieved through a performance of language without secure semantic value. The witness is the host and bearer of a tenanted but inoperative language, conveying only the fact that language is happening, discrete from its signification.

The transitory subjectivity elicited through the sound more than the semiotics of language is a fundamental part of the precarious existential condition of Beckett's creatures. The relationship between speaking and subjectivity recurs most plainly in the fourth text of Beckett's *Texts for Nothing* (*TN*, 2010b), a series of thirteen short texts originally written in French between 1950 and 1951. Coming shortly after the trilogy, these texts are equally concerned with the means to go on speaking, but since they average a couple of pages in length, the subjects they depict are remarkably evanescent. Nevertheless, Beckett's narrator in the fourth text identifies the fact that the act of speaking appears to imply a 'life': 'There's my life, why not, it is one if you like, if you must, I don't say no, this evening. There has to be one, it seems, once there is speech, no need of a story, story is not compulsory' (*TN*, 18). The meaning of a story is unrequired since the words themselves manage to convey someone speaking. Enunciation continues to intimate a life despite the fact that who is speaking or what is spoken is unknowable. The resultant subject exists in the moment of language even as the source and substance of speech is divested from the narrative.

However, since the subject is native to enunciation but devoid of the individuality achieved through story, the act of bearing witness injects a complex double movement into the first-person pronoun. To an extent, the witness is present in the 'I' as the subject of speech, but this 'I' also conveys the distance required to refer to the self, thus making the subject a perceived object. Beckett refers to the flimsy identity invested into 'I' in his correspondence with Duthuit when he writes: 'I cycle frantically, I, that is the person who is supposed to represent me' (2011: 150). The personal pronoun does indeed 're-present', in at least venturing to make presence again, which calls attention to the estranged perspective adopted towards oneself, as Richard Begam notes: 'the subject can know itself only by becoming the object of its own consciousness; but in becoming the object of its own consciousness it ceases to be itself, which is to say a subject' (1996: 69). Furthermore, this universal and anonymous pronoun only ever replaces a more personal appellation, and is consequently an impersonal signifier used in lieu of the ability to speak from a position of complete identity. Hence, Catherine Mills describes the phenomenon of the pronoun as a synchronous possession and dispossession: 'the "I" marks the simultaneous appropriation and expropriation of the living being in language and their irreducible disjuncture' (2005: 205). The first-person pronoun always betrays the connection and disconnection inherent to self-referential speech.

Beckett offers a distillation of this double movement in the opening lines of *The Unnamable*. The phrase 'I say I' (*T*, 293) intimates both an owned and borrowed 'I', the second of which serves to impair the authority of the initial utterance, thereby causing each to be marred by doubt. While the initial self-reference implies an attachment to a person, the second 'I' is detached as a figure of speech, which uncovers the representational function of both pronouns. The narrator expresses this destabilization shortly after, saying 'I seem to speak, it is not I, about me, it is not about me' (*T*, 293). Despite this, the phrase 'I say I' shows that the word 'say' remains in between the two damaged self-referential pronouns. By situating the enunciating 'mouth' in the middle of two 'eyes', Beckett appears to reveal the countenance of testimony. This face places emphasis on utterance, which is an activity that allows the speaker to discern the tenuous connection between pronoun and person, but also bears witness to this broken state of self-reflection. As a result, the witness demonstrates that testimony cannot achieve the unity of self and speech, and subsists instead as a residual subject that articulates the inability to speak.

For Beckett's narrators, the use of language and the moment of utterance, alongside the recognition of these occurring activities, mark a tension between identification and alienation. His narrators are preoccupied with the self-constructing and self-erasing movement of enunciation in which each moment of utterance raises a speaker but, as a transient activity, cannot be easily possessed. The lack of a proper system of semantics to allow narrative an accumulation of signification means enunciation yields a rather different view of self-identification because it relies on the present context and immediacy of speech, which discontinues reflection.

On the doomed metaphysical task of returning language to its
subject, Agamben writes that, 'precisely this impossibility of
conjoining the living being and language, *phone* and *logos*, the
inhuman and the human – far from authorizing the infinite deferral
of signification – is what allows for testimony' (2002: 142, 130).
Agamben perceives the human subject overcoming and surviving
the partition between self and expression or, more acutely, being
partially constituted by a realization of non-identity. He infers that
the figure of testimony is a 'subject to desubjectification' and
'witness to its own disorder' (Agamben 2002: 106). As we have
seen, there is 'intimate extraneousness implicit in the act of speech'
(Agamben 2002: 117), as the subject is at once part of and apart
from the spoken word. This means that the speaking witness is
being oneself and at the same time knowing oneself as an other,
thereby effectively 'giving an account of its own ruin' (Agamben
2002: 117). The subject perceives the loss of self and is reconstituted
by this process, which makes testimony possible and accounts for a
unique type of subjectivity that resonates with Beckett's creatures.
Images of ruin pervade Beckett's trilogy to convey the psychological
and physical conditions of the characters, and also echo the ability
to reflect on inability that absorbs Beckett's (in)sovereign narrators.
The impotent-potent hybrid returns in the identity of ruins as the
creatures acknowledge themselves as splintered figures.

In *Malone Dies*, the bedridden narrator presents an arresting
image of decay as both body and spirit are failing: 'give my body the
old orders I know it cannot obey, turn to my spirit gone to rack and
ruin' (*T*, 189). Malone resorts to stories to distract him from this
deterioration, and yet he repeatedly recognizes this division between
reality and fiction as an aspect of his ruin. After a lengthy exposition
of Sapo's encounter with the Lamberts, Malone remarks: 'I shall
hear myself talking, afar off, from my far mind, talking of the
Lamberts, talking of myself, my mind wandering, far from here,
among its ruin' (*T*, 216–17). The Beckettian vestige of subjectivity
is realized through this perpetual rambling, in both senses of the
word, about the dilapidated self. Malone's self-portrait of a detached
other, talking and walking in the distance, effectively says 'I am not
here', which demonstrates the concomitant presence and absence of
self that causes Agamben to define testimony as that which bears
witness to its own disorder. Malone frequently points out this
disappointed self-discovery: 'That which is seen, that which cries

and writhes, my witless remains. Somewhere in this turmoil thought struggles on, it too wide of the mark. It too seeks me, as it always has, where I am not to be found' (*T*, 187). Though the self is elusive, Malone continues to recognize a self that can be missed, and this kind of reflection on his state of ruin reveals traces of a subject privy to its own desubjectification.

Malone's perspicacity on his ruined identity recurs in *The Unnamable*. The narrator explains how the value of words vanishes because he is no longer present in his thoughts: 'To tell the truth, let us be honest at least, it is some considerable time now since I last knew what I was talking about. It is because my thoughts are elsewhere. I am therefore forgiven. So long as one's thoughts are somewhere everything is permitted' (*T*, 325). As with Malone, the narrator's self-presence is split into the current speaker and the thinker elsewhere. Nevertheless, the very possibility of thought residing in a remote place means the speaker belongs to its constituent other, which sustains the narrator's partial existence as a ruin. That is, the narrator's recognition of absence preserves the sense of presence. It is this coincidental dynamic that makes the art of failure, pure enunciation and ruined identity central to testimony in that these accounts always stipulate a kind of dissociation that at least alludes to the participating subject. The identity in ruins in Beckett is the residual subjectivity from articulating the inability to speak, whereby the fracture of self becomes the substance of testimony.

Testimony of fiction

While reflection fails to unite the speaking subject and the perceived object, the continuing acts of testimony outline the absent self, or 'not-I', to throw up an impression of self that is always short of totality. This is a creaturely dimension because the subject is an identity in action, exposed to the process of creation and, moreover, because it involves conceiving self alongside other creations or projections of the self. The circumnavigation of complete self-identification in *The Unnamable* inspires fictional elements, which in turn contribute to the narrator's disintegration, 'ruined as I am and still young in this abjection they have brought me to' (*T*, 354). In these figments of the imagination is the implicit sign of testimony generated through creativity, yet authorial creation is always both an adumbration of the creator and, as Anat Pick suggests, 'an abdication' (2011: 16). As with the ruinous personal pronoun, creativity is dissociated from and associated with the creator, as it concedes presence to recalcitrant creations that also vouch for the creator, albeit in their usurpation. In actively expressing and dethroning authorial creativity, fiction doubly *describes,* in the sense of 'writing down' as well as 'removing the scribe'.

Beckett's demonstration of the creaturely subjectivity actively ruined and realized in the making intersects with deconstruction's interrogation of the subject. In an interview with Jean-Luc Nancy, Derrida defines the subject as a 'finite experience of non-identity to self' (Derrida 1991: 104). However, in keeping with his philosophy of presence, which takes issue with this finitude, Derrida adopts Antonin Artaud's rubric 'subjectile' as a term that evinces the intermediate site of difference and the division of identity (Derrida 1994: 154). For Asja Szafraniec, the narrator of *The Unnamable* is a victim of the subjectile's helical infinity, condemned to a futile search for self that spawns and depletes two prosthetic guises, namely Mahood's eternal self-reflection, or not dying, and Worm's complete lack of reflection, or not being born (2007: 130). If, as Szafraniec affirms, *The Unnamable* is the text closest to undoing the system of identity through fictional works because it is '[u]nable to close the circuit, not even by prosthesis' (2007: 127), the conclusion must be that these fictional edifices obscure the 'real' identity that fabricates them, that these voices are simply an annex and not part of the subject. In what remains of this chapter, the contention is that fictional constructs are fundamental to the ruins of subjectivity in Beckett. The author-narrators gift a voice to others in a critical attempt to efface and desubjectify themselves. Thus, the internal avatars offer the opportunity to reinforce the divided nature of enunciation. They perform the crucial role of fabling in the sense of generating speech and encourage the important state of mediation within writing that is a condition of the personal and impersonal relationship with language.

Beckett attends to the filtered and kaleidoscopic composition of the subject in *Molloy*: 'Chameleon in spite of himself, there you have Molloy, viewed from a certain angle' (*T*, 30). Beckett refers to a changeable identity, capable of assuming different forms, all of which are components of the subject, despite the lack of a core self.

Each new guise is not the sum of the authorial 'I', or a route to self-knowledge, but necessarily a persona, a manifestation of the partially desubjectified state of identity. The multiple and often fictional voices that invade Beckett's narrators are a failing gesture in the totalized vision of the subject, but it is a failure that serves a purpose in the study of the self-conscious experience of the subject. The subject must surrender its totality to self-reflectively fold back on oneself, not in a psychoanalytical sense of working through layers and depths, but in a relational sense, in order to realize the estranged coordinates of the subject. As such, this act is a detachment from self to be with self, a veritable 'inclusive exclusion' (Agamben 1995: 27), which is exemplified by the double nature of the word 'cleave': bound by an incision, intimate at the site of rupture.[5]

The polyphony apparent in Beckett's trilogy is the principal focus in the late prose text, *Company* (C [1980] 2009a), and it is worth a brief detour into this dissection of inner voices before returning to the trilogy to see how fictional voices can contribute to testimony. In *Company*, the narrator attempts to bear witness to the act of one's own speaking by detaching the speaking self from the spoken self. The narrator materializes in dual form through a 'pronominal *pas de deux*' (Ackerley and Gontarski 2004: 107), as he speaks in second person to a companion who symbolizes the narrator also. By announcing his inventions and being announced as that invention, this bifurcated perspective amounts to a comprehensive self-projection since both act and subject matter are directed towards a veiled self-reflection, or rather, self-creation. Beckett essentially offers another variation of the author as creature theme since the narrator acknowledges that he is a 'Devised deviser devising it all for company' (C, 30). Although the narrator is able to utter himself into existence and compose a vision of himself as the subject of language, the two – act and content – remain separate. By necessity, the narrator is internally alienated, keeping a united identity at arm's length and re-imagining himself before articulating the 'you' that he deceptively inhabits.

The narrator of *Company* effectively assumes roles as author and character, developing a speaking voice and listening confidante to objectify the story. The narrator's process is often available to him: 'Might not the hearer be improved? Made more companionable if not downright human. Mentally perhaps there is room for enlivenment. An attempt at reflexion at least. At recall. At speech even. Conation of some kind however feeble. A trace of emotion. Signs of distress. A sense of failure. Without loss of character' (C, 17). This characterization is also a study of character; it is criteria for self-assessment as well as creation. In satisfying each of the specifications (reflexion, conation, emotion), the narrator improves his three-dimensional portrait and brings his ipseity into focus, revealing to himself his own capacities. *Company*, then, has the peculiar effect of presenting and effacing its subject. It throws its voice and creates the illusion of multiple presences when, in fact, a single presence has been split to establish a conversation between its constituent parts. As such, the 'I', the enunciating person, is absent: 'Nowhere to be found. Nowhere to be sought. The unthinkable last of all. Unnamable. Last person. I' (C, 15). In turn, the narrator largely refrains from using the first-person pronoun to avoid phrases such as 'I said', which would suggest a more obvious autobiographical mode that neatly connects the present and past.

Beckett presents a narrator who inserts biographical vignettes and studies himself in a kind of schizophrenic projection of self, yet filters this sense of identity with a framework of otherness that dislocates the announcing 'I', displaces the sovereign author and demands the text's autonomy. The text is oddly autobiographical, but in a way that foregrounds the ruinous dynamics of self-reflective partitioning and fictional constructs as opposed to a direct correlation between the writing and the self. Jean-Luc Nancy proposes that 'there is not, nor has there ever been any presence-to-self that would not call into question the distance from self that this presence demands' (Derrida 1991: 102). It is this paradoxical nature of identity, always constituted by the space between presences, that Beckett hits upon in the last word of *Company*: 'Alone' (C, 42). In this recognition of isolation, the self divides into object and subject, observed and observer, pointing out the necessary severance of self that such a self-conscious assertion would require. In effect, the narrator is making company up to and including the final utterance of the text.

In its exploration of the implicit distance within self-presence, *Company* is comparable to Maurice Blanchot's 1994 text *The Instant of My Death* ([1994] 2000). Set in 1944, the narrator in Blanchot's text reflects on a young man's narrow escape from execution at the hands of what first appear to be German soldiers but, as it transpires, are members of the Vlassov army, allies of the

Nazis. Yet, as Derrida makes known in *Demeure* with the aid of a personal letter from Blanchot, the narrative viewpoint in *The Instant of My Death* suggests a familiarity or intimacy with the protagonist's episode and implies that the two presences have a single source in Blanchot's own biography. Far from suggesting unity, however, this short text offers a representation of memory and autobiography by evoking the distance between the present and the said event or remembered self. As a result, Derrida recognizes the liminal space between testimony and literature, and later, testimony and fiction. He writes: '[I]f testimony thereby became proof, information, certainty, or archive, it would lose its function as testimony. In order to remain testimony, it must therefore allow itself to be haunted. It must allow itself to be parasitized by precisely what it excludes from its inner depths, the *possibility*, at least, of literature' (2000: 30).

As previously mentioned, testimony is rooted in uncertainty for Derrida. A witness can swear an oath, yet his or her deposition is not purely objective or direct knowledge; testimony is always the retrospective act of bearing witness encumbered by fallacy. Blanchot's evocation of this distinction encourages Derrida to trace 'the meshes of the net formed by the limits *between* fiction and testimony, which are also *interior* each to the other' (Derrida 2000: 56). According to Derrida, there is fiction within testimony and testimony within fiction. The crossover takes place due to the testifying 'I's inability to account for what the pronoun signifies without becoming, in some sense, a fictional 'I'. As Jennifer Yusin suggests, testimony reveals 'the failure of autobiography to maintain its status as biography. It would seem, then, that any attempt at autobiography becomes fiction as the I announces, as Blanchot claims, its inherent failure and absence' (2005: 137). The error of testimony emerges in the intervals between experience, memory and enunciation, meaning that the language of testimony will always be in excess of its motivation and imply a degree of fiction.

In relation to Beckett's trilogy, the crucial point of interest in Derrida's reading of Blanchot is the way in which testimony might figure in fiction and the resultant possibility of tracing the fictional reconstruction of self – the young man or the 'he' in Blanchot – back to a testifying voice of sorts as a manifestation of the suppressed author-narrator. The possibility of identifying an originary voice amongst a cast of figments queries whether the substitute voices in

Beckett's trilogy are figures of prosopopoeia (a rhetorical device by which an imaginary, absent or dead person is represented as speaking or acting), or rather heteronyms (voices imagined by a writer to produce idiomatic writing styles), as David Jones proposes. Prosopopoeia essentially gives a mask and thus a 'face' to a source, while heteronym poses 'other' constructed voices. Jones opts for heteronym because '[p]rosopopoeia may ultimately promise a return to intelligibility; as a rhetoric figure adopted by a particular speaker, it looks forward to the moment at which the mask will be lowered and the speaker's "true" voice restored' (2011: 21). Beckett's narrators exert themselves to consolidate the multiplicity of voices and return to the singular subject but, strictly speaking, this endeavour is in vain if subjectivity is considered as a complete identification with self. In this latter respect, Jones' adoption of heteronym to describe the narrative dynamic in Beckett's work is a prudent position.

However, prosopopoeia remains relevant as a term that emphasizes the ownership between creator and creature, ventriloquist and dummy, rather than suggesting that these voices are completely discrete and individual, which is not always the impression gleaned from Beckett's work. Daniel Katz, to name one Beckett scholar, recognizes the ambivalent position assumed throughout the trilogy, in which "'stories of others" are told "as if" they belonged to oneself' (1999: 91). It is questionable whether the stories are really about or belong to others, commandeered as one's own, or actually about and belong to the teller. This creates a conflict in which the distinction between self and other is obscured for the sake of discourse. Accordingly, it might be more accurate to say that prosopopoeia and heteronymy clash in Beckett's work and in doing so, maintain an indecisive narrative, with the former fundamentally inspiring a pursuit of the host and the latter destabilizing that single identity. Malone suggests as much in one of his many returns from the fictional world of Macmann back to the self-awareness of his position as a writer in the hospital room:

> perhaps we'll all come back, reunited, done with parting, done with prying on one another, back to this foul little den all dirty white and vaulted, as though hollowed out of ivory, an old rotten tooth. Or alone, back alone, as alone as when I went, but I doubt

it, I can hear them from here, clamouring after me down the
corridors, stumbling through the rubble, beseeching me to take
them with me (*T*, 237).

Malone realizes the possibility of assembling the constituent voices
in his mind and also abandoning the voices to reveal his solitariness.
As the 'Murphys, Merciers, Molloys, Morans and Malones' (*T*,
237) continue to implore the narrator, the image of ruins appears
through the 'rubble' to suggest a demolished subject. By observing
his ruins overrun with figments, however, some part of the self is
reflecting on the uncertainty over self-presence that the voices
precipitate and thus bearing witness to its own disorder. This
creaturely subjectivity means that the fictional beings can act as
figures of alterity that offer the host a relative value, even if his
central position is inaccessible or untenable. By saying these voices
do not amount to self, it seems that, rather than overwhelm the
narrator, Malone gets a sustained view of himself as a deferred
presence. Although the voices may stem from the narrator as figures
of prosopopoeia that act in his absence, they also show that Malone
is not completely absorbed in them and so these heteronymic voices
are different to him, which ultimately helps to satisfy the *cogito*.

By the time Beckett reaches *The Unnamable*, he has the narrator
experience a range of different relationships with the figments that
emerge. The initial reason for developing these fictional voices is to
achieve the one true voice preserved in prosopopoeia. The possibility
of retrieving an originary identity is the motivation behind the
narrator's attempt to indulge and subsequently disband surplus
voices, which would re-establish the site of creation. In a precursor
to the 'Alone' of *Company*, the narrator of *The Unnamable*
recognizes his precarious position from the outset: 'I shall not be
alone in the beginning. I am of course alone. Alone. That is soon
said. Things can be soon said. And how can one be sure, in such
darkness? I shall have company. In the beginning. A few puppets.
Then I'll scatter them, to the winds, if I can' (*T*, 294). The narrator
is uncertain whether he is alone and therefore resolves to have
company. It is only the dissolution of other voices that will confirm
the solitariness of the narrator in the end. That is, only after his
company has departed will he recognize the vacillations of his
aporetic and ephectic discourse as himself alone. As such, the
narrator contemplates the crowd of past protagonists and, in an

echo of the earlier lines, remarks: 'I'll scatter them, and their miscreated puppets. Perhaps I'll find traces of myself' (*T*, 327). In this formulation, the voices cover a subject that lies beneath or behind their activity, but dispersing these creatures will help to identify the creator.

The narrator is impelled to refer to his fictional constructs in order to undertake a process of elimination that will recognize and dispel fiction in order to identify his reality negatively. The narrator states: 'First I'll say what I'm not, that's how they taught me to proceed, then what I am' (*T*, 328). The oppressive 'they' that lurk in this passage and insist that their negative technique is a passage to self-discovery is the same cohort of voices that move to usurp the narrator's presence. The upshot of the narrator's impression of reality against the touchstone of fiction is that the faintest knowledge of his situation cannot be achieved or expressed without a degree of fiction: 'All these Murphys, Molloys and Malones do not fool me. They have made me waste my time, suffer for nothing, speak of them when, in order to stop speaking, I should have spoken of me and of me alone. But I just said I have spoken of me, am speaking of me' (*T*, 305). The contemplation of his puppets here means the narrator inadvertently stumbles upon a passage dedicated to him. Thus, the narrator of *The Unnamable* can only attest to himself through the portal of fiction.

The prevalence of surrogate voices means the narrator is caught up in fiction for lengthy periods, to the extent that the voices encroach upon his identity. By focusing on what he is not, the narrator invests himself into the cohort of voices, moving from the negative identification of the elimination project to a sustained confabulation alongside heteronymic voices. It is therefore imperative that the narrator recognizes these voices as substitutes if he is to maintain the possibility of an independent identity, as when he reflects: 'I thought I was right in enlisting these sufferers of my pains. I was wrong. They never suffered my pains, their pains are nothing, compared to me, a mere tittle of mine, the tittle I thought I could put from me, in order to witness it' (*T*, 305). The narrator clearly attempts to transfer his issues to the prosthetic figures, but fortuitously they cannot be employed as like-for-like replacements. The consolation is that the incompatibility of the fictional voices allows the narrator to comprehend the identity crisis that is undoubtedly his own.

The narrator also suggests that although the fictional voices tend to efface the single authorial voice, they might also demonstrate his character in action. Rather than use the creatures as fictional others to offset his real voice, this 'dirty pack of fake maniacs' (*T*, 371) are reduced to a facet of the narrator's own personality, namely his 'inaptitude'. He says, 'Perhaps all they have told me has reference to a single existence, the confusion of identities being merely apparent and due to my inaptitude to assume any' (*T*, 333). It is significant that the narrator should take ownership of inaptitude because it means that although his creatures consume him, his subjectivity can consist in his being consumed, aware of himself buried 'behind my mannikins' (*T*, 308). The more these figures take over in *The Unnamable*, then, the more the narrator realizes this invasion as a repercussion of his defining property. Effectively, the narrator can testify to his role in his own ruin at the hands of his interlocutors.

As encounters with non-identity become increasingly relevant to the experience of subjectivity, the multitude of occasions in which Beckett's narrators claim that self-knowledge is banished from them and that speech is 'not-I' take on new significance. Towards the end of his assignment, Moran feels a 'growing resignation to being dispossessed of self' (*T*, 149) as he gradually deteriorates to resemble his target Molloy. Curiously, however, this transformation would not only inadvertently complete Moran's investigation by 'discovering' a Molloy-like condition, but also improve his sense of identity precisely by assimilating the stranger:

> Physically speaking it seemed to me I was now becoming rapidly unrecognisable. And when I passed my hands over my face, in a characteristic and now more than ever pardonable gesture, the face my hands felt was not my face any more, and the hands my face felt were my hands no longer. [. . .] And this belly I did not know remained my belly, my old belly, thanks to I know not what intuition. And to tell the truth I not only knew who I was, but I had a sharper and clearer sense of my identity than ever before, in spite of its deep lesions and the wounds with which it was covered (*T*, 170–1).

Previously, Moran had prided himself on a disciplined mind-set founded on sovereignty over self and authority over his son. Yet, the more Moran's impression of his outward appearance slips and he

loses grip of his regimented self-image, the more these ephemeral
façades give way to a profound recognition of the self that lies
beneath. In other words, as he becomes a ruin of his previous state
he can come to recognize a constitutive difference between the
ordered past and disordered present.

It is a paradoxical event in which contact with an unfamiliar
version of oneself induces a strong sense of identity. Such a moment,
it can be suggested, implies that the experience of desubjectification
is the key component of the fictional prostheses and their oppressive
voices in Beckett's work. This is a feature that doubles strikingly as
a passage into testimony in that only through speaking about an
other will the identity in ruins be available. In Yusin's essay on
Blanchot, she goes as far as to claim that '[a]s much as testimony
may assume the autobiographical voice that writes about a singular
experience, it is fiction that opens the creative space in which the I
is able to write as an I' (2005: 142). Fiction indicates an acceptance
of the pronoun's personal and impersonal characteristics, it
confesses and performs its inherent failure, which, on the contrary,
testimony tries to eschew when it employs the 'I'. As such, testimony
is the bedfellow of fiction, despite its prefigured attempts to conceal
this proximity; fiction haunts every attempt at testimony and that
creativity is the necessary ingredient in realizing the unattainability
of truth. The same holds true for Beckett, whose texts bear witness
to the fact that the mediatory practice of writing as an 'I' attests to
the failure of testimony. Nevertheless, Beckett's narrators come to
rely on fiction for any recognition or documentation of their
existence, despite it being permeated by the exclusion and
desubjectification not usually related to judicial testimony.

Beckett's trilogy resonates with rather unorthodox concepts of
testimony that focus on the spaces between seeing and saying, event
and account. The fallibility of the witness and the dissociation
inherent to retrospect are most intense in Holocaust testimony, but
the same issues apply to Beckett's author-narrators to render them
both ignorant and impotent, and yet oddly cognizant of their
deficiencies. Beckett's thorough engagement with an art of failure
precipitates contingent narrative and fractious subjective conditions
that show up the inefficacy of epistemological and expressive modes
proper to the human. The obligation to speak and inability to speak
conspire to make Beckett's author-narrators creaturely subjects,
bound to creation. The term (in)sovereignty describes the

concomitant potency and impotence that makes up Beckett's creaturely aesthetic, and a similar duality contributes to the identity in ruins that describes the simultaneous possession and dispossession of self that marks Beckett's creatures. Although the creaturely dynamics I have traced depart from the standards notion of a sovereign witness and human subject, Beckett's creatures offer an ontological position that retains testimonial value and subjective viability despite the crises in language and identity. Bearing witness to the event and the self inevitably leaves things unsaid or incomplete, but it is an awareness of the impossibility of speaking and knowing through the performance of language and trying to understand that attests to the lacunae left by the thing itself.

2

Power:

Master–servant relationships

Beckett's creaturely aesthetic undermines the artistic foundations of sovereign power and reconstitutes testimonial value from the detritus of competent practice. In the wartime and post-war context of physical hardship, ideological destabilization and artistic inadequacy, Beckett's engagement with ignorance and impotence offers an apt focus on powerlessness. Testimony in Beckett's trilogy includes a 'sovereign as creature' dynamic that impacts individual characters, yet it is possible to trace the abject state of Beckett's creatures back to other figures of power to explicate what it means to be a subject and a fellow creature. Rather than focusing exclusively on author-narrators, Beckett develops a series of attachments and confrontations between characters, or master and servant relationships, to exercise, challenge and neutralize power and authoritative creation. These master–servant relationships show how figures of authority are preserved to keep stable identities based on binaries, but also that power is frequently destabilized in co-dependent relationships.

G. W. F. Hegel explicates the co-dependency between lord and bondsman in relation to identity thinking in the seminal chapter 'Independence and Dependence of Self-Consciousness: Lordship and Bondage' in his first major work *Phenomenology of Spirit* ([1807] 1998). Hegel explains how consciousness must escape itself to gain knowledge of itself and that this '[s]elf-consciousness achieves its satisfaction only in another self-consciousness' ([1807] 1998: 91). The meeting of two self-conscious beings triggers a struggle for superiority that aims to prove the value and freedom of the self. Ironically, the victorious lord becomes a dependent force, reliant on the bondsman to mediate his self-consciousness. However, for Hegel, the struggle engineers the extreme conditions of 'dread' and 'fear' in which threat allows the bondsman to recognize himself. Furthermore, the bondsman's work objectifies his being, thereby allowing him to 'possess his independence in thinghood' (Hegel [1807] 1998: 95). Antibiosis, according to Hegel, presents a kind of symbiosis whereby antagonisms between two foreign bodies reveal the self to consciousness, causing identity to thrive.

This 'self-will, a freedom which is still enmeshed in servitude' is a significant repercussion that justifies the use of the master–servant coupling over master–slave and lord–bondsman variations since it highlights the strength a servant can extract from work (Hegel [1807] 1998: 98). The OED defines 'servant' as '[o]ne who is under the obligation to render certain services to, and to obey the orders of, a person or a body of persons, especially in return for wages or salary'. This payment is one motivation to offer service, yet the servant's usefulness to a master lends this subordinate role a power of its own. The servant has the ability to unsettle power roles, both coincidentally, as Hegel shows, and through voluntary submission, as typified by the ascetic servant of God whose self-discipline and abstention offers purpose while inducing reverence from others. The term 'servant' thus comes to 'express a relation to the Sovereign', as in 'servant of the state' or a 'public servant'. The servant effectively has a dual level as both anonymous worker subject to the master and influential counterpart through his or her indispensible service.

Master and servant identities are unstable, and liable to oscillate or have a contradictory nature. As such, the narrative condition of (in)sovereignty, in which a position of power enfolds a position of impotence, finds an equivalent in the master–servant relationship. Walter Benjamin asserts that the sovereign power to decide and override decisions means the sovereign is 'confined to the world of creation; he is the lord of creatures, but he remains a creature' (1977: 85). In carrying out a narrative, this 'sovereign as creature' simultaneously occupies the peak of power and trough of impotence. But the sovereign creature also emerges as a social dynamic when the master relies on the servant for distinction and, in extreme cases, resorts to inhuman or monstrous levels of brutality in order to dominate an other. The master is degraded in order to rule; he is a creature simultaneously amongst and above creatures. In this way, the master–servant binary is destabilized to the extent that sovereign power encloses creaturely weaknesses and vice versa. The co-dependency between master and servant essentially marks a point of tension in the power struggle that can decentre power altogether.

After an exposition of the socio-political and artistic transitions in France during the early years of the Second World War, the opening sections of this chapter interpret the service granted to patriarchal forms of mastery in Beckett's *Watt* and the creaturely state of melancholy in *Waiting for Godot*. Not only do these texts represent Beckett's steps towards refreshing literary styles and content in prose and drama respectively, they also share an interest in how single figures of authority sustain power systems and dictate narrative momentum. Read together, the two texts convey the influence of absent others and the habit of projecting and preserving masters to combat the fear of abandonment. Beckett's work both invokes and undermines transcendental authority, but while he deprecates metanarratives, they nevertheless remain as a potential to govern his characters.

The stability that an overarching narrative offers is found to a lesser extent in the distinction of binary roles. The second half of the chapter follows the movement from superhuman to subhuman others, considering the complex identity issues between the Nazis and Jews, and how the resulting conflicts relate to deep-rooted tensions between human and animal identities, to comment upon the necessary alterity in Beckett's work. As the impossibility of self-identity denies independence, Beckett's characters attempt to develop identity through externalized conflicts. In turn, the pseudo-couples are deprived of singularity and are subject to neighbourly co-dependency. The biopolitical tensions of these antagonistic and compulsory power struggles are the primary focus of the later sections of the chapter, which move to expound the multifaceted apparatus of authority. With reference to Michel Foucault's readings of sovereign power and Agamben's analysis of the biopolitics of the Third Reich, I address issues of territory and care in examples from a number of Beckett's texts from the immediate post-war period, including *The Expelled* (French 1946; English 1962), *The End*, *Mercier and Camier* (written in French in 1946; French 1970; English 1974) and *Molloy*. The organization of space in Beckett reveals a political juncture at which welfare for the same crosses into violence towards the other. By bringing Beckett's master–servant relationships into view alongside the context of the Second World War and the Holocaust, this chapter on power serves to illuminate the artistic and extra-literary axis where compositional tensions meet socio-political and ethical issues.

Exercising writing in *Watt* the fungible and Knott there

Beckett was very much a struggling writer before the war and, besides developing an artistic network, Beckett's formative years were spent negotiating the shadow of his artistic precursors and the contemporaneous literary voices after the Great War. Shortly prior to the outbreak of the Second World War, Beckett visited Germany, during which he visited many art galleries and made friends with several artists including Karl Ballmer and Willem Grimm. Beckett wrote to Thomas MacGreevy during this 1936–1937 trip, noting: 'the campaign against "Art-Bolshevism" is only just beginning' (2009e: 387). He anticipated what he was to witness first-hand during his stay: the diminishing presence of art that failed to support the ideals of the totalitarian state. The Third Reich's censorship of 'degenerate' art, particularly the Commission of Confiscation of July 1937, was enforced by the *Reichskulturkammer* to temper liberal dissent. For David Weisberg, the Fascist regime called for the 'destruction of cultural freedom in order to consolidate social control and maintain the repression of democratic dissent' (2006: 43–4). He argues that this suppression of artistic freethinking conditions Beckett's political outlook since 'it threatened the only social matrix in which his writing might make sense' (Weisberg 2006: 43). It is curious, then, that it is in the context of Beckett's clandestine existence in the rural south of France during the Nazi occupation of Paris that his literary approach acquired an immediacy and significance that was missing prior to the start of the Second World War. The strict censorship and ideological conformity enforced during the Nazi occupation make the formal and thematic levels of mastery and service in a text such as *Watt* appear all the more apparent, innovative and radical. At a time when art is forced to fortify political ends as another vehicle for propaganda, Beckett's text refuses such systematization by absorbing and obscuring notions of authority, order and control to deliver a defiantly experimental retort to the sanitized works that the Nazi regime approved, such as Adolf Wissel's bucolic paintings and Adolf Bartels' *völkisch* poetry.

As much as the writing is diffusely political, it is necessarily personal. Beckett mainly wrote his experimental novel *Watt* while taking refuge in La Croix, near the unoccupied village of Roussillon. Naturally, in the early to mid-1940s, Beckett's writing was secondary to his work with the French Resistance and his manual labour on the Audes' farm (Knowlson 1997: 324–5). Yet the fact that Beckett continued to write suggests that creativity is a required act; it is imperative to exercise the ability to write. He later recognized how important writing was for his spell in the Vaucluse region, pointing out the mental succour it provided: 'Without my writing I would have gone mad' (Beckett quoted in Lamont 2001: 135). It seems that writing fiction allowed Beckett to keep his bearings on reality and act as a private resistance to the maddening wartime conditions. Beckett also described *Watt* as 'an exercise' (quoted in Cohn 2001: 112), which implies that, at this point, the question for Beckett is not how to respond artistically to world events, but how to save one's creative faculties in critical times. Accordingly, the word 'exercise' can be taken in a number of ways to mark *Watt* as a fulcrum in Beckett's career. It suggests that he is maintaining a practice of the past, in a conveyance of writing as a relic through the period of turmoil, or even a melancholic lingering over writing. It also suggests that Beckett is improving his practice, working out his method to craft a new approach. In this sense, the exercise is an experimental activity. In addition, the homonymic value of the word also suggests 'exorcise', and this 'driving out' or 'getting rid' of style, convention and the sedimented idea of writing as a writer is contrary to the sense of exercising a well-established skill. Taken together, however, Beckett's approach to his novel elicits the tensions between the expressive freedom of yesteryears, the present task of maintaining his creativity and the direction to transform literature for the future.

The eight-year period of inactivity and transition during the war, punctuated only by *Watt*, ultimately led to Beckett's turn to the French language and his foray into drama, which are the outstanding changes to his artistic practice. At the same time, he was also quietly developing his understanding and integration of the relations between power and compulsion, freedom and thraldom, in the process and product of his writing. Beckett was deliberating the pitfalls of poetics based on sovereignty, complete with a masterful author, and moving into hitherto unexplored forms of incompetence. His focus on incompetence, however, does not occlude the influence of rigid backgrounds or strict structures, like tradition, sovereignty and reason. As he was completing *Watt*, Beckett was subject to the Vichy regime, which replaced the Republican motto '*Liberté, Egalité, Fraternité*' (Freedom, Equality, Fraternity) with '*Travail, Famille, Patrie*' (Work, Family, Homeland). Although several commentators, most notably John P. Harrington in *The Irish Beckett* (1991), have pointed out the novel's local Irish colour and debts to Anglo-Irish tradition, particularly the Big House novel (Harrington 1991: 109–42), the Vichy regime's throwback to the feudal system also offers a productive context in which to read the novel.

Watt and his superior Erskine are one combination of manservant pairs from a continuous stream of servants that enter the Knott household, work for the mysterious master Mr Knott and eventually leave having rarely witnessed their employer. Watt is a pensive character who carries out protracted analyses of the house rules and servants' duties in a bid to make sense of his role. Notwithstanding *Watt*'s recognizably Irish locale and allusions to Irish culture, the changes to the political slogans in France during the early 1940s help to illuminate the dynamics of the Knott household. Anthony Uhlmann suggests the National Revolution's new motto evokes 'a more medieval idea of a ' "natural" order' (1999: 95). It replaces the responsibility of 'freedom' in the original Republican motto with the more physical obligation to 'work', which transforms the citizen into a human resource, not unlike the peasants paying homage to the owners of Anglo-Irish big houses. The change from 'equality' to 'family' in the motto stresses the domestic hierarchical structure, headed by the patriarch and founded on service to the 'house'. While the word 'house' promotes the idea of a small, close-knit community, or social microcosm, it also connotes a designated zone of governance – the decisive house rules under the roof. This principle also has an affinity with the greater levels of autonomy afforded to the self-sustaining estates of the Irish landed class. 'Family' itself derives from *famulus* meaning servant, and the combination of work, house and servant clearly points to the duties that Watt performs. The fact that 'fraternity' is exchanged for 'homeland' expands the idea of household servants to a national level, with the government acting as the noble or patriarch, hence 'fatherland'. The implication of the Vichy motto for Watt, then, is the reduction of his individual identity, as he becomes part of a system. Watt's place in the Knott house is emblematic of the individual's role in a socio-political mechanism that has reduced its democratic, egalitarian values and accentuated sovereign, dynastic rule, which gathers impersonalized subjects together to work for the benefit of a master.

The contexts of the Vichy regime and Anglo-Irish aristocratic rule in relation to *Watt* imply specific systems of order based on the assumption of more intrinsic power positions. Friedrich Nietzsche uses the terms 'noble' and 'servile' in his philosophy to describe the roles underpinning the will to power. But as with Uhlmann's acknowledgement of the Vichy regime's appeal to a 'natural order', Nietzsche adopts these categories from the feudal politico-economic system and naturalizes them. In his philosophical bestiary, these terms come to form a fundamental dichotomy in power relations between the courageous nobility and gregarious animals that depend on others. As Alphonso Lingis recognizes, in Nietzsche, 'eagles, lions and serpents are noble; sheep, cattle and poultry are servile' (2004: 9). Nietzsche employs these classifications not in an allegorical way, but in a kind of zoomorphic process that draws a line of continuity between humans and other species. The inherent nature of the noble and servile roles is significant in Beckett's text since, before his entrance into the Knott household, the first appearance of the eponymous protagonist gestures towards Watt's identity as an object, a thing to be used, which is a status he acquires at the expense of human semblance and attributes.

Beckett's exposition of Watt is through the eyes of three observers, Mr Hackett and Goff and Tetty Nixon. As Watt disembarks from a tram, the reader is told that 'Tetty was not sure whether it was a man or a woman' (*W*, 11). This thinghood, the questionable status of 'it-ness' that is Watt, applies to a number of sexually ambiguous and sexless creatures in Beckett's work that reveal the author's distrust of pronouns. His writing, Beckett says, 'has to do with a fugitive "I" [. . .]. It's an embarrassment of pronouns. I'm searching for the non-pronounial. [. . .] [I]t seems a betrayal to say "he" or

"she"' (quoted in Shainberg 1987: 134). This viewpoint leads
Beckett to drop sex altogether in *The Unnamable*, for example, in
which the lack of a name destabilizes other referential determinations
and becomes palpable in the redundancy of sexual classification.
The initial portrait of Watt as a sexless creature then devolves to an
inanimate item, with Beckett extending Nietzsche's line of servility
from human to animal to inorganic matter: 'Mr Hackett was not
sure whether it was not a parcel, a carpet for example, or a roll of
tarpaulin, wrapped up in dark paper and tied about the middle with
a cord' (W, 11).[1] An anthropomorphized version of this image
introduces Watt as a tall, clownish oddity, anticipating the stiff
'funambulistic stagger' (W, 24) depicted later. But it is the actual
objects that Mr Hackett sees that hold more significance for Watt as
a servant. He is a carpet to be walked over, which suggests his
submissiveness, or a tarpaulin used to cover up, which implies a
practical quality. As a mundane object, Watt is set up as an article
of service belonging to a domestic setting.

In Watt's likeness to a roll of carpet or tarpaulin, Beckett conveys
his character's inertia, as a thing brought into service by an external
force. Such articles are defined by a function assigned to them,
which is a particularly creaturely state that recalls the definition of
the creature as subject to another's control. The passivity of an
inanimate item corresponds with the docile disposition of the
creature, which is reinforced shortly after Watt's objectification: 'a
milder, more inoffensive creature does not exist' (W, 14). Given his
enigmatic introduction, there is a question mark over Watt and he
is doubly 'inoffensive' as a result of this blankness as an
uncharacterized character. While the reader learns that Watt is
intriguing to Mr Hackett and in debt to Goff Nixon, his destination
is indecipherable and the trio of onlookers are ignorant of all other
means of identification, such as Watt's 'Nationality, family,
birthplace, confession, occupation, means of existence, distinctive
signs' (W, 16). In this way, Beckett alludes to the very composition
of his protagonist in that Watt seems to have materialized from
nowhere, having no traceable origins or background. Furthermore,
when Goff Nixon finally does recall a physical feature, 'a huge big
red nose' (W, 26), it is in keeping with master Knott's criteria for
'the two types of men' to serve him (W, 51). Watt fits the physical
description Knott stipulates and therefore this telling first
appearance defines Watt as an archetypal servant. Beckett's

exposition acts as a kind of job interview conducted through the public reconnaissance between Mr Hackett and the Nixons, and Watt's indistinctness makes him a suitable candidate for the servile herd that continuously passes through Knott's house.

It is apt that Watt arrives as a nondescript entity since he is appointed to fill the vacancy that Arsene leaves in the Knott house, and this process of replacement stipulates a level of homogeneity and adaptability to achieve a seamless transition. Watt's emptiness, as it transpires, is occupied by the inscrutable organization and structure of the household tasks. His inability to comprehend menial duties, such as feeding the dogs, causes him to serve blindly, in one sense, in that he satisfies his designated function without an explanation or justification of the reasoning behind it. Yet his quest for lucidity through self-reflection also results in a second blindness, which causes his provisional status as a being continually under question. Watt repeatedly fails in his attempts to name exactly what he is and he effectively remains a mystery to himself. Since Watt is an enigmatic figure preoccupied with the enigmas of the house, he decides to consider himself a man for convenience. This gendered existence offers him little comfort and is tantamount to his objectified status. The narrator says that 'for all the relief that this afforded him, he might just as well have thought of himself as a box, or an urn' (W, 69). Watt identifies with receptacles as much as humanity. He is equally a hollow container loaded with cremated remains, operating as a holder of nothingness.

The protean identity that amounts to naught is ideal for Watt's induction into a servile role moulded by the needs of a master since, crucially, he does not have to change or conform drastically to be assimilated into the system. He can perform his job without a massive overhaul of his personality. It is also significant that Arsene initiates Watt, with 'information of a practical nature to impart' (W, 37) in his twenty-three page 'short statement' (W, 31–54), because it imposes the established order onto the new generation, thus allowing the ground-floor operations to uphold the routines of the Knott household upstairs and maintain the illusion of constancy. Despite the changes in personnel, with Watt for Arsene, Arthur for Erskine and Micks for Watt, Beckett focuses on the synchronicity of this interchange. In a rich image that offers multiple opportunities for interpretation, Beckett writes: 'for the coming is in the shadow of the going, and the going in the shadow of the coming' (W, 48).

The seamless transitions between arrivals and departures show that the servants are fungible, trading places with one another and presumably passing on responsibilities, such as preparing, serving and collecting Mr Knott's dinner before giving the leftovers to the dogs. Bequeathing duties in this way mimics the heritage of an ancestral house but, for the workforce, it is the post itself that takes priority over the person that fills it, thereby withholding individuality from the servants that receive the role.

The 'shadow' of the going also suggests an inherited ignorance towards the duties the servants perform. When Watt sees 'a figure, human apparently' (W, 194) on his departure from the Knott house, this new figure is described in remarkably similar terms to Watt: 'a sheet, or a sack, or a quilt, or a rug' (W, 195). The arriving servant appears as a new inanimate object to replace the old object it resembles. As Richard Begam points out, 'Watt finally confronts an image of himself – meets himself, so to speak, face to face' (1996: 96). Begam accentuates the self-knowledge of this meeting, yet the fact that Beckett offers four variations in the description to place emphasis on alternatives indicates that this is not a positively recognizable mirror image of Watt that offers him a reliable reflection of himself. Although he encounters a similarly indeterminate figure, any sense of identification is through their mutual anonymity, which stresses a connection based on their unknowable selves. Indeed, Watt's inability to fathom the meaning of his actions, along with the lack of teleology in his daily undertakings, suggest that these domestic items confer nothing of his own true function, or rather, the reason for his docile performance. In effect, Watt is a servant simply because he serves, but the nature of his service is not disclosed to him. His status as a thing overwhelms his self-knowledge and yet denies any understanding of his role in the wider scheme. Watt remains unaware of the principles that govern the strict instructions of the eccentric Mr Knott. As a result, the lack of context and cause that Watt endures divests him of an accumulative identity or idea of self, other than in the actual performance of his duties.

While intimating his place in a series of characters in Beckett's corpus, Watt's position as a device in a concatenation of devices also represents the lineal arrangement of life itself. The novel begins and ends at stations that resonate on a religious level, alluding to the 'Stations of the Cross' that depict the Passion of Christ and provide a vision of life and death characterized by the throes of service.[2] The stations in *Watt* suggest that the novel's setting is a temporary one, with a stream of travellers entering and exiting by similar means. The sequential aspect of rail transit is apparent in the connecting shadows of the 'coming' and 'going', which imply birth and death, particularly since the shadows cast in this image would require a light source from the direction of arrival and the direction of departure. This spiritual representation of mortality, with divine light symbolizing the passage in and out of transient earthly life, attributes a figurative value to the house, portraying it as the locale of lifetime. It also suggests that, paradigmatically, existence falls into a pattern of service to an overseeing but often unseen master, while the exact purpose of the routines and responsibilities continue to perplex. As Arsene informs Watt, 'in truth the same things happen to us all, especially to men in our situation, whatever that is, if we only chose to know it' (W, 37). In this way, the Knott house is an analogy for existence, but, more acutely, it conveys a way of life administered by 'top-down' systems, such as the religious and parliamentary 'houses' that govern and dispatch servants. Beckett's domestic setting illustrates the individual's disposable role as a puppet manipulated by the strings of obscure forces, such as the habitual routines of life and the prescience of mortality, while simultaneously alluding to social, political and military power structures.

Whereas servants are succeeded, the sempiternal head of the house Mr Knott remains fixed. Before Arsene exits, the servant says that 'there is one that neither comes nor goes, I refer I need hardly say to my late employer, but seems to abide in his place, for the time being at any rate, like an oak, an elm, a beech or an ash, and we rest for a little while in his branches' (W, 48). Knott is the enduring pillar of the household; he is a lord who watches ephemeral bodies pass through. As the employer, he also ordains the rules that engage the subordinates, so that he looms over the house as 'the shadow of purpose' (W, 48). Knott's lordship evokes an ecclesiastical model of patriarchal guidance, not dissimilar to the shepherd template of Judeo-Christian scripture that organizes a flock behind a leader, and is adopted by the clergy. For instance, David's psalm 'The Lord is my Shepherd' speaks of the path to righteousness and residing in the house of the Lord (Psalms 23), which details a sense of direction and belonging. In the Gospel of John, 'I am the good shepherd: the good shepherd giveth his life for the sheep' (John 10.11) asserts that the leader protects and is responsible for his followers, and, in true pastoral service, willing to sacrifice himself. In this proverbial formulation, the shepherd and the flock supposedly offer purpose to one another and embark on an identification process that collapses the master–servant dichotomy to instil the principles of mutuality. Despite this, the flock is homogenized while the shepherd is individualized, which elevates a single figure above a general group. It is clear that, as a result, service is appropriated as a means to power.

For Derrida, the human organization of power does not merely resemble a religious hierarchy, but rather supplants that former system. There is an 'onto-theologico-political structure of sovereignty', he writes in *The Beast and the Sovereign*, in which '[t]he human sovereign takes place as place-taking [lieu-tenant], he takes place the place standing in for the absolute sovereign: God' (Derrida 2009: 47, 54). In adopting authority, man is a substitute for, not a servant of, the divine power; the 'stand-in' underlines the absence of the Absolute and foregrounds its replaceability. This theocratic dynamic presents itself as servitude, with the monarch acting *Dei gratia* (by the grace of God) and the cleric preaching in the name of God, but the service is in name only since the divine power is not active and actually usurped by the 'assistance' of the representative. This deiformity is particularly pronounced in the apostleship and papal jurisdiction of Catholicism, in which appointed figures assume authority, even infallibility, in translating and disseminating holy dogma. In this cynical reading, the *servus servorum dei* (servant of the servants of God) papal tradition tarnishes servitude with the possibility of power in the guise of humility. Service effectively leads to responsibility, which in turn leads to authority.

Knott's mastery over his servants conveys a similar expropriation of authority, in which he assumes a likeness to God, but also becomes a god in the monotheistic dimensions of the cloistered household. As master of the house, Knott owns the living space, defines the hierarchical boundaries, dictates the diurnal rhythms of the staff and controls the domestic atmosphere. His power indicates a strong presence, and yet his authority is not enforced explicitly through physical or verbal means. Ironically, it is Knott's absence that confirms his godliness. In Exodus, for example, the Lord promises his presence but not in the form of pure theophany: 'Thou canst not see my face: for there shall no man see me, and live' (Exodus 33.20). Likewise, Watt has 'no direct dealings with Mr Knott' (*W*, 55) and, throughout his stay in the house, 'Of the nature of Mr Knott himself Watt remained in particular ignorance' (*W*, 172). When Watt does see Knott in the flower garden, the master is still strangely aloof, with head bowed and eyes closed. This rare encounter leaves Watt sorry and glad at once: sorry that his wish of 'seeing Mr Knott face to face' (*W*, 145) does not materialize but glad that his fear of doing so is not confronted. The equilibrium between desire and distance sustains Knott; a combination of fascination and mystique promotes his influence but also ensures his longevity.

The manner in which Knott remotely impels the activities in the house is a precursor to the phantom Godot from Beckett's most famous play *Waiting for Godot*. The two vagabonds Vladimir and Estragon stand by a tree on a country lane, occupying themselves with idle chatter in anticipation of a figure named Godot. The tension of the drama rests on the nonattendance of its *deus ex machina*, and Godot remains the cardinal power in the proceedings due to this tantalizing absence. In a similar manner to Godot, the master of the house in *Watt* is also influential in a negative way, as the name 'Knott' implies. He exists for the most part as an invisible force, absent in body but present as potential. Knott is defined by the presence of the things he is not and for this reason he is effectively implied in every sight and situation. For Jeremy Parrott, the dialectical relationship between presence and absence means Knott is pervasive everywhere: '[W]ithin the residual negation at the name's core nestles the plenum-void, 0/zero, whence all matter comes and whither it will once again return. [. . .] He may therefore be considered like an endless knot in the shape of a sideways figure 8 – the symbol of infinity – comprehending within himself all possibilities' (Parrott 2003: 93).

Knott's name brings to mind the nothingness that marks the beginning and end of everything. He represents the complete absence to which all presence is bound. When divided into its constituent parts, 'no-thing-ness' sees the master as the intangible opposite of the servant as a 'thing'. Therefore, Watt is mindful of his counterpart Knott while unable to receive communion with him. This curious concomitance of absence and presence, or psychological presence despite physical absence, is harboured within the subject to uphold an objectifying other. The unseen master is a diffuse figure of faith that exists as an active rule in the mind of the servant.

The association between Knott's absence and divinity is reflected in the inability to summon or obligate a deity. In 'God is a witness that cannot be sworn' (W, 4), Beckett's pun on swearing refers to profanity, and serves to evoke the overlap between common law and canon law in the condemnation of blasphemy. Furthermore, the judicial surface meaning of Beckett's line, in which God is a witness that cannot bear witness, compares religious and legal orders to demonstrate the prevailing judgement that takes effect *de facto*. The tribunal system establishes truth beyond reasonable doubt and delivers rulings in the absence of God's verdict, despite its reverence for religious law. Yet, as with Knott, being elsewhere means the deity is perpetually unseen and potentially anywhere. As such, God comes to represent a ubiquitous force, transmuting into moral conscience and subsisting in the subject's doubt, guilt or fear. This compunction is replicated in the Knott household when Watt transgresses the house rules. Beckett writes: 'No punishment fell on Watt, no thunderbolt' (W, 98), which is redolent of a wrathful deity, 'But he was not so foolish as to found in this a principle of conduct, or a precedent of rebelliousness, ho no, for Watt was only too willing to do as he was told' (W, 98). The lack of discipline and reference to folly here indicate an approach that encourages self-government, in a kind of imposed autonomy produced by the absent but influential nature of Mr Knott. Subsequently, Watt appears to conform on his own volition, freely obeying orders, and although he questions his duties, he does not actively challenge them. In effect, Beckett shows that compliant but ostensibly independent subjects can preserve the power of absent lords.[3]

Watt's and the other servants' concurrent subjection to an absent ruler and ability to exercise autonomy conveys a state of creatureliness under a godly creator, or autocratic creation. It is a divisive position for the creature: adhering to the absent figure of meaning, yet largely as a free agent; predicating order upon a metaphysical power, yet resorting to the observable physical world to glean the import of it all. Anat Pick defines such a predicament as one of the key tensions for the creature: 'the creaturely is not simply a synonym for the material and corporeal. It carries within it (as inflection, as horizon) an opening unto a religious vocabulary of creation and created, and so attempts a rapprochement between the material and the sacred' (2011: 17). In Beckett's *Watt*, the servant creature is emblematic of the relationship between the everyday, mortal life and a governing body or spiritual guide. The 'harmonious relation' between the material and the sacred, though, is limited to the fact that the household routines are upheld even though the system's significance is unfathomable. As the potential and responsibility for self-realization dawns, the creature remains bound to the absent creator and abides by the nebulous operations of its original dictates.

'A vague supplication': Melancholy in *Waiting for Godot*

In order for the 'absence' of Knott and Godot to become 'non-existence', the servants, or 'waiters', have to be immune or ignorant to the master's influence and cease to preserve divine power by refusing to submit to it. As in *Act Without Words I* (1958), Beckett's protagonists must finally resist the goading master, remain unmoved and instead take the Promethean plunge to assert *non serviam*, akin to Milton's quasi-heroic Satan. Yet, in terms of the identification of being, George Berkeley's principle *esse est aut percipi aut percipere* (to be is both to be perceived and to perceive) (Berkeley 1999: 25–7) continues to inform Watt and the pair Vladimir and Estragon, which stresses the reliance on witnessing and, crucially, witnessing being witnessed. As I have argued above, this relationship of perception can partially survive through a projected master, such as the faith in the absent Knott and Godot. However, Beckett's creatures desire more than the spiritual guarantee of deism, and, as with the intervention of theism, wish to summon the master and seek confirmation of the materiality of both their service and superior, which locks them into a state of deferral, questioning and waiting. They cannot wholly achieve or accept the mantle of individual freedom and responsibility. On the contrary, Beckett's characters continually fear the creaturely state of abandonment – analogous to existential angst – that comes in the wake of familiar ideological and identity structures.

With Watt, the nostalgia for conventional order extends into a reliance on alternative determining processes, such as rational thought and 'a pillow of old words' (*W*, 99). Despite his attempts to understand the workings of the house, he is repeatedly baffled and denied access to a prevailing order. To return to the domestic metaphor, Watt suffers a kind of 'homesickness' since he is estranged from the systems of organization that should offer him stability. In rigorously testing variations and possible solutions, he consistently turns to familiar methods, processes he is *at home with*, but this loyalty leaves him without satisfactory answers. Watt clearly yearns for reliable figures and forms of judgement, but is left with unwieldy meditations and errant signifiers. Similarly, Jeffrey Nealon's essay on *Waiting for Godot* asserts that language is the substance of Vladimir and Estragon's being. They are subject to the infinite extemporization of words, not an engineered overarching narrative. Nealon writes: 'it is the play of Vladimir and Estragon's words, not any agreed-upon meaning for them, which constitutes their social bond. Waiting for legitimation of their society in Godot is, from the beginning, unnecessary' (Nealon 1988: 520). Beckett's two creatures each perceive and are perceived by the other, and the contradistinction of their lively verbal exchanges reinforces these processes. Nevertheless, their words continue to address and anticipate a higher, more established form of validation, and the interaction that sustains the couple is deemed a temporary measure prior to the genuine purpose that the master promises.

It is evident that Beckett's characters have epistemological allegiances and are committed to progressing through customary practices, despite the pitfalls of ratiocination, logocentric cognition and sovereign monocracy. Peter Barry discusses the implicit postmodern threshold that Nealon sees in *Waiting for Godot*, noting that Vladimir and Estragon 'are trapped at the modernist stage, and hence riven with nostalgia for the whole lostness of the past' (2002: 89). Initially, the terms 'nostalgia' and 'lostness' appear incongruous to a play fueled by the dramatic tension of an imminent arrival. Given that the pair persistently wait to meet Godot, and in conjunction with the fact that Beckett employs dramatic irony to elicit the tragedy of the forlorn situation, the characters appear to be trapped in a delusional state of postponed realization. The lost is not acknowledged as gone and, accordingly, the tense is not retrospective. Instead, the past is conducted in the present, with the characters subscribing to prospective events while the audience is wise to the tragic emptiness of their situation. For the majority of the play, then, the characters' 'nostalgia' – which suggests memory, or a 'return back' – lacks the closure of the mourning process to give it historical distance. Godot remains a prospect not yet arrived, and therefore a possibility still.

However, a sense of nostalgia is included in the play retrospectively when Vladimir appears to awaken from the enduring past and allude to the dramatic irony at work. As Pozzo exits, Vladimir briefly suspects that Lucky's blind master was Godot after all, before entering into a rare soliloquy:

> But habit is a great deadener. (*He looks again at Estragon.*) At me too someone is looking, of me too someone is saying, he is sleeping, he knows nothing, let him sleep on. (*Pause.*) I can't go on! (*Pause.*) What have I said? (*He goes feverishly to and fro, halts finally at extreme left, broods*) (*WFG*, 83).

As the idea of the absent master becomes unmoored, mobile and transposed through the initial confusion between Godot and Pozzo, Vladimir subsequently assumes the role of overseeing Estragon. While he watches over his companion, Vladimir also continues to imagine a witness overseeing himself, as though the patriarchal model inspired by the God of the Old Testament, or God(OT), is an inveterate default. Despite that, in this glimpse into his own somnolent state, Vladimir detaches from self to contemplate self, becoming at once observer and observed. The two final utterances in the above example – the statement 'I can't go on!' and question 'What have I said?' – serve to condense the process of reflection through which Vladimir finds an apprehending counterpart in himself. By responding to his own statement, Vladimir effectively shifts the focus of mastery once more. Having contemplated Godot, Pozzo and himself as masters over others, Vladimir realizes that he is his own master or at least the maker of his master. His self-examination allows him to realize the fact that the idea of mastery is located or created internally, within the self, which briefly deposes the original idea of Godot from a privileged position.

Vladimir's move into soliloquy during this section of the play accentuates his independence and as the stage becomes an arena for his short-lived self-analysis, his internal drama comes to dominate the attention of the viewing audience. His momentary detachment from the others onstage means that the singular speaker briefly assumes a more direct command of the audience's focus. Although

draped in the poetics of self-reflection here, Vladimir treads the thin
line between introspection and public speaking. By talking to
himself alone and simultaneously selling his thoughts to the
audience, the soliloquy clearly fixates on the individual while
disseminating the individual's view in the process. When Vladimir
rejoins the antics, signposted by the remark 'Off we go again'
(WFG, 84), there is a subtle but noticeable shift in Beckett's
dramaturgy from a more candid tone to the inconsequential register
that characterizes the play. As a mode of address, the soliloquy
highlights the power relations between the speaker and the audience
in the playhouse, signalling a level of servile passivity from the
audience and the speaker's capacity to capture, persuade and
instruct the listener. Therefore, this episode alludes to the word
'propaganda' itself in the sense of a religious 'congregation for the
propagation of the faith', and indicates the uncomfortable proximity
between dramatic conventions and political communication.

Despite dethroning Godot, Vladimir's inward gaze fails to supply
a *telos* that would provide a definitive meaning and purpose to life.
While Vladimir's speech intimates his oratorical power, he is not in
a sovereign position. His internal division marks the threshold to
the infinite problem of apperception in which the subject is unable
to perceive selfhood transcendentally, at least other than as a
perceiver. As with the identity in ruins discussed in the previous
chapter, in which any knowable subjectivity is based on a
simultaneous possession and dispossession of self, Vladimir's self-
mastery appears to cause an internal subject-object rupture. Beckett
explores this problem of self-knowledge most directly in his 1965
motion picture *Film*, directed by Alan Schneider and starring Buster
Keaton. In Beckett's visual piece, '[l]ike Godot the camera never
appears, but as a metaphor of self-perception, the camera
photographing itself photographing itself becomes a trope for the
paradox of apperception' (Ackerley and Gontarski 2004: 194). The
absent onlooker, or eye (E), pursues and is part of the self, or object
(O), that takes flight and is pursued. This insurmountable
disjunction, visualized as a steady distance between camera and
actor in Beckett's film, inserts a barrier of alterity for Vladimir that
can be projected back onto a transcendental figure in an attempt to
reconsolidate the individual. The absent master, as such, becomes a
representation of everything the subject cannot perceive or confront
through reflection.

In contrast to Vladimir's inescapable mirroring, the absent master promises a totalizing narrative extraneous to the characters that can redeem the ruined subject. Through Vladimir's return to the 'Godot' paradigm, he holds onto the original state of potential objectification and continues to cultivate a buried prospect. When Godot's messenger boy arrives to inform the pair the master will not be coming, it is Vladimir who pre-empts him saying, 'He won't be coming this evening', but who also states, 'But he'll come tomorrow' (WFG, 84). Vladimir does not accept Godot as a manifestation of the desire for wholeness, but as a real validating figure who will complete him. Vladimir turns back to the tree and country lane overshadowed by Godot, 'to remain mad' as Beckett's famous maxim suggests (WFG, 73). As a consequence, the couple Vladimir and Estragon reactivate a ruined history, they 'keep their appointment', and return to a relative comfort zone: 'Yes, one thing in this immense confusion is clear. We are waiting for Godot to come' (WFG, 72). Having peered through the artifice at his ignorant self, Vladimir immediately reverts to an unconscious condition now consigned to the past. Thus, these Beckettian creatures refuse to accept their identity in ruins or the testimony of fiction since they re-subscribe to a soteriological solution to their plight in the guise of the saviour Godot.

As a result of Vladimir's brush with clarity, it is clear that throughout the play Vladimir and Estragon wish to incarnate a lost idea, and in doing so endure what Walter Benjamin calls 'melancholy immersion' (1977: 232). In *The Origin of German Tragic Drama*, Benjamin focuses a section on melancholy, describing how 'in its tenacious self-absorption it embraces dead objects in its contemplation, in order to redeem them' (1977: 157). Although Benjamin's melancholy resembles a nostalgic preoccupation with the past, it places emphasis on the proximity and immediacy in reanimating bygone material. In *Waiting for Godot*, this reconnection with the past catapults Vladimir beyond waiting towards an active desire for the lost authority that could validate his existence. He becomes a victim of the rosy retrospection principle *memoria praeteritorum bonorum* (the past is always well remembered) that he previously called 'unpleasant' (WFG, 79), perhaps because it ensnares people in reflection and replicates the kind of static nostalgia that Vichy France held for agrarian life (Fogg 2009: 33). Accordingly, Vladimir swiftly begins to resurrect a familiar wrathful figure, stating that Godot will punish them if he is dropped and save them when he arrives (*WFG*, 86–7).

Melancholic fixations are a component of the creature for Eric Santner. In particular, he highlights the pause over absence in his study of creaturely life: 'melancholy retards adaptation, attaches itself *to* loss; it says no! to life without the object (or ideal)' (2006: 89). The ideal for Vladimir and Estragon is a figure of meaning for their future and the charade that Godot embodies provides a suitable distraction from their abandoned state. For them, holding on to Godot preserves the idea of a natural order that would offer intrinsic meaning for their lives. Vladimir therefore refuses to take on the existential angst that realizes the artificiality of this order. He would rather believe in the construction than be cast adrift into a physical life without the possibility of higher meaning. Vladimir's deflection of abandonment ironically continues to retrieve a sense of genesis and original motivation from Godot, rather than recognize himself as a co-creator of a play of language that ultimately generates their melancholy condition.

Vladimir does not acknowledge himself as a free agent because his play of language with Estragon cannot deliver this revelation in an intelligible way. As Nealon goes on to discuss in his essay, Lucky's tirade parodies the idea of a totalizing narrative that could perceive and express the manifold complexities of ontology (1988: 523). Lucky's final thought on the fragments of academic and philosophical dross is 'unfinished . . .' (*WFG*, 38), and this open end implies that the incomplete account will recommence, that further attempts will be made to 'think' the conclusion. The deluge of words and thoughts in Lucky's sustained form, but also the pseudo-couples' rapid-fire crosstalk and Watt's permutations, shows that the silence of metaphysical realization cannot be finally articulated or brought into being as part of the narrative, but only experienced as abandonment. Although the creatures exist through their words, they cannot use words to apprehend the conditions of their existence once and for all.

The covenant of totality subsists in the absence of Godot, yet when the reality of their orphanhood beckons, Beckett's characters cannot provide an alternative unifying structure through self-reflection and self-expression. Consequently, they slide back into the creaturely space of melancholy immersion. Andrew Slade's description of melancholy elucidates this relapse that Beckett's characters experience: 'a melancholic subjectivity remains bound to the lost object of its history resolutely holding to the traces of its memory and seeking to find it again, repetitively missing it' (2007: 3). This recurring lack inflicts a cycle of loss, retrieval and belief that unfolds in the struggle to express and understand in Beckett. These creatures are exposed to an enterprise that refuses to accept the loss of the desired state and therefore protracts the unspoken entropy that remains underneath.

Godot does not positively represent, but instead elicits a constant lack, a lacuna that is unable to be tenanted or assimilated into the characters' knowledge. Beckett's depiction of absent masters illustrates that, for him, the idea of a transcendental vantage lingers in and around the problematic of subjectivity that denies oneness and resorts to contingent, albeit hollow, safety measures. His creatures are bound to decrepit conventions, feeding nostalgia for the ruined past. They are abandoned at a point of interregnum, but claw their way back from this bewildering state to enter a survival state with the hangover of previous orders of authority. In the face of a lawless, meaningless existence, *Watt* and the pair in *Waiting for Godot* continue to subscribe to the established illusions of a truant figure. Beckett's creatures project a master figure to fill the gap that they inevitably confront in self-reflection and self-expression.

Master–servant context: The Holocaust and the Jewish creature

A master narrative that rises above disparate perspectives to arrange an objective whole is a dangerous concept according to Beckett. During his time in Germany, he was wary of this totalizing presentation of history and commented to Axel Kaun:

> I am not interested in a 'unification' of the historical chaos any more than I am in the 'clarification' of the individual chaos, and still less with the anthropomorphism of the inhuman necessities that provoke the chaos. What I want is the straws, flotsam, etc., names, dates, births and deaths, because that is all I can know. [...] Rationalism is the last form of animism (quoted in Knowlson 1997: 244).

Beckett suggests that a single explanatory account of reality is akin to an inflexible worldview anchored by supernatural powers. The fastidious diary that Beckett kept during his Germany trip is testament to these misgivings, as he prefers to note empirical details without arranging them into a coherent account. Beckett found that the Nazi tendency to totalize history, particularly the 'interminable harangues' of Hitler and Goering, eclipsed the reductive accounts he saw in German history books (quoted in Knowlson 1997: 238). For Beckett, these oratory displays had the ring of faith-mongering. Mark Nixon notes that 'Beckett's correlation between Nazi discourse and biblical "truth" appears several times in the pages of his diary' (2011: 85). In Beckett's references to animism and truth, then, he identifies a messiah complex in Nazi historiography and political addresses. Beckett compares political propaganda to religious dogma to suggest that the polemical and rhetorical style of the Nazi campaign against racial intermixture invokes the supreme judgement of divinity.

Although Beckett's observations predate the Nazis' so-called Final Solution, the correlation between autocratic and biblical authority is most evident in the sovereign power applied against the Jews. James McNaughton argues that the 'anthropomorphism of inhuman necessities' to which Beckett refers 'was in its worst allegorical simplification the Jew, who was the necessary scapegoat for a rational system of history that could not reconcile Germany's supposedly divine Germanic destiny with its egregious historical failures, such as losing World War I' (2005: 107). The Nazis created a palpable figure of German downfall, a diabolic figure stemming from 2,000-year-old anti-Semitic prejudices, to provide a readily digestible narrative that would explain German history and determine their future actions. As Victor Klemperer attests, 'the Jew is in every respect the center of the LTI (*lingua tertii imperii* or language of the Third Reich), indeed of its whole view of the epoch' (1999: 321). In its singular, reductive approach, Nazi anti-Semitism indoctrinated a holistic view of history that was expedient to inculcate as the definitive account. This tactic contributes to Beckett's mistrust of master narratives, which is clearly seen in his derisive jab at the Führer's messianic position. In a 1938 letter to George Reavey, he writes 'I heard Adolf the Peacemaker on the wireless last night. And thought I heard the air escaping – a slow puncture' (Beckett 2009e: 642). Beckett refers to Hitler's 'peace or war' ultimatum to Czechoslovakia here and recognizes the hostility behind the Nazi rhetoric on protection and intervention. He also wryly implies that Hitler's speech is hot air and that the Führer is slowly deflating under the pressure of his own fanaticism. Beckett sees through this narrative, then, but he also recognizes that Hitler's political front is collapsing into all-out war.

Beckett's (in)sovereignty largely undermines the veracity of master narratives, and yet, as in *Watt* and *Waiting for Godot*, the authority of a panoptic perspective has a residual influence in his work. Whereas author-narrators such as Molloy, Moran and Malone struggle to produce sovereign narratives, Watt, Vladimir and Estragon appeal to others in order to maintain the idea of absolute rule. As such, the aspiration towards testimonial and ideological authority continues as an oppressive fixture. Parallel to these influential conceptual structures, however, is a more physical version of the master–servant relationship. After the war, as the iron-fisted biopolitical nature of the Nazis' *Blut und Boden* (Blood and Soil) policy seeps into public consciousness, Beckett's creatures also display more rudimentary power struggles based on territory and violence. Mastery persists as an abstract presence in the guise of obscure voices and imperatives, but Beckett often depicts the corporeality of power. These bodily tensions begin with the organization of space, as living environments and social domains are limited to distinct groups, and this segregation culminates in the violent application of sovereign power. In a harrowing echo of Nazi radicalization, the master Pozzo from *Waiting for Godot* points out the move from expulsion to extermination. Referring to Lucky, Pozzo says: 'The truth is you can't drive such creatures away. The best thing would be to kill them' (*WFG*, 25). It appears that the pursuit of power and the racial hierarchy that gripped Europe in the middle of the twentieth century gave Beckett an acute awareness of the more aggressive aspects of social and political relations.

The nadir of the catastrophe, the Holocaust, is an extreme example of the antibiosis between masters and underlings. The systematic nature of the killing, the efficiency with which modern technology terminated life and transformed the intimacy of death into a shared experience, in conjunction with the sheer amount of casualties, sets its scale and intent apart from previous mass murders. The Nazis reasoned that the genocide of the Jews, alongside gypsies, homosexuals and the mentally and physical disabled, was necessary to eliminate inferior beings, regarded as a drain on resources, as well as a social and genetic dilution of the superior race (Bergen 2003: 1–28). It is not clear what knowledge Beckett had of the Nazi rationale behind the concentration and extermination camps, but it is probable that he was aware of the German persecution of Jews from radio broadcasts and newspapers. Lois Gordon's biographical text on Beckett offers some assessment of the sources and experiences that informed his view. She notes that Beckett's half-Jewish uncle Boss Sinclair had left Germany for Dublin by 1933 owing to safety concerns, and she goes on to suggest that Beckett's enduring compassion towards downtrodden Jews was instilled prior to the war through his friendship with James Joyce:

> That Beckett was interested in the Jewish plight is certain; as Richard Ellmann notes, forty years after the war the subject of Jewish suffering made Beckett weep. That Beckett would have empathized with the Jews as a persecuted people even before his London days is also likely. In addition to his general 'sensitiv[ity] to the suffering around him', his friend and hero James Joyce, who had forged an epic figure in the Jew Leopold Bloom, often spoke of himself as a Jew. Joyce equated the Jews and Irish as persecuted peoples ('Israelite-Irish') (Gordon 1998: 106).

Although Gordon settles for a simple equation of Jewish and Irish persecution, Joyce's depiction of Jews in *Ulysses* (1922) remains a contested issue. Despite Joyce claiming to 'have written with the greatest sympathy about the Jews' (quoted in Ellman 1982: 709), it is clear from the nationalist citizen's mockery of Bloom and the Jewish faith in the 'Cyclops' episode of *Ulysses* that Joyce also risks reinforcing anti-Semitic Jewish stereotypes in his writing. It is fair to say, however, that Beckett shares Joyce's fascination, if not identification, with Jewish culture and the Jews as a persecuted people. The Nazis' treatment of Beckett's Jewish friend Paul Léon (who was Joyce's personal assistant) certainly serves to galvanize Beckett's empathic leaning towards oppressed communities. Tellingly, Beckett joined the Resistance in 1941, the month after the Gestapo arrested, starved and tortured Léon (Knowlson 1997: 304).

However, despite any historical insight into persecution or personal affinity with the persecuted, Beckett's knowledge of the

Holocaust itself is dominated by the death of a key figure in his Resistance cell, Alfred Péron. Beckett's friend was arrested by the Gestapo in 1942, deported to the Mauthausen concentration camp in north Austria and died in Switzerland shortly after liberation in 1945 (Beckett 2011: 16). Beckett quite possibly discovered more about Péron's ordeal at Mauthausen from Georges Loustaunau-Lacau's first-hand account of the camps entitled *Chiens maudits: Souvenirs d'un rescapé des bagnes hitleriens* (Cursed Dogs: Memories of a Survivor of Nazi Labour Camps), which was published in 1945 and therefore one of the earliest Holocaust accounts available to the public (Knowlson 1997: 381). As a non-Jewish civilian who escaped deportation, Beckett could only imagine the physical and emotional suffering based on the limited information he could access, including reports and tributes in *The Irish Times*. Yet as a friend, sympathizer and resistance member, it is legitimate to claim that the Holocaust profoundly affected Beckett on a specific, personal level as well as a broader anthropological level. Not only did he witness the disaster's demolition of the idea of humanity, his way of life had also changed and cherished people were now gone.

In 1983, Rosette Lamont asked Beckett about the political connotations of his literary imagery in relation to Auschwitz and, although the author avoided the direct enquiry, he spoke of Péron: 'At the time of liberation he was still alive. He started on a trek in the direction of France. On the roads, survivors resorted to cannibalism. Péron died of exhaustion and starvation' (quoted in Lamont 1990: 43). Beckett describes the transformation of humans into desperate competitors stripped of civilized standards as they struggle to return to the normality of home. The horrific image of enervated and emaciated figures feeding on the dead or dying shows a cruel twist of irony in that the ingestion of the human produces a savage inhuman other. Beckett's sympathy goes out to these suffering creaturely victims as they journey back to humanity. It is significant that Beckett should concentrate on this particularly inhuman experience because this reduction was at the centre of the Nazis' ambition. The incarnation of the inhuman other from the human goes back to the original devaluation of egalitarianism in the concentration and death camps. The Nuremberg Laws of 1935 that culminated in genocide present a clinical endeavour to confirm the status and improve the security of the self-identified master race.

The legislation effectively divided people into orders of worth, divested human life of its universal sanctity and reserved importance for a designated group. This filtering of life, predicated upon the developed and sophisticated social and medical science of modern civilization, boils down to a biopolitical activity that introduces sovereign political calculations into the materiality of life.

In Giorgio Agamben's terms, biopolitics means to invest *zoē* – the term used to describe life outside a particular way of life – into the sphere of *polis* (Agamben 1995: 4). This implies that there is a political dimension to 'bare life' at a point where the simple fact of living is transformed into a totalized version of life, such as the concentration and extermination camps as the consequence of Fascism. In these conditions, the lifestyles and cultures known as *bios* are funnelled into a single vision of *zoē*. For Agamben, these exemplary biopolitical sites cast judgements on types of life to pursue a supreme version of life worth living. Sovereign power over life considers undeserving beings exempt from the political measures for preserving and improving the quality of life, thus rendering the Jews outlaws. In its most extreme form, this political neglect develops into biopolitical activity, whereby the extermination camps enforce the notion of 'life that does not deserve to live' (Agamben 1995: 136). The philosopher Roberto Esposito, a key exponent of biopolitical concepts, propounds the magnitude of this decision:

> Human life here becomes the terrain of decisions that have to do with not only its external thresholds – that is, what distinguishes it from animal or vegetal life, for example – but also inner thresholds. This means that politics will be allowed to, will even be asked to, decide what is a biologically better life, and also how to strengthen it through the use, the exploitation, or, when necessary, the death of a 'worse' life (2012: 72–3).

Groups designated as subaltern are separated from the master race, distinguished as biopolitical material and thus rendered expendable creatures, in an act that challenges the inalienable human status.

On a biopolitical level, the Nazis' sovereign decision on the fate of the Jewish people elevates and asserts the claims of the Aryan 'race'. Since the superiority of one cannot be confirmed without the inferiority of the other, the Nazi propaganda campaign constructed an image of the Jew as an infectious disease ('racial tuberculosis') and commensal organism ('world parasite') (Otto 1943). In the 1940 Fritz Hippler propaganda film *The Eternal Jew*, Jewish people are depicted as rats, with the Nazis battling an infestation of unclean vermin. Whilst presuming supremacy over the target, Nazi propaganda is also replete with fear-mongering images of threat and corruption. This use of animal symbolism in a hierarchical method of identification, and the extermination that sought to concretize the supposed superiority, appropriates the human–animal binary to reinforce the relationship between superior masters and subordinates. One particularly contentious debate arising from this parallel is the extent to which the Holocaust is comparable to livestock slaughter. A thorough examination of the differences and similarities in the relationship between the Nazis' treatment of the Jews in the Holocaust and human treatment of animals in factory farming is beyond the scope of this book. Such ethically sensitive material is rightly the subject of several dedicated monographs and articles.[4] However, the fact remains that the very existence of this debate means that the human–animal polarity in the Nazi invectives against Jewish people, particularly the association with primitive, hidden or rapidly breeding creatures, highlights a familiar identification tactic that focuses on heterogeneity to allay the uncomfortable proximity with a perceived other.

In order to link Beckett's creatures with the contemporaneous dehumanization properly, it is worth stressing how, in the most general sense, alterity positions are exploited to promote individuality and gain status in identity struggles. The idea of an identity in ruins and the author-narrators' fictional prostheses found in Beckett's trilogy show that the acknowledgement of an other retains a sense of subjectivity for the individual, albeit through a necessary experience of desubjectivity. That is, a part of the subject is dispossessed in order to preserve a relative coordinate with which to partially identify oneself. The examples of division noted in Chapter 1 occur within the individual but, in a more tangible way, they translate into the power dynamics between characters in Beckett's texts. It is not difficult to see the lordly Pozzo and his slave creature Lucky in *Waiting for Godot* as an instance of how masters rely on the possible subordination of an other to elevate themselves and dispel any parity. Pozzo laughs at the idea that Vladimir and Estragon are of his own kind: 'You are human beings none the less.

As far as one can see. Of the same species as myself. (*Laughs.*) Of the same species as Pozzo!' (*WFG*, 15). While it is amusing for Pozzo to think of himself on a par with these poor creatures, he does not extend the same status to Lucky. Knowlson notes the contextual significance of this identification tactic: 'Pozzo's treatment of Lucky reminded some of the earliest critics of a *capo* in a concentration camp brutalising his victim with his whip' (1997: 380). Pozzo's whip certainly recalls the head prison guards in the Nazi camps and the violence used to assert their authority. I would add that, alongside the rope passed around Lucky's neck, Pozzo's treatment of Lucky also illustrates how the slave recalls the animal. Whereas Lucky is a 'human being' (*WFG*, 20), or at least a 'cretin' to Vladimir and Estragon (*WFG*, 18), he is a dancing 'hog' and a thinking 'pig' to his master (*WFG*, 16). Therefore, Pozzo's lordship over Lucky evokes human mastery over animals and applies to the power hierarchies between human others. The power dynamic in Beckett's *Waiting for Godot* traces human social tensions as well as interspecies relationships. This ambivalence creates a plausible comparison to the Nazis' persecution of Jewish people, in which the phenomenon of radical difference has passed from anthropocentric identification into racial persecution.

The Nazis' extreme separation of identities is physically enforced to reinstate a master–servant binary. In a crude and selfish protection of individuality, the peril of conflated identities and reshuffled boundaries initiates a return to a fixed monadic state through dependable polarized roles. However, while the endeavour to elevate a group in this way echoes the anthropocentric project to distinguish humans from animals, the warped Nazi perspective does not exactly promote the Holocaust and livestock slaughter analogy since the value of noble animals often exceeds that of the Jews in Nazi ideology. In a massive contravention of the Hippocratic oath, Nazi doctors used prisoners as *Versuchspersonen*, test subjects or human guinea pigs, often in place of animals. Medical professionals justified this type of treatment with biopolitical rhetoric, as physician Fritz Klein exemplifies when he infers, '[t]he Jew is the gangrenous appendix in the body of humankind' (quoted in Rees 2005: 185). The Third Reich also introduced a range of measures to ensure that animals were respected and killed humanely (Sax 2000: 35). Furthermore, as a dog owner and a vegetarian himself, Hitler contributed practically to animal liberation, as Peter

Singer relates: 'Becoming a vegetarian is a highly practical and effective step one can take toward ending both the killing of nonhuman animals and the infliction of suffering upon them' (1995: 161). In keeping with the ethical treatment of animals, but also a discriminating view of life worth living, the Nazis extend compassion to nonhuman animals while inflicting severe human suffering.

The expulsion and extermination of the Jews is not repeated in kind for animals, which indicates that Nazi ideology is comfortable with the stability of the human–animal distinction, or rather, it lauds particular qualities in living creatures to shift the self–other boundaries. Boria Sax suggests that the species difference was not a primary concern for the Nazis: 'In their nihilistic perspective the important distinction was not between "humans" and "animals", at least in any traditional way. It was between victor and vanquished, between master and slave' (2000: 23). The peculiar implication is that Nazi animal rights convert inhumane forms of mastery over animal commodities into a guardianship that promotes animal husbandry and the master–pet intimacy for certain noble animals. The treatment of the Jews, then, can be considered a pursuit of otherness within humans that modifies anthropocentrism to revolve around the Aryan, while the human–animal alterity is secure enough to grant custody to an equivalent class of animal. This view holds that modern violence does not treat people like animals identically, but that human groups are exposed to the same compulsion to assert identity that delineated humans from the base collective term 'animal'. From a Nazi perspective, the Jew is part of a new inferior class that includes servile animals and constitutes the necessary other. The focus on identifying *against* as opposed to identifying *with* means the aspiring power imposes a state of otherness on the counterpart in an attempt to gain distinction and organize difference hierarchically.

It is this sense of a necessary other that is intrinsic to the power politics of Beckett's co-dependent pseudo-couples, and the grotesque relation and revulsion that informs the biopolitical exclusion of his characters. Before discussing the biopolitical struggles that appear in Beckett's work, it is worth reiterating the claim that the concept of animality consistently haunts the alterity thinking behind social and racial identification. In *Malone Dies*, Beckett offers a most explicit reference to how human mastery over animals is reflected in the human mastery over other humans. Malone himself relies on

the 'goodness' of his nurse (*T*, 185) and Malone's character
Macmann is under the charge of 'his keeper' Moll (*T*, 261). It is the
relationship between Macmann and Moll that conveys the
subordination of animals that underlies human power struggles.
Malone writes that 'Moll's lips puffed and parted in a dreadful
smile, which made Macmann's eyes waver like those of an animal
glared on by its master and compelled then finally to look away'
(*T*, 260). Moll's intimidating expression reveals Macmann's
vulnerability, which makes him distinctly animal-like under her
control. This type of reaction shows how the animal other is invoked
as the subject is dehumanized by another in the pursuit of power. As
such, the victim is made to feel like an animal because the master
wants to be dissociated from that status. As soon as human weakness
is exposed or exploited, the human is redolent of the animal.
Agamben asserts that animality remains an ineradicable element of
the human's composition and that the Jew, as 'the non-man
produced within the man', is synonymous with 'the slave, the
barbarian, and the foreigner, as figures of an animal in human form'
(2003: 37). Like Foucault before him, who argued that 'it is
animality that reveals the dark rage, the sterile madness that lie in
men's hearts' (2001: 18), Agamben suggests that the animal
continues to exist as a trope for the deplorable and errant aspects of
human behaviour. In conjunction, Foucault and Agamben recognize
how the well-rehearsed human–animal divide is interior to the
human and reproduced in society; the animal's legacy continues
between humans and within humans riven by identity wars.

Biopolitical struggles: Territory and custody

Beckett's master–servant relationships present both the corporal
battles of social nature and the internal battles held within the self.
The hostility and dependency between his characters depicts the
physical conflicts between adversaries and counterparts, and alludes
to individual psychological conflicts in a purgatorial state of
subjectivity. Adorno mentions how these internal affairs spill over
into the external world in his essay on *Endgame*: 'As soon as the
subject is no longer doubtlessly self-identical, no longer a closed

structure of meaning, the line of demarcation with the exterior becomes blurred, and the situations of inwardness become at the same time physical ones' (1982: 129). As noted above, in *Watt*, this overlap causes the protagonist to confuse his identity with objects, namely a pot. In Beckett's master–servant relationships, the psychological disunity in self is also manifest as domination over another, often in the form of violence and abuse, but also custody and service. Hence, Beckett's term 'pseudo-couples', which he uses to describe Mercier and Camier in *The Unnamable* (*T*, 299), encapsulates the bind and bond of the necessary other. The term implies a problematic togetherness between two entities, since the relationship is at once required and antagonistic. Adorno goes so far as to argue that the pseudo-couple in *Endgame* lack independence and are therefore without personal distinction. He writes that '[e]ven the outlines of Hamm and Clov are one; they are denied the individuation of a tidily independent monad' (Adorno 1982: 144). In other words, they are a veritable pseudo-couple, a false twosome, in the sense that they constitute a bipartite singular. Esslin's more explicit reading in *The Theatre of the Absurd* compares *Endgame* to Nikolai Evreinov's *The Theatre of the Soul* (1915) to suggest that Beckett's play is a monodrama, which represents 'different aspects of a single personality' (2001: 66). The ambiguity over the physical denotation or psychological connotation of Beckett's plays appears to support the idea that issues of subjectivity and identity are local to both body and mind. Since it is difficult to determine whether the pseudo-couple are real people in a room or abstractions in a 'skullscape' (Ben-Zvi 1986: 4), the result is that the self–other binary pervades public and private spheres. In this way, Beckett's pseudo-couples act as a device to convey psychological duality and its propagation in social interaction.

As beings subject to the non-synthesis of self that leads to subsequent pursuits of difference amongst others, Beckett's creatures do not exactly conflate the homo–hetero tensions seen in either internal self-consciousness or the external human–animal divide. Contrary to hybrid figures that emerge as the original progeny of two distinct parents, Beckett's characters are vessels for duality to co-exist and they reveal this schism within the self in their antibiosis with others. Molloy recognizes the interplay between his more autotelic animal self and idealistic human self: 'For in me there have always been two fools, among others, one asking nothing better

than to stay where he is and the other imagining that life might be
slightly less horrible further on. [. . .] And these inseparable fools I
indulged turn about, that they might understand their foolishness'
(*T*, 48). Molloy's selves jostle within him, with the prospect of
knowing only the asininity of their condition. This tension between
the static and progressive sides of Molloy is reflected in his dealings
with external others. When he meets the charcoal-burner in the
forest towards the end of his narrative, there is a conflict of interests
as Molloy wants to continue on his quest and the stranger wants
him to stay. Their inability to communicate verbally underlines the
antibiosis between them: 'Either I didn't understand a word he said,
or he didn't understand a word I said, or he knew nothing, or he
wanted to keep me near him' (*T*, 84). Molloy resolves this conflict
through violence, kicking the charcoal-burner to death and thereby
mastering a situation he could not master internally. In this way,
there is a correlation between the identity tensions of the internal
sphere and the tensions surrounding the pursuit of difference
between humans and animals, or self and other. The symbolic
human and animal *within* each individual is illustrated *between*
individuals.

The basic theme of elevating and demarcating one's individual or
group identity translates from primal creatures to modern power
struggles. The executions of power that stalk distinction are
an intrinsic part of a bioprocess: the survival of self. In the movement from raw life material to a refined elite, from anonymity
to sovereignty, the self is perennially detaching from peers
and emphatically reforming itself anew. In *Strangers, Gods, and
Monsters* (2003), Richard Kearney studies how alien, divine and
grotesque others satisfy the necessary alterity that grants the subject
identity by virtue of relativity. In his discussion of Heidegger,
Kearney notes that 'each mortal remains a cleft creature with one
eye on its terrestrial genesis, the other on its celestial aspirations'
(2003: 167). Caught between earth and sky, 'mud and mind, dust
and dream' (Lupton 2000: 5), this cleft creature struggles with its
lowly past and inglorious beginnings while striving towards its
divine end. As such, the pursuit of power over difference is a process
that appears as a step in evolution; it is a way of advancing, defining
or safeguarding oneself or one's group.

Fin de siècle social Darwinism took this biological connection to
affirm that the laws of natural selection explain human hierarchies

as well as plants and animals. The shift from terrestrial to celestial spheres is most apparent when the Nazis integrate notions of selectivity and evolution – particularly the theories of biologist Ernst Haeckel – into their political policies, thereby turning natural selection into the active *Selektion* of the death camps: 'Their political dictionary was replete with words like space, struggle, selection, and extinction (*Ausmerzen*). The syllogism of their logic was clearly stated: The world is a jungle in which different nations struggle for space. The stronger win, the weaker die or are killed' (Tenenbaum 1956: 211).[5] The continuity between humans and animal ancestors in Charles Darwin's *The Descent of Man* (1871), for example, shows that 'man is descended from some less highly organized form' but 'if he is to advance still higher he must remain subject to a severe struggle' (Darwin 2008: 319, 331). While these power dynamics become more complicated and obscure as psychological, social, political, ethical and metaphysical tensions, they continue to hark back to a primordial struggle. Each onward step evokes primitive competitions and early forms of domination.

For Beckett, however, who considered Darwin's *The Origin of Species* (1859) 'badly written catlap' (2009e: 111), the Victorian idea of evolution as a narrative of improvement is false. These on-going, animalistic struggles are not directed towards idealism, but instead signal a kind of biotic stasis since the ever-present contest for power arrests the humanist vision of development. In *How It Is* (*HII* [French 1961; English 1964] 2009g), Beckett highlights the retrogression that attends the pursuit of advancement through his explicit portrayal of the exertion of power and violent control in the master–servant relationship between the narrator and Pim. Beckett began writing what turned out to be his last novel-length work the year after *Fin de Partie* was published in 1957, and completed it two years later in 1960. In a letter to Donald McWhinnie, Beckett explains the basic premise: 'A "man" is lying in the mud and dark murmuring his "life" as he hears it obscurely uttered by a voice inside him' (quoted in Knowlson 1997: 461). It is tempting to interpret this imagery, as Gary Adelman does, as 'an apocalyptic world like that of soldiers dying in the mud of no-man's land between the trenches, murmuring their prayers' (2004: 199). Despite this, Beckett's inverted commas suggest that the narrator is not exactly a 'man' or a figure with a recognizably human 'life', and that these terms are only employed to refer to some relatable form of being.

Although Beckett's imagery recalls the barbarism of war, its primitivism also stretches back through 'vast tracts of time' (*HII*, 3). The narrator's description of crawling in the mud, 'the cord sawing my neck the sack jolting my side' (*HII*, 39) evokes the depiction of Lucky from *Waiting for Godot*, tethered and equally bogged down by the bag, basket and stool. These afflictions connect the narrator of *How It Is* with the animal-like treatment and oppressive situations that Beckett's other creaturely servants endure. As a result, the narrator, the eventual master, first appears as a similarly primitive, browbeaten creature, and this reminds the reader that the narrator and his eventual servant Pim are essentially of the same primordial origin. Consequently, the narrator's sovereignty over Pim is an imperious display of power over his own kin, which signals a pivotal stage in the development of differentiation and individuality. Since verbal communication between the pair appears to be beyond their capability, the narrator stabs, thumps and scratches his counterpart to physically assert his superiority. As mud dwellers, both the narrator and Pim resemble mudskipper fish, or Gobies, and this reinforces Beckett's nod to evolution in that these animals neatly illustrate the step from a purely aquatic life to an amphibious one. The narrator displays this evolutionary process in his belief that although he is a creature, he can at least be less of a creature than Pim: 'the wish to be less wretched a little less' (*HII*, 8). Despite this, the pursuit of highness appears bound up with downfall: 'progress properly so called ruins in prospect' (*HII*, 17). This is not the upward trajectory of historical progress, but a progress that incorporates its own decline. It seems Beckett is undeterred by the epic scale of this principle so long as it undercuts itself, predicting its own collapse. In kind, the title *How It Is* itself suggests both an axiomatic statement and the contingency of the present tense.

Despite Beckett's distrust of master narratives, then, his narrators evidently lodge views of a similarly grand magnitude and survey immense temporal and historical patterns. Prior to *How It Is*, the unnamed narrator in the seventh text of *Texts for Nothing* refers to the cycles of memory as 'the same return, like the spokes of a turning wheel' (*TN*, 30) and later, in text nine, the narrator briefly dollies back from the busy foreground of existence to perceive a permanent backdrop when he utters 'what vicissitudes within what changelessness' (*TN*, 37). These phrases have a profound resonance, and yet Beckett often faces the scale of philosophical thinking while refusing the authority of the philosophical form. His narrators are tasked with untangling the bewildering human condition from within that bewildering human condition. That is to say, the characters are unable to transcend themselves to reflect on an ontological axiom. The narrators in both *Texts for Nothing* and *How It Is* are consumed by an insistent performance, evidenced by the line 'I say it as I hear it' (*TN*, 22; *HII*, 3), and this overwhelms the possibility of any indubitable wisdom. As such, these passing insights do not allow them to improve their knowledge, alter their approach, surpass their constitutive conditions or gain a metaphysical truth, but rather haunt and ruin them periodically. It appears that Beckett's clearest glance at a master narrative is in its repeated return and collapse.

The idea that ancient traits remain in the present, lingering and resurfacing, is noticeable in the images of crawling and creeping figures in Beckett's post-war writing. These depictions serve to prostrate the upright human and reduce him to a primitive creature. For example, Beckett describes Molloy 'crawling on his belly like a reptile' (*T*, 90) and bluntly calls to mind lice in the name Lousse (*T*, 33). The word 'reptile' itself stems from the Latin for 'crawled' while the alternative name given for Lousse in *Molloy*, Sophie Loy, gives credence to the idea that civilization is a façade for barbarism. 'Sophie' derives from the Greek for wisdom, as in philosophy, and the Irish pronunciation of 'lie' reads phonetically 'loy'. The lie of wisdom therefore gives way to Lousse, or louse, suggesting the primacy of parasitic insects, or contemptible and unpleasant creatures. Estragon brings these crawling and louse images together in *Waiting for Godot* when he exclaims 'All my lousy life I've crawled about in the mud!' (*WFG*, 52). Furthermore, in *Endgame*, Clov discovers a flea, or crablouse, from which humanity might start again (*E*, 22) and Hamm says: 'Dig my nails into the cracks and drag myself forward with my fingers' (*E*, 41). Although moving forward, crawling is an undignified and taxing mode of transit that betrays a constant barbarity and therefore declines the idea of evolution as progress to suggest that primitivism accompanies humanity's onward trajectory. In this way, the Nazis' depiction of the Jew as a primitive being, as the 1941 propaganda poster exclaims 'Jews are lice; they cause typhus', backfires onto humanity in general for Beckett. His creatures effectively carry the evolutionary archive with them as baggage into an unavoidably ancient modernity.

Beckett's portrayal of master–servant relationships points to basic and chronic systems of governance, such as physical strength and intimidation, as well as the primal psychology behind these systems, such as self-interest. Although his depictions of power avoid a specific political critique, he nevertheless grasps the drives at the core of governance and ascendancy that find their epitome in the Holocaust. Beckett includes various encounters with authority that display a level of order and control based on territory – on making and managing space. In the first volume of *The History of Sexuality* (1978), Foucault makes a clear distinction between territorial sovereignty, which allows life and threatens death, and biopower, which allows death and fosters life ([1978] 1990: 135–45). Despite this, policed spaces are a preliminary step towards a biopolitical level when considered as part of the Nazis' determination to create *Lebensraum* (living room) for their people. As the state nurtures the select population, it produces the adverse effect of excluding others from the political, and eventually the physical, territory. Agamben points out such an overlap in which 'an unprecedented absolutization of the biopower to *make live* intersects with an equally absolute generalization of the sovereign power to *make die*, such that biopolitics coincides immediately with thanatopolitics' (2002: 83). As people exiled and displaced from the governed space, Beckett's creatures illustrate the biopolitical threshold that appends passive neglect and active abuse.

Beckett's narrators in *The End* and *The Expelled* are never settled in their surroundings or belong to a place. Written in the year immediately after the war, these novellas follow the narrators as they are evicted from homes and gradually ostracized from society. The final act of charity towards the narrator in *The End* suggests the beginnings of isolation and self-sufficiency: 'This is a charitable institution, he said, and the money is a gift you receive when you leave. When it is gone you will have to get more, if you want to go on. Never come back here whatever you do, you would not be let in' (*FN*, 39). Beckett's narrator is a subject of territorial sovereignty since the state has abandoned him. He is no longer a concern for the welfare system and thus left to fend for himself independently. However, this end of care is the start of his voyage out of society altogether, which surely guarantees his demise. The narrator is told that he 'must not loiter in the cloister' (*FN*, 39), that he is not welcome in the sheltered space. Moreover, the word 'loiter' resonates on both a narrative and physical level, implying that the idea of nomadic progression is paramount, as his wonderings and wanderings are enforced as a result of a sovereign decision. Hence, his peripatetic movements are administered firstly and then monitored: 'One day I had a visit from a policeman. He said I had to be watched, without explaining why. Suspicious, that was it, he told me I was suspicious' (*FN*, 43). This vague oppressive authority serves to coerce the threatening narrator out of the governed sphere and make him a vulnerable outlaw. At times, the public is complicit in this banishment, and even prioritize their useful animals over fellow human beings. A landlord ejects the narrator from his home for this reason: 'He said he needed the room for his pig which even as he spoke was catching cold in a cart before the door and no one to look after him' (*FN*, 44). Although this kind of human devaluation is outrageous, the domestic and social spaces in *The End* are nevertheless the domain of a discriminate sovereign rule that orders humans into types and excludes its deviant subjects.

The policing of territory is more punctilious in *The Expelled*, which is a text that bears the status of Beckett's homeless figures in its title. The narrator is evicted from his house in the opening pages in a manner that recalls pest control: 'A thorough cleansing was in full swing. In a few hours they would close the window, draw the curtains and spray the whole place with disinfectant' (*FN*, 5–6). The extent of this purification suggests that the authorities wish to erase the narrator's filthy presence and that he is a stain upon society. Once expelled, the narrator decides to walk on the road so as not to inconvenience the people on the pavement. He says, 'A policeman stopped me and said, The street for vehicles, the sidewalk for pedestrians. Like a bit of Old Testament' (*FN*, 8). This blunt rule resounds like a biblical commandment, as though it is an elemental law that also applies to the narrator for his safety. Yet a second policeman approaches: 'He pointed out to me that the sidewalk was for everyone, as if it was quite obvious that I could not be assimilated to that category' (*FN*, 8). The narrator is not included in the precise organization of space, diverted from the street to the sidewalk, but is instead dissociated from the public in general. He is alienated from the community and sundered from the Everyman as an aberration. This ideological separation is later enacted as a bodily distance when the narrator spends a night in the stables with a cab horse and finally retreats into the sunset until he is 'down among the dead' (FN, 16). Beckett's itinerant narrator lacks the solicitude granted to the working animal and is banished to the dark periphery of biopolitical responsibility. As a subject of territorial sovereignty, he is initially a black sheep, a disgrace to the social group, but as he becomes an isolated biopolitical pariah, he is a scapegoat in the wilderness beyond provisions.

The comparisons between unassimilated beings and animals complicate Beckett's marginalized figures, notably in *Mercier and Camier* (MC, 2010c). Written around the same time as the four *nouvelles* in 1946, this text shares the same movement between city and countryside. In a public garden, a ranger referred to as a 'maleficent being' (MC, 8) drives two copulating dogs away from the pagoda. He proceeds to order Mercier and Camier to move on from the shelter, thus creating a parallel between the animals and the men. The law rather comically interferes with the dogs on a biological level, stopping them in the act of procreation, and the government of territory suggests a similar, yet subtler, biopolitical action towards the men. Mercier and Camier initially think the ranger does the dogs a 'service', and question whether he has served them also. Mercier says 'Can it I wonder be the fillip we needed, to get us moving?' (MC, 9), which implies that petty rules and regulations keep the social mechanism turning, in the same way that they ensure Mercier and Camier's narrative unfolds. But, as with the dogs pulling in opposite directions, Beckett's original pseudo-couple are sent off without a sure purpose and ultimately meander aimlessly to a bridge on the edge of the town, where they remember the animals they have recently encountered. They think back on Helen's talking parrot, which is a peculiarly liminal being as an animal capable of mimicking human speech. This parrot coincides with the bridge as an interstitial structure to reflect the pseudo-couple's own ambivalence and mobility between the suburban fringes and the rural hinterlands. Furthermore, the liminal creature and interstitial structure signify the pair's crossover into a state of biopolitical vulnerability. Mercier claims the parrot 'will haunt me till my dying day' (MC, 20), thus suggesting that the present memory of the bird might portend his imminent demise. Ominously, the parrot is remembered at the point Mercier approaches the countryside in the dark, where he says 'I have a feeling he was dead the day she told us she had put him out in the country' (MC, 100). Like abandoned domesticated animals, it seems

Mercier and Camier stray onto the edges of an abject and fatal state that the absence of biopolitical guardianship induces.

Beckett's vagrants are subject to more indirect forms of power that benefit appointed social circles but cause inequity, limit opportunities and restrict the well-being of others. This idea of control expresses the crux of power for Foucault: 'In effect what defines a relationship of power is that it is a mode of action that does not act directly and immediately on others. Instead, it acts upon their actions: an action upon an action, on possible or actual future or present actions' (2002: 340). The dominant force divests the other of influence and efficacy, and effectively monopolizes active power. In *Molloy*, this 'action upon an action' renders Beckett's protagonist a social misfit. When Molloy rests on his bicycle, a policeman asks 'what are you doing there?' (*T*, 20) and suggests that Molloy's inert occupation of valuable space is a 'violation of [. . .] public order, public decency' (*T*, 20). Molloy's mere presence transgresses the law and, in a physical sense, he is clearly refused sanctuary. He is also excluded from the bureaucratic system because he is literally 'without papers' (*T*, 24) and is therefore effectively without certain human rights but not totally without human support.

As a result of the vague oppression of biopolitical power, Molloy receives his care elsewhere, namely through Lousse. Nevertheless, Lousse's brief custody of Molloy is also entangled in a Foucauldian sense of power as care becomes an act that must be accepted. Molloy points out that beggars cannot be choosers: 'Against the charitable gesture there is no defence, that I know of. [. . .] To him who has nothing it is forbidden not to relish filth' (*T*, 24). The needy are at the mercy of their benefactors and are predominantly biddable subordinates, expected to abide by the established protocols. This influence takes on a more forceful, sinister hue when Molloy attempts to depart the house: 'doubtless she had poisoned my beer with something intended to mollify me, to mollify Molloy' (*T*, 47). Lousse tries to make Molloy a more malleable, submissive patient, which suggests that care is an alternative means of controlling people. It is evident that custody is integral to the anatomy of power when Molloy resists Lousse's supervision, and that her matronly control attempts to acquire the type of dedication that Molloy displays in the dogged pursuit of his mother. Molloy's custody at Lousse's home presents maternal care as a veiled form of dominance that reveals the intimacy between mastery and service.

The power dynamics raised in Molloy's encounter with a figure of care corresponds with the relationship between pets and owners to further elucidate the master–servant binary. Judging by Lousse's adoption of Molloy, it appears that indigents and domestic pets are incapacitated with support; they are helped to the point of subordination. Molloy is associated with dogs in particular, as he effectively replaces Lousse's pet dog Teddy, having accidentally killed him. The parallel is confirmed at the dog's interment when Molloy thinks, 'On the whole I was a mere spectator, I contributed my presence. As if it had been my own burial. And it was' (T, 37). Molloy implies that the dog's passing marks his own death and the birth of Lousse's dog-man. In place of Teddy, Molloy is a human pet, a creature to care for and lord over through a coinciding sense of responsibility and ownership.

Notably, Molloy's own obligation to replace Teddy and the resulting '[s]pecies anxiety – the dilemma of what it is to be human' (Wheatley 2013: 59) evokes the Irish mythological figure Cuchulain. While maintaining the human–canine proximity, this legend balances the scales of power considerably given that Setanta, the warrior son of the god of light Lug, volunteers to act as Culain's guard in place of the hound he killed in self-defence. The legend retains ideas of servitude and ownership since Setanta becomes Cuchulain, which literally means 'Hound of Culain'. Considering the gregarious nature of the human–canine relationship, the legend also reflects loyalty, friendship and mutuality. The power of care appears to extend both ways here, and thus the dog is 'the animal that perhaps more than any other runs to and fro between the human and animal worlds, simultaneously marking and crossing the boundary between them' (Armstrong 2008: 17). Such is the mobility of canine company between civilization and savagery that commander Kurt Franz ordered his dog to attack prisoners at the Treblinka death camp using the words 'Man, bite the dog' (Sax 2000: 22). Here, in a reversal of lycanthropy, the hierarchy is thoroughly confused, treating the dog as a man and elevating the animal to the level of a loyal fellow, and at the same time deriding the prisoners with the derogatory term 'dog'.

In Beckett, the dog's ability to traverse human and animal worlds brings together the two distinct spheres to show that power is shared between master and servant. Returning to *Molloy*, Lousse needs to care for Molloy to feel purpose and belonging. Molloy explains, 'I would take the place of the dog I had killed, as it for her had taken the place of a child' (*T*, 47). This sequence of replacement aligns Molloy with both animal and infantile dependents, but it also highlights how Lousse requires a dependent subject. Her gain from the caregiving role is made clear when Molloy observes how Lousse sells 'the benefits for both of us if I would make my home with her' (*T*, 48). The suggestion that the arrangement is mutually beneficial indicates how the subordinate provides a vital service to the master that leaves the master in debt to and reliant on the subordinate. Giving care is akin to gaining responsibility, but receiving care means to inherit the status of the necessary other and therefore an oddly powerful role as an identity position. The effect is that Beckett's pseudo-couples develop a level of co-dependency that obfuscates the boundaries between mastery, service and companionship.

Control and dependence are similarly inextricable in Beckett's *Endgame*, which results in a deadlock between the pseudo-couple Hamm and Clov. Santner points out that the title of this play evokes the 'turbulence of sovereignty, the rise and fall of kings and queens (on the chessboard of battle)' (2011: 251). In this sense, *Endgame* also suggests the strategic contest for territory, although these sovereign struggles are in a stalemate. On one hand, the blind master Hamm has the trump card in the larder combination and its contents, and therefore has a dependent subject in Clov. On the other, the lame but motile Clov has the power of care, symbolized by the painkillers, and therefore takes control in making Hamm dependent on his service. Their relative identity is notable when Hamm demands to be 'Bang in the centre' of the room (*E*, 19). Although it posits Hamm as the primary focus of attention, the audience witness that Clov places him there, which centres the master only in relation to his satellite servant. As Adorno puts it, 'Hamm is the king, about whom everything turns and who can do nothing himself' (1982: 146). This turnaround in the master–servant relationship discloses the power of the other and accentuates the co-dependency that unsettles the power distribution.

The ruling force requires a subordinate to actualize the hierarchy and, without a reference point, the master lacks an outlet to exercise such power and is only theoretically potent. The toy Pomeranian, for example, whose servitude and obedience are very much illusory, reveals the falsity of Hamm's position without Clov. In an exhibition of megalomania, Hamm believes the stuffed dog is gazing at him and begging for food: 'Leave him like that, standing there imploring me. (*Clov straightens up. The dog falls on its side*)' (*E*, 26). Beckett's stage directions show that the inanimate toy is beyond the realms of authority, whereas Clov duly follows orders. Unlike Gertrude Stein's 'I am I because my little dog knows me' (1973: 111), Beckett's formulation sees Clov become Hamm's little dog as he sits the prop up. But like Stein's insight, the subordinate position becomes key to identity. Maud Ellmann explains that '[i]f the "I" depends upon the knowledge of a little dog, this is not a neuter, neutral universal I, but a contingent subject rooted in relations with human and inhuman others' (Ellmann 2006: 83). In this respect, the master relies on the servant to give dominance meaning; there is no dominion without a minion. Separately, each party lacks the context, the gaze, or the all-important dialogue that the other affords. As a result, Beckett's pairs are contracted to one another in mutual dependence. Before Clov halts at the door, they verbalize their bind:

> **Hamm**   I'm obliged to you, Clov. For your services.
>
> **Clov**   (*turning, sharply*) Ah pardon, it's I am obliged to you.
>
> **Hamm**   It's we are obliged to each other (*E*, 48).

This obligation has the double sense of requirement and service, 'I oblige you' and 'I am obliged to you'. At once, Hamm and Clov show their needs and know they are needed in a bind that both gives and takes power. The hierarchical master–servant relationship, in which the sovereign power produces a creature subject, effectively divulges an altogether more performative becoming that disrupts the creator–created binary. As forms of power run both ways, the co-dependency dynamic evokes a lateral 'rhizomatic' relation. Deleuze and Guattari explain that '[a] rhizome has no beginning or end; it is always in the middle, between things, interbeing, intermezzo' (1988: 25). Similarly, in Beckett's play, the vertical tree-like axis of power (one over another), unfolds its latent horizontal axis (each obliged to the other), where ostensibly oppositional forces draw and are drawn ceaselessly into reciprocation, thereby conflating the binary and leaving no party more privileged. It is a tension of the master–servant relationship that Beckett captures in Clov's suspended departure in the final tableau of *Endgame*.

Beckett's portrayal of power struggles between masters and servants navigates religious models, social relations, evolutionary processes and biopolitical activity. These tensions and conflicts are destined to continue in Beckett's vision since they search for a centred unity that is essentially non-existent; the necessity of the contest itself disputes such a sovereign reconciliation. Despite this, his figures refuse to renounce the possibility of polarized identities, and are therefore imprisoned in a melancholic state of relative being and the act of relation – in dialectical modes that govern their social and experiential narratives. The various figures of superiority and inferiority covered in this chapter, expressed in terms of human and animal figures, self and other, master and servant, reveal a paradoxical relationship that is antagonistic and yet loaded with elements of compatibility, cohabitation and collaboration. Although control and degradation make creaturely figures in the hands of power, riving a lowly and lofty binary, the real creaturely state is trapped in the process of being made, in the interminable clash of required alterity and the on-going failure to tessellate. The transcendent level of power, while an aspiration still, is a myth that leaves Beckett's creatures redrawing the lines of territory, identity and fellowship.

3

Humour:

Failure and degradation

When addressing the humour in Beckett's work in relation to the Second World War and the Holocaust, it might seem proper to claim that its most vital value is in resisting totalizing systems. Beckett turned to humour in this spirit in his pre-war letters occasionally to address Nazi Germany and its intransigent ideologies. For example, as early as 1934, he labelled Hitler's *Mein Kampf* – a book Beckett studied seriously in 1942 according to Lois Gordon – 'Mein Krampf [My Cramp]' to poke fun at its rigid worldview (quoted in Gordon 1998: 138). In a letter to Arland Usher in 1938, Beckett also noted wryly that the perfect Aryan 'must be blond like Hitler, thin like Goering, handsome like Goebbels, virile like Roehm – and be called Rosenberg' (quoted in Knowlson 1997: 297). These cutting jokes fly in the face of the injustices emerging in Europe and illustrate the celebrated acerbic aspect of humour in times of tyranny. Yet laughter cannot overthrow the fascist behemoth and is rather more serviceable as an outlet to withstand flux, in the way Terrence Des Pres speaks about humour's temporary relief from the maelstrom of the Holocaust: 'humour counts most in precisely those situations where more decisive remedies fail' (1988: 217–18). It is not only the looming presence of totality that humour can undermine, but also deep inefficacy and radical uncertainty, which were in abundance during Beckett's most fertile creative period. With the physical destruction and death toll of the war years came the threat to the edifices of human life. The historian Tony Judt notes that '[f]or most Europeans in the years

1939–45 rights – civil, legal political – no longer existed' (2007: 38). Socio-political and ideological structures were in disarray as the conflict unfolded and returning to former values afterwards was not straightforward as '[w]hat was not utterly discredited was irretrievably damaged' (Judt 2007: 40). Furthermore, the cranking of an anthropological machine that decides what is and is not human severely endangered the viability of an essentialist human being. In this context, the dark humour of Beckett's post-war work stands out as both a product and preservative of the contingency exposed after the devastation of Western humanist codifications, and assumes a salient role in the reassessment of the human.

Aristotle claimed that no animal but man ever laughs (2001: 70), and although this assertion has not gone without dispute, humour has long been perceived as a component of the human, the *homo ridens*. In Beckett's earliest post-war writing, the breakdown or inefficacy of human rationality sits alongside persistent human indignity and atrophy as common sources of humour at the expense of the human. As such, Beckett's humour takes account of the wider schema of ignorance, impotence and indigence that dehumanizes the human being. Several critics, most notably Simon Critchley (2002: 111), cite humour as a consolation to the received nihilism of Beckett's literary world, with laughter offering a form of boundary and resistance. In an essay on the laughable but persistent negativity in Beckett, Suzanne Dow acknowledges this tendency to view humour's utility on the outer reaches of human comprehensibility. She writes that 'Beckett's humour is often taken to be a lucid reckoning with a horizon, the taking cognizance of a limit' (Dow 2011: 122). In this respect, humour in Beckett's work is deemed to be an instrument of human perseverance, called upon in humanity's continual confrontations with the harsh realities of mortal life. For Laura Salisbury, Beckett's humour is also far from frivolous, as it is through humour that a vision of human survival emerges amidst the obliteration of human faculties: 'it is not a question of the work providing a little comic relief; it is more that, through humour, shards of humanity and dignity are still to be found amid the ruins of narrative and the detritus of a post-apocalyptic theatre space' (2012: 5). At the precarious extremes of narratological, cognitive, cultural and anthropological meaning, humour is seemingly a sign of human fragility that simultaneously reaffirms humanity.

If humour confirms or at least salvages traces of the human, it does so through the failure and degradation of the human that betrays its creaturely dimension. This contradiction in Beckett's humour stems from the fact he engages with and problematizes the rather stifling theories of superiority, relief and incongruity laughter in order to obscure or multiply the targets of humour and complicate the relationship between the audience and the character. Thomas Hobbes gives an early definition of superiority laughter as he surveys human passions in *The Elements of Law, Natural and Politic* (1640). In a rare mention of laughter, Hobbes says it is 'nothing else but *sudden Glory* arising from a sudden conception of some Eminency in ourselves, by comparison with the Infirmity of others, or with our own formerly' (1999: 54). Alexander Bain reconsiders this definition of laughter to focus on the degradation and relief that superiority implies and, furthermore, to consider ideas, practices and organizations as targets of derision. In *The Emotions and the Will* ([1859] 1899), Bain asserts that 'Laughter is connected with an outburst of the sense of Power or superiority, and also with a sudden Release from a state of constraint' ([1859] 1899: 259). Beckett's humour certainly engages with the infirmity and constraint in these theories of laughter, although the eminency and power indicate a detachment from the object of humour that conflicts with Beckett's effectively self-deprecating humour against the species. One of the questions Beckett asks about the status of the human as he interrogates the motives and meaning behind laughter is whether the reading and viewing audience can associate with and dissociate from Beckett's creatures concurrently to feel both impotent and powerful.

Bain's contemporary, Herbert Spencer, concentrates on the notion of release in his theory of relief laughter in 'On the Physiology of Laughter' ([1860] 1911). Spencer describes laughter as a means of channelling excess nervous energy and notes that 'laughter naturally results only when consciousness is unawares transferred from great things to small – only when there is what we may call a descending incongruity' ([1860] 1911: 310). This type of relief is clearly connected with the incongruity humour advanced by Immanuel Kant in his famous definition of the laugh in 1790 as '*an affect arising from a strained expectation being suddenly reduced to nothing*' (italics in original) ([1790] 2007: 161). Beckett would have been familiar with the incongruity theory having read

Schopenhauer's work in the 1930s. In a brief chapter on laughter in *The World as Will and Representation* ([1818] 1969), the German philosopher claims that it is simple and easy to understand that 'laughter results from nothing but the suddenly perceived incongruity between a concept and the real objects that had been thought through it in some relation' (Schopenhauer [1818] 1969: 59). The notion of descending incongruity in the shift from high expectations to base revelations is closer to Beckett's post-war humour. As we shall see, Beckett produces some sophisticated incongruity humour by pairing technical language, spiritual ideas or cultured references with descriptions of orifices and their workings. This dichotomy between the products of the mind and the processes of the body relies partially on privileging the mind over the body. As Ruby Cohn notes with reference to Flemish philosopher Arnold Geulincx in her second monograph on Beckett: 'The Mind alone is rich and graceful, adds Geulincx, but it is fastened to a dying animal' (1973: 5). This view holds that the human mind occupies a powerful, elevated position while the body is a lowly biological vessel prone to decay. For Beckett, however, it seems the mind–body duality is unstable and that the psyche is as equally fallible and fragile as the physical self. Beckett's depiction of the mind often involves equalizing the levels between the cerebral and the terrestrial, which means embodying the processes of the mind, situating signs of intelligence alongside depictions of the vulgar body and highlighting language's contribution to physical humour.

While there are certainly instances of the sword, shield and succour of humour in Beckett's work, in the context of his netherworld in which going on is never particularly desired, humour's actual incapacity to change or cleanse negativity make it strangely complicit in incarcerating the human. The dark underbelly of humour has the potential to compromise the supposedly defiant laugh sounded in Beckett and the neat formulation of humour as a resistant or subversive force, thereby intimating an altogether more affirmative negative, which actually accepts, confirms and reinforces misery. It is this humour that suggests a creaturely element in that the laugh no longer merely reflects on the human predicament but contributes to it. The detached assessment of the world slides into an actual experience of that world. In this way, humour is 'the exploration of the break between nature and culture, which reveals the human to be not so much a category by itself as a negotiation between categories' (Critchley 2002: 29). In revealing and responding to unhappiness, Beckett's humour reveals the paradoxical moment in which the laugh is both a conscious recognition of the situation, as though an interruption of life as a result of perceiving life, and an action indistinct from the situation, as though laughter is another part of the life to which it supposedly responds. It is this limbo of indeterminacy that engenders the concomitance of the highly comic and deeply tragic in Beckett's work.

In its 'amphibious' (Critchley 2002: 36) traversal of the limits of the human and its transient assuaging of incomprehensibility, humour appears to slip between human cognition and animal immersion, between meaning and living. Humour therefore realizes the creaturely dynamic of continual creation that occurs on the edge of self-knowledge and immanence. It thrives on what exceeds other human faculties: it parries human degradation and suffering, mitigates the overwhelming pressure of mortality and sounds out against the ineffable. In turn, humour offers a means to exist in contiguity with negativity, alterity, non-being and silence, in a kind of renewable subjection to desubjectification. This negotiation of susceptibility links to recent theories of laughter that understand the phenomenon as 'a vocal affirmation of mutual vulnerability' common to both human and nonhuman animals (Simon 2008: 46). Vulnerability is a lodestar in the pursuit of definitions of creaturely life, particularly Pick's emphasis on material vulnerability, Santner's sense of ontological vulnerability and Lupton's allusion to the vulnerability of the provisional. It is through laughter as a shared expression of precariousness that Beckett's work also intersects with a creaturely dimension. As Beckett's creatures endure their failing narratives and the plight of their meaningful being, laughter figures as an affirmation of the perceived threat to the symbolical significance of the subject and increased exposure to the bareness of material necessity.

This chapter retraces the themes of testimony and power to reframe issues of failure and degradation in light of Beckett's humour. Drawing on a number of influential theories on humour, including the work of Mikhail Bakhtin, Henri Bergson and Sigmund Freud, I interpret the degrading elements of Beckett's humour in which comic failures bring communication into the realm of slapstick comedy to deride diegetic modes of storytelling, and produce a series of textual spectacles that narrow the gap between the mind and the body, and between subject matter and formal considerations. Beckett's humour, I argue, is an expression of the unspeakability that emerges in the breakdown of language and should therefore be considered in relation to the Beckettian pursuit of silence. The following sections analyse how language materializes as a component of the physical humour of the *Endgame* through the joke of Hamm and Clov's bodily entrapment, or creaturely suspension, and how Beckett's metanarrative techniques produce a creaturely movement between captivation and realization that embroils the audience in the profound joke of being. Finally, Beckett's version of gallows humour poses the idea that laughter, as both a gesture of resistance and preservation, is conducive to endurance for Beckett as it defies despair and sustains unhappiness.

Humour in failure

Much of the literature Beckett produces during the post-war period revolves around destitute figures in scenes characterized by failure and disappointment. Even so, Beckett's work is not oblivious to the humour in failure, despite being unremitting in its immersion in protracted failure. His texts are funny because his author-narrators often imitate the idea of the human in their struggles with reason, language, narrative and consciousness. As these faculties are exaggerated, misused and ultimately broken in the hands of Beckett's creatures, the image of the human is destabilized, and yet the creatures largely persist with this paragon, continuing with properties they demonstratively lambaste, which engenders a grotesque version of the human, at once disconcertingly familiar and amusingly different. Andrew Gibson notes that in the 'Three Dialogues' with Georges Duthuit, Beckett 'makes it quite clear that he is consciously rejecting an art that "pretends to be able"' (1985: 116). Wearing incapacity on its sleeve, Beckett's post-war work follows trying creatures beset with expressive and epistemological difficulties. This introduces a sense of humour on a narrative level through what Gibson describes as a 'comedy of description' or simply 'wastage', which protracts the problems in employing language and the difficulties in relating information (1985: 118).

Although intensifying this profligacy in his post-war work, before embarking on increasingly severe attenuation, Beckett's early use of pun contains the rudiments of this foolish narrative excess and highlights his rapid evolution after 1945.

In paronomastic humour, the polysemy of language opens up multiple significations for each word, whereby a comic alternative undercuts the expected meaning. In the 1938 novel *Murphy*, Beckett presents a protagonist particularly receptive to puns owing to his deep thoughtfulness and great erudition. The narrator remarks that Murphy studied under Neary, a philosopher who can stop his heart at will, and that 'Murphy was one of the elect, who require everything to remind them of something else' (*M*, 42). Murphy is clearly attuned to the allusive quality of words yet, as Ruby Cohn notes, of the 124 puns included in the novel, the majority come from the narrator (2001: 82). It is Beckett's narrator who embraces the pun as a fundamental part of the world when he says, 'In the beginning was the pun' (*M*, 43). This joke mimics the first verse of the book of John to mock the idea of a stable, pre-created meaning grounded in God. It suggests that using 'Word' as a metonym for 'God' already entails the unpredictability of language. However, Beckett's narrator in *Murphy* tends to exploit the proliferation of meaning for comic effect in a conscious way in this early novel. The narrator can draw on language's capacity for other meaning privately, without allowing the narrative to digress. For example, he says that Neary's servant 'Cooper never sat, his acathisia was deep-seated and of long standing' (*M*, 76). The use of a medical term here makes this an esoteric pun, causing the joke to rely heavily on the reader's vocabulary or willingness to consult a dictionary. It suggests that Cooper's restlessness is well established while implying the symptoms. This type of highly intellectual display in *Murphy* shows a more personal type of humour that can exclude the reading audience. Murphy exemplifies a similar self-satisfying humour when he tells his partner Celia a joke:

'Why did the barmaid champagne?' he said. 'Do you give it up?'
'Yes,' said Celia.
'Because the stout porter bitter,' said Murphy.
This was a joke that did not amuse Celia, at the best of times and places it could not have amused her. That did not matter. So far from being adapted to her, it was not addressed to her. It amused Murphy, that was all that mattered (*M*, 88).

Murphy pleases himself with the wordplay but Celia does not appreciate this linguistic humour. He delights in the joke's homophonic value and neglects the fact that it lacks sense. The question 'Do you give it up?' also reveals Murphy's smug victory in revealing the punch line. Together, the medical pun and this aural pun show that certain information and tastes must be shared in order for the pun to avoid alienating the audience.

Whereas the arcane pun in *Murphy* shows a competent narrative voice conducting a level of humour that can exclude the reader, Beckett's later puns in *Molloy* reserve the knowing grin for the reader and for Beckett. In the second part, for example, Moran encounters a dim man one evening and describes how the man's face and body are appropriately matched. Moran notes, 'If I could have seen his arse, I do not doubt I should have found it on a par with the whole' (*T*, 150). Beckett increases the crudity of his humour as he turns to the monologue. The verbal dexterity displayed in *Murphy* is reduced in this instance and the lack of a third-person narrator generally ensures that puns no longer occur from such a position of sovereignty over possible meaning. Instead, the alternative meaning appears accidental and serves to divert the intention of the sentence towards new and unwanted significance, without the smile of omniscience. This type of ignorant pun that avoids esoteric words and resorts to crudity is easier to detect for the reader.

Although Beckett tones down the erudition of his humour in the example above, he continues to employ cultured references and learned ideas to produce an eclectic, and indeed comic, mix of highbrow thinking and bodily reality. In Cartesian dualism, the body is distinct from the superior component of being, the mind. It is the mind, or the *res cogitans*, that constitutes the person fundamentally while the body, or the *res extensa*, is a sensory machine (Descartes 2008: 51–64). The French philosopher Henri Bergson addresses a similarly hierarchical conception in his study *Laughter*. He writes: 'When we see only gracefulness and suppleness in the living body, it is because we disregard elements of weight, of resistance, and, in a word, of matter; we forget its materiality and think only of its vitality which we regard as derived from the very principle of intellectual and moral life' (Bergson [1911] 1999: 49). This positive image of the body is actually achieved by seeing past the normal properties of the material form, but when the body *qua* matter is recognized, it is a source of laughter: 'No sooner does the

anxiety about the body manifest itself than the intrusion of a comic
element is to be feared' (Bergson [1911] 1999: 51). These basic
anxieties about the body are widespread and do not necessarily rely
on access to specific cultural codes or social conceptions of the
body. The physical state is a shared condition and therefore a
common source of humour. From a later anthropocentric
perspective, the mind remains the pride of the human, capable of
symbolic thought and language systems far in advance of the
capacity of nonhuman animals. The body, on the other hand,
reminds us of the shared materiality of living things and what Judith
Butler describes as 'mortality, vulnerability, agency' (2004: 26),
which should be extended to the animal kingdom, as Cary Wolfe
has pointed out (2013: 18–21).

Since Beckett's humour navigates between, on the one side, elite
language and learned culture and, on the other, the universal fact of
the body as matter and process, Beckett offers a sophisticated
juxtaposition of mind and body that not only involves the nuanced
texture of supposedly high and low subjects, but also conveys the
tensions of a duality that makes up the human being. As Agamben
suggests, 'man has always been thought of as the articulation and
conjunction of a body and a soul, of a living thing and a *logos*, of a
natural (or animal) element and a supernatural or social or divine
element' whereas we should 'think of man as what results from the
incongruity of these two elements' (2003: 16). In this context,
Beckett's humour involves 'degradation' or 'debasement' in the
sense of situating the abstract or superior alongside the physical or
natural. That is, in terms of deposing the human mind from its
pedestal and bringing the immaterial back to down to earth.
Whereas the pun in *Murphy* uses a technical term to make a joke
about a physical condition, Beckett undermines elevated language
in *Molloy* by pairing it with base content for a bathetic comic effect.
This paves the way for a marginally more magnanimous approach
to humour since the cruder material gives the audience a common
ground in the 'horrors of the body and its functions' (*T*, 118). There
nevertheless remains an intellectually demanding aspect to Beckett's
incongruity humour as his candid assessments of the body and
bodily processes are often filtered through or placed alongside
technical language and erudite material.

On entering the forest, Molloy contemplates his physical
weaknesses and refers to his 'arse-hole' before long: 'Jesus-Christ,

it's much worse than yesterday I can hardly believe it's the same hole' (*T*, 79). The use of a spiritual icon stands out as a humorous, and indeed blasphemous, outburst in the context of Molloy's bodily issues. Molloy appears to recognize the crudeness of this topic, only to replace the religious reference with an artistic tradition: 'I apologise for having to revert to this lewd orifice, 'tis my muse will have it so' (*T*, 79). Beckett juxtaposes a vulgar reference to the body with the romantic notion of a creative inspiration that recalls the daughters of Zeus in Greek mythology. Since Molloy implies, scurrilously, that the 'muse' is fixated on his arsehole, Beckett effectively connects a figure of inspiration to a site of expulsion for a comic sense of incongruity. As Molloy continues to list his bodily afflictions, he also employs medical and scholarly language: 'But my prepuce, sat verbum, oozes urine, day and night, at least I think it's urine, it smells of kidney. What's all this, I thought I had lost the sense of smell. Can one speak of pissing, under these conditions? Rubbish!' (*T*, 81). By employing the technical name for foreskin and following it with the Latin adage meaning 'a word to the wise is sufficient', Molloy signals the obscurity of his wording through an equally elitist phrase. Hence, Beckett still demands a high level of knowledge from the reader for the incongruity between the technical language and body part to be fully understood. The difference here is that 'oozes urine', 'kidney' and 'pissing' make the missing subject relatively obvious. Beckett applies sophisticated language to a more vulgar scene to make a mockery of the cultured style while allowing the gist of the humour to be recognized. This incongruity is itself a sophisticated form of humour about the body, although the intellectual weight of 'prepuce' or 'sat verbum' is less in light of the more plainspoken later parts of the passage. Beckett effectively retains the difficulty of the high modernist imperative in his use of cultured references and bookish terms to depict the body, but also includes more vernacular descriptions to produce challenging and surprising comical contrasts.

Beckett's art of failure complements these humorous juxtapositions as the narrators often respond with confusion to their own fragments of intellect. Obscure words are still deployed but their meanings are not definite, so that esoteric language is subsequently filtered through the narrator's uncertainty. At the beginning of *Malone Dies*, after the repeated use of 'perhaps' when Malone is devising his writing plan, he employs a technical word but is unsure whether it is appropriate. Malone surmises, 'There I am back at my old aporetics. Is that the word? I don't know' (*T*, 181). There is a double sense of humour in this line in that Malone's narrative incompetence is amusing for uninformed readers whereas informed readers recognize that the 'I don't know' reinforces the 'aporia' of the text. Beckett returns to this comic illustration of an apparently unknown word in *The Unnamable*. Again, Beckett's narrator uses the technique at the beginning while deliberating how to proceed: 'I should mention before going any further – any further on – that I say "aporia" without knowing what it means' (*T*, 293). The narrator dwells on an empty word that actually develops the static conditions he is attempting to identify with 'aporia'. His use of the word without knowing its meaning contributes to the impassable path that involves speaking despite the inability to positively communicate. In this turn to ignorance, Beckett opens up his imitation of narrative and linguistic frailties to the audience, directing the confusion away from the reader and towards the narrator. He therefore focuses on bodily materiality in two ways that each democratize his humour: directly referring to the body, which draws attention to a shared condition, and subverting mental faculties, which lessens the alienating effect of erudite language. Beckett diminishes the authorial intelligence seen in *Murphy* through an emphasis on trying to employ words in a state of common ignorance in the trilogy to make the humour more accessible. Nevertheless, the sophisticated subject matter that Beckett addresses ensures an intellectual and textured sense of humour.

The pun is effectively a microcosm of Beckett's amusing narrative tone, or 'syntax of weakness' as he described it, that developed in the 1940s and 1950s (Beckett quoted in Harvey 1970: 445). The reader is frequently invited to observe the humorous potential of language while Beckett's narrators are excluded from the joke in their attempts to relate stories sincerely. Sigmund Freud calls this type of inadvertent humour '*naïve*' in his 1905 study *Jokes and their Relation to the Unconscious*. Freud's analysis of humour builds on Spencer's relief theory but suggests, in part, that humour is either 'tendentious' or 'non-tendentious'. The former is the product of an aggressive impulse that engages oppressive or forbidden material to grant a psychological release. Non-tendentious humour on the other hand lacks the same hostile drive, and is therefore tame or innocent. Freud defines this division through the phrase '[a] joke is made, the comic is found', although he does suggest that naive humour can sound like a joke despite lacking intention (1976: 239–40). On occasion, Beckett's narrators chance upon what they consider to be a joke but is actually closer to the comic in the Freudian sense, such as when Malone vows to write his memoirs despite his short memory: 'When I have completed my inventory, if my death is not ready for me then, I shall write my memoirs. That's funny, I have made a joke. No matter. There is a cupboard I have never looked in' (*T*, 184). Malone has not made a joke here, but rather found the comic element of his naivety. This seldom occurs in Beckett's first-person narratives, and humorous moments are frequently left undetected or unremarked. Malone's reflections are in fact littered with humorous glitches in language and thought, such as 'My body does not yet make up its mind' (*T*, 198) and 'let us leave these morbid matters and get on with that of my demise' (*T*, 236). Despite this, Beckett's characters largely fail to appreciate or construct humour, and tellingly, a distracted Malone indicates that jokes might be another unexplored 'cupboard'.

The reader's vantage of knowledge in the comprehension of a joke, or the 'in-joke' at the narrator's expense, injects a voyeuristic aspect into the relationship between teller and receiver, which exposes the narrator's awkward communication and fumbling narrative style. The inefficiency with which Beckett's narrators conduct their stories is paramount to his humour in the prose. Gibson recognizes that the narrators 'refuse to conform to the convention of salience which so often governs description in the classic text. Salience becomes a pose, adopted only to be travestied' (1985: 118). This digressive technique halts the action to dwell on a single, often superfluous, piece of information. Aporia stifles any possibility of developing significant events and the narrative progression ebbs as a consequence. Three examples across Beckett's work serve to highlight humour's presence in the exercise and interrogation of reason and language in his narrative form. First, in *Watt*, Arsene's lengthy induction of the new arrival Watt shares the title character's penchant for permutations and commitment to excessive explanation. As Arsene traces their predecessors in the Knott house, he follows a logical process but forgets the content:

For Vincent and Walter were not the first, ho, no, but before them were Vincent and another whose name I forget, and before them that other whose name I forget and another whose name I forget, and before them that other whose name I forget and another whose name I never knew, and before them that other whose name I never knew and another whose name Walter could not recall (*W*, 50).

The sustained attention to variations in *Watt* satirizes the attempt to present information comprehensively. Arsene is unable to retrieve the names of the servants as he concentrates on the system. The repetition of 'forget' in the above example parodies the repetition of 'begat' in the first chapter of the gospel of Matthew to show how a repetitive form can supplant meaning. In the Bible, Matthew employs the word 'begat' thirty-nine times over fifteen lines, moving forward in time from Abraham to trace Christ's ancestry (Matthew 1.2–16). This fixation on one word suggests a type of pedantry, which Schopenhauer describes as 'that clinging to form, the manner, the expression and the word that is peculiar to pedantry, and with it takes the place of the real essence of the matter' (1969: 60). Similarly, in Beckett, the process overwhelms the point of the passage. Beckett's text echoes the advancing 'begat' with the receding 'forget', thereby reversing the flow of time as it moves back into an increasingly obscure past while maintaining the pattern of thought. He shuns the implicit etcetera that conscientious readers would expect with repetition and patterns and, instead, the rigorous mental practice replaces elliptical spaces, which effectively fills the text with hollow, predictable and unnecessary passages. These exhaustive attempts at explanation are a waste of effort and comic in their ignorance of sufficiency.

Beckett (*MC*, 4) develops these textual shortcomings for comic effect in *Mercier and Camier* when the two heroes repeatedly miss one another having appointed a meeting time and place. Beckett writes out the scene in full, before summarizing:

In other words:

	Arr.	Dep.	Arr.	Dep.	Arr.	Dep.	Arr.
Mercier	9.05	9.10	9.25	9.30	9.40	9.45	9.50
Camier	9.15	9.20	9.35	9.40	9.50		

Evidently, the 'other words' to which Beckett resorts is a timetable. The reason for Mercier and Camier's failure to meet is simple: one waits while the other walks, the other waits while the first one walks. Despite that, the written description complicates the scene, making it difficult to track the characters' movements. The table elucidates the matter with more efficiency and signals the failure of description in words, but the narrator is not content with this perspective, suggesting it is overly contrived when he says 'What stink of artifice' (*MC*, 4). Indeed, timetables are devised to organize and be efficient and, as Foucault affirms, serve to 'establish rhythms, impose particular occupations, [and] regulate the cycles of repetition' (1991: 149). This type of structured layout certainly clears up the scene but also makes it sterile, which implies that, although the written description fails to elucidate the sequence of their non-coincidence, it is at least a more organic expression of the wayward protagonists. The contrast between convoluted prose and clear tabulation is a patent source of humour that allows the narrative to move forward while heralding the inadequacy of this compromised mode of 'progression'.

Molloy also resorts to numbers to surmount a narrative impasse and proceed with his ramblings. Beckett's narrator hibernates for winter in swathes of newspaper, noting 'The Times Literary Supplement was admirably adapted to this purpose, of a never failing toughness and impermeability. Even farts made no impression on it' (*T*, 30). The implication is that literary criticism is stringent and closed off, but also flatulent in the figurative sense. In any case, Molloy is not concerned with the written content of the book review and values it only for the insulating properties of the paper it is printed on, perhaps sharing the disdain of Vladimir's cutting retort 'Crritic!' in *Waiting for Godot* (*WFG*, 67). On the other hand, mathematics offers Molloy a reliable insight into himself, although this science is merely used to calculate the rate of his flatulence:

> Three hundred and fifteen farts in nineteen hours, or an average of over sixteen farts an hour. After all it's not excessive. Four farts every fifteen minutes. It's nothing. Not even one fart every four minutes. It's unbelievable. Damn it, I hardly fart at all, I should never have mentioned it. Extraordinary how mathematics help you to know yourself (*T*, 30).

Mathematics is used to analyse his past and is preferred over language alone. The numbers have fixed values and, in relation to the scale of time, Molloy can quantify and contextualize his being using averages to divide periods of existence into fathomable parts and thus gain a level of perspective. Words are laborious and confusing whereas mathematics acts as reliable shorthand and is an appropriate, efficient mode of expression for problems and solutions. Despite all this, Beckett's creatures persevere with words and consign scientific thought to the vulgar body. Molloy reduces mathematics to mere 'trumpery' as he uses his show of arithmetic to discuss trivial matters. In this way, Beckett confronts 'the vile suggestion that art has nothing to do with clarity, does not dabble in the clear and does not make clear' (quoted in Topsfield 1988: 25–6). This humorous degradation of language into lengthy digressions and the use of rational thinking for base subject matter shows that Beckett situates sophisticated disciplines alongside a benighted dimension of the human that society tries hard to censor. Beckett's humour of failure indulges ineffective narrative techniques that mimic human modes of meaning to present a distorted caricature of the classic author.

Textual performances

Beckett degrades language and evinces the petty utility of words through the incongruity between high intellect or mental rigor and the minor or base material to which it is directed. The mind's abstract constructions and conceptual powers may offer sanctuary from the physical world, but these illusions merely set up the mind to plummet back to a recognition of its weak corporal vessel and poor expressive vehicles. However, the point stressed in the following section is not the body as a site of finitude, but how the body is invoked at the limits of communicative language to express a language of its own, a body language so to speak. The tension between content and form in Beckett helps to produce a level of humour that traces the limits of the word while continuing to traverse them *in corpore*, thereby deferring the complete failure of language and the complete acceptance of physical finitude. In short, Beckett's language–body formulation creates a creaturely state of suspension as laughter occurs at the limit of the language performance, but it does not realize the dream of transcendence.

Mikhail Bakhtin discusses the downward movement from the elevated, abstract level to the lowly, bodily level in *Rabelais and his World* ([1965] 1984). His work on the carnival and grotesque realism holds degradation as an essential principle. Bakhtin's notion of the 'carnivalesque' describes the humorous festivities of the people as they unite against the official culture. The community resort to the grotesque to resist the governed world, which 'exaggerates and caricatures the negative, the inappropriate' (Bakhtin [1965] 1984: 303). This subversion of power promotes the lower stratum, associated with 'food, drink, defecation, and sexual life', which is easily understood and shared by others in order to produce a collective atmosphere ([1965] 1984: 18). Bakhtin explains that this rebellion against authority is a form of 'grotesque realism', which entails 'the lowering of all that is high, spiritual, ideal, abstract' ([1965] 1984: 19) so that symbols of the upper stratum, such as the heavens, the face and the mind are reduced to the lower stratum of the earth, the genitals and the buttocks. In this respect, the bodily element is 'deeply positive' since it is 'something universal, representing all people' ([1965] 1984: 19). In Beckett's world, the cerebral level is also equal to the terrestrial, although the downward movement of degradation in Bakhtin has a purely 'topographical meaning' ([1965] 1984: 21), whereas Beckett's humbles the elevated sphere of the mind that anthropocentricism and humanism privileges. Reason, consciousness, language and narrative prove to be as ineffective as the body, but suffer a steeper degradation in comparison with the already 'grounded' physical self. As Beckett explores the weaknesses of the metaphysical alongside the physical, and effectively amalgamates the mental sphere of his monologues and the bodily sphere of his drama, his humour of failure disrupts the mind–matter duality. The bathetic interplay between the mind's faculties and the body's crude workings suggests that the noble is reduced to the common, and that 'laughter degrades and materialises' ([1965] 1984: 20).

The degradation from the upper to the lower strata indicates a parallel between Beckett's prose and drama. Although Beckett resorts to actual performances on stage, the appearance of his texts on the page and the experience of reading the prose offer textual equivalents to the physical clowning he explores in the drama.

Much has been written about the physical humour of Beckett's prose and drama, particularly the ribald and scatological sides of the imperfect body.[1] On separate occasions, both Shane Weller and David Houston Jones have also examined the point of crossover between physical abjection and textual abjection. In Weller's book *Beckett, Literature, and the Ethics of Alterity* (2006a), for instance, he introduces the idea that laughter *at the other* is always the laughter *of the other* to assess the extent to which Beckett's humour includes an ethical principle. Weller rightly suggests that the abject body in Beckett 'does not possess the power of resistance to the official or normative that Bakhtin claims for the Rabelaisian body' (2006a: 115–16). Beckett does not celebrate the body nor grant it the unifying or subversive quality of the carnival. If the body is a common ground for people, it is also an embarrassing fact that is socially repressed and a burden for Beckett's decaying creatures. Nevertheless, Weller does briefly follow the idea that in Beckett's brand of 'wordshit' (2006a: 116), literature itself becomes an abject body.[2] Beckett's prose gives physicality to intellectual processes inasmuch as his narratives deliver a formal impact that renders and imposes cognitive movements through amusing textual performances. Watt's lexical loops, Mercier and Camier's timetable and Molloy's calculations are all textual spectacles, whereby linguistic forms translate the metaphysics of reason into a visual and experiential substance. These passages fall short when transmitting information through the semantic value of language, and yet each example continues to offer a textual embodiment of the mind since they execute language's execution. As such, language is a suitable tool to demonstrate the inability to communicate effectively as it bears out its own deficiency. Beckett effectively presents a grotesque and abject *textual* body.

As with the crude humour of the wretched body, the textual performance of the grotesque and abject in Beckett carries humorous undertones. Molloy's attempt to solve the problem of his sucking-stones is a prime example of how Beckett causes words to appear virtually senseless through an excess of reason and at the same time offer a humorous formal display. As Molloy attempts to find a way of sucking each stone in turn by circulating them around his various pockets, his description of this process mimics the rearrangement of the stones. Words too are rearranged into similar but different patterns as he replaces 'left' with 'right' and 'greatcoat' with 'trousers'

(T, 69). Molloy's 'Watch me closely' (T, 72) marks the beginning of his show, implying that the solution he describes is a kind of close-up magic trick that necessitates eagle-eyed vigilance to follow. On stage, the rotation of Molloy's sucking-stones would equate to Vladimir and Estragon's hat-cycle skit. As it is, Molloy's fidelity to logic verges on nonsense since the profusion of repeated words and recycled syntax largely makes his reasoning confusing for the reader. Molloy's careful and extended consideration of the rearrangement of his sucking-stones is at once amusing and frustrating. Molloy appears to recognize as much when he says 'Do I need to go on?' and replies 'No', and yet he does persist with his maddening reasoning. Crucially, immediately after this scene, Molloy remembers a woman who approached him on the beach and then returned to her companions 'Huddled together like sheep [. . .] laughing no doubt, I seem to hear laughter far away' (T, 75). This laughter suggests a sardonic reaction to Molloy in the context of his performance and the reference to 'huddled sheep' indicates a crowd, particularly a mindless or biddable audience. In the same way that theatre audiences laugh at the pratfalls and slapstick antics of *Waiting for Godot*, Molloy perceives a plausible group reaction to his own performance and, by implication, him as a person. This laughter of superiority highlights the failure of Molloy's intended explanation, indicating that his attempt to elucidate in fact achieves the opposite and is therefore risible. The distance of the laughter after Molloy's sucking-stones performance suggests it is from an outsider and not from the implied spectator that he initially addresses. The audience is no longer in league with the performer, but rather laughing from afar in a detached, judgemental way. More than this, the distance of the laughter and the uncertainty in the word 'seem' implies that Molloy is paranoid about his performance; that he reflects mentally on the impression he gives to others and imagines an obscure laughter directed at himself. The failure of Molloy's reason actually provokes a self-conscious reaction, a kind of phantom laughter analogous to feelings of embarrassment and shame. Therefore, this distant laughter anticipates the reading audience's laughter at Molloy's textual acrobatics and conveys the laughter that Molloy imposes upon himself. The result is that Molloy becomes a part of the crowd that closely watches his performance.

Beckett's bedridden protagonist in *Malone Dies* reinforces the human mind's relationship with the physical self that Molloy introduces. Malone describes how Macmann's carer, Lemuel, strikes himself on the skull with a hammer because the head is 'the seat of all the shit and misery' (*T*, 269). With allusions to the Roman physician Galen, who considered the head the source of reason, and parodying the birth of the Goddess of wisdom Athena from the head of Zeus in Greek mythology, Beckett's reference to the head as 'seat' conjures a clever depiction of the degradation of the mind, playing on the term to indicate buttocks, which marries the head and arse to create a comic image of the headspring of worthless and contemptible drivel. The lofty head is at once the seat, or the centre, and the bottom, or the butt of the joke. In addition, 'seat' refers to the sedentary position and intimates a viewer. As with Molloy's distant laughter, the seat has double relevance as source and audience, culprit and witness, as though the brain sits and observes the misery of the body it controls and to which it belongs. The head is therefore implicated in the plight of the human as the seat of nonsensical reason, the coordinating centre of the wretched body and the reflective capacity that laughs at it all.

In Beckett's prose and plays alike, humour stems from the rigidity of the respective targets, with physical humour exposing the inflexibility of the body while textual humour unhinges the systematic rational mind and contorts narrative conventions. In his study *Laughter*, Bergson theorizes rigidity as a source of humour, focusing chiefly on physical humour. He writes: 'We laugh every time a person gives us the impression of being a thing' ([1911] 1999: 56). Bergson's example is the inability to adapt when falling over, noting that the body appears simply as an object in time and space, subject to physics, and thus stripping the human momentarily of an ideological value and anthropocentric ascendency. He proposes that absent-mindedness and ignorance of self are measures of humour and, in this state, human agency collapses into automatism: 'The attitudes, gestures and movements of the human body are laughable in exact proportion as that body reminds us of a mere machine' (Bergson [1911] 1999: 32). This 'thingness' extends to human faculties and their limits for Beckett, which reduces modes of thought and expression to empty frameworks and redundant customs. Hence his characters trip up figuratively in the prose, stumbling on epistemological and communicative obstacles. Beckett applies Bergson's mechanics of the body to the mind's operations, presenting automatic, lengthy and unsuccessful workings of rationality in a laughable attempt to resolve contradictions and settle on reliable information.

However, from the trilogy onwards, Beckett's narrative mode offers a further alternative version of Bergson's notion of absent-mindedness. The monologues are self-conscious and self-reflexive projects, situated within the individual mind. Despite this introspection, the inward glance in Beckett withholds complete self-knowledge and preserves psychological blind spots so that, in effect, levels of the mind remain absent. This principle is noticeable in Molloy's contemplation of the dog in the A and C scene. Molloy is perched high on the hill, overlooking two men walking in opposite directions. Man A or man C (Molloy is unsure which) is walking a small dog: 'a pomeranian I think, but I don't think so. I wasn't sure at the time and I'm still not sure, though I've hardly thought about it. [. . .] Yes, it was an orange pomeranian, the less I think of it the more certain I am. And yet' (*T*, 12). Doubt repeatedly returns to make Molloy a casualty of the voices in his mind and the more he thinks, the further he is dragged into a cognitive oblivion. The humour of absent-mindedness in Beckett's version is that vacuity is demonstrated through the narrator's psychological self-examinations. The narrator of *The Unnamable*, for example, is entangled in a web of contradictions in the attempt to unravel his meditations on the self: 'If I say anything to the contrary I was mistaken. If I say anything to the contrary again I shall be mistaken. Unless I am mistaken now' (*T*, 347). For all of the narrator's efforts to make sense of experience, pay attention to detail, be alert to one's position and invest in the structures of language and logic, the result is a humorous circumnavigation of the crux, which amounts to a lacuna akin to Bergson's absent-mindedness. Essentially, the failures enclosed within the body of the text emerge as the concretized evidence of the mind's presence, but only in its inefficacy.

The Beckettian creature is a degraded version of the humanistic ideal in both body and mind; he is *Homo incapacitus*. By reducing the constitutional properties of humankind, typically held as evidence of human supremacy, Beckett presents an altered vision of humanity that cannot be considered elite. The humour inherent to this failing figure rests on the detritus of epistemology and expression that foregrounds the lower stratum of the body. In turn, the attention to degradation in Beckett's humour of failure conveys his resistance to signification in favour of aesthetic impact, or what Adorno calls the 'shock of the unintelligible' (2003a: 243). The prominence given to form and enactment in Beckett's work encourages Adorno's reading of *Endgame* as a profoundly senseless formal experience that rejects the transmission of explicit meaning through diegetic content. However, Simon Critchley argues that Adorno consistently underestimates comedy, to the extent that Beckett can 'make a philosopher as subtle and intelligent as Adorno appear slightly maladroit and flat-footed' (1997: 160). Adorno states bluntly that, in Beckett's *Endgame*, 'the only comical thing remaining is that along with the sense of the punchline, comedy itself has evaporated' (1982: 135). Critchley focuses heavily on this statement and asserts that 'humour is this very experience of evaporation, which is the evaporation of a certain philosophical seriousness and interpretative earnestness. Humour does not evaporate in Beckett; rather laughter is the sound of language trying to commit suicide but being unable to do so, which is what is so tragically comic' (1997: 157). Humour is not evaporated altogether in Beckett, according to Critchley. It remains as language attempts to mute itself, as an employed language tries to articulate and theorize its own end, never satisfying the teleological goal of philosophical seriousness and interpretative earnestness. The laugh, as 'the sound of language trying to commit suicide', implies that language is still active and valuable, albeit preoccupied with self-obliteration. Therefore, the laugh is not the end of language, but the perpetual coda of language. It is the interstice between the termination of language and the goal of Beckett's language, namely silence. As a vocalization that is anchored in the on-going reduction of language structures, the laugh in Beckett's work is taken as a product of language as it tries to silence itself.

Laughter's advent on the edge of silence is marked as Beckett returns to textual performance in *The Unnamable* in order to convey language's disintegration into a more primitive, visceral semantic code:

> that's how it will end, in heart-rending cries, inarticulate murmurs, to be invented, as I go along, improvised, as I groan along, I'll laugh that's how it will end, in a chuckle, chuck chuck, ow, ha, pa, I'll practise, nyum, hoo, plop, psss, nothing but emotion, bing bang, that's blows, ugh, pooh, what else, oooh, aaah, that's love, enough, it's tiring, hee hee, that's the Abderite,

no, the other, in the end, it's the end, the ending end, it's the silence (*T*, 412).

The narrator disgorges a range of inarticulate but emotionally charged sounds. He predicts that the laugh will finally burst out and signal the end of the expressive dilemma, but evidently the art of laughter requires skill and must be rehearsed. Ironically, the curtailed chuckle released here is precisely an art; it is artificial or 'invented', which suggests that the narrator actually requires a more spontaneous or 'improvised' laugh that responds to the situation without hesitation or contrivance. He needs a laugh that sidles towards the end of language and in closer proximity with silence. Tellingly, the narrator's reference to the Abderite invokes the Ancient Greek philosopher Democritus, commonly known as the laughing philosopher, associated with 'scoffing' and who famously pronounced 'no thing is more real than nothing'.[3] In this allusion to 'scoffing' and 'nothing' in *The Unnamable*, Beckett intimates laughter's role in mocking language to get closer to the vacuum of silence on the other side.

Critchley's notion of 'laughter as the sound of language trying to commit suicide' also evokes Walter Benjamin's aphorism in *The Arcades Project*: 'Laughter is shattered articulation' (1999: 325). Far from being altogether unintelligible, Benjamin suggests that laughter is the breakdown of the formerly successful, stable and clarified structures of communication. The laugh is not the after-effect of shattered articulation either, but is itself a gesture of lucidity in pieces. Although Critchley forwards a more dilated and dramatic version of Benjamin's phrase, both emphasize that laughter does convey meaning, however scantly. Similarly, the narrator of *The Unnamable* pronounces how the end will occur but nevertheless continues to emit a series of rudimentary sounds that have expressive value. As Sara Crangle points out in her chapter on laughter in *Prosaic Desires* (2010), sound 'is an expression of knowledge, meaning, or emotion and, fundamentally, meets a basic and continuous human longing for communication' (2010: 130). The narrator of *The Unnamable* bypasses knowledge and meaning to an extent to insist upon 'nothing but emotion', and yet these sounds have the intention of silence behind them and are therefore related to the thousands of words uttered before, each aiming to say the end. But even the most reduced forms of expression, including outbursts of emotion, contain a paronomastic quality of excess. As Beckett himself exemplifies when he explains to Alan Schneider that his work is 'a matter of fundamental sounds (no joke intended)' (quoted in Harmon 1998: 24), sounds, like words, reveal more or other than intended. They fill the void with a parenthetic supplement that holds off the nothingness of silence.

However, the narrator of *The Unnamable* is correct in suggesting that laughter is related to the end of language, and it is particularly noticeable in the term 'gag'. Referring to Shakespeare's *Titus Andronicus* (1594), Manfred Pfister picks up on laughter's relation to silence:

> It is a laugh beyond, or at the far side of, tears, a pathological laughter. And what it expresses – like the silence, like being struck dumb, to which it is closely related and which it disrupts – is utter helplessness and the most radical protest against the horrors of existence and the failure of language to express them discursively (2002: 185).

Laughter, like silence, is expressive, but laughter is also an incursion on silence and, as such, it denies the absence of sound. The laugh can therefore be valid as a non-discursive expression that reacts to context and indicates a communicative value. It can also desecrate silence to help punctuate and perpetuate the obligation to speak. As the voice in *The Unnamable* demonstrates in its spluttering and coughing performance, words and sound partake in the unending end of language in an attempt to claw towards the final expression of utter silence. The paradox here is that the act of speaking is motivated towards the silence that it also denies. Adorno is well aware of this insurmountable problem: 'The words resound like merely makeshift ones because silence is not yet entirely successful, like voices accompanying and disturbing it' (1982: 137). These words, like the obscure sound of laughter, say the unsayable, but are not a guillotine for expression as a whole. They postpone complete silence with the remnants of meaning to sustain the impact of degradation and failure. Indeed, Beckett realizes that 'every word is like an unnecessary stain on silence and nothingness' (quoted in Bryden 1997: 279) and yet he also knows he 'could not have gone through the awful wretched mess of life without having left a stain upon the silence' (quoted in Bair 1990: 681). Since silence is not entirely successful, the fundamental joke of Beckett's humour of failure is that the failure is never complete. Laughter, as the shattered and suicidal throes of language, fails to achieve the silence and is unable to cease staining silence. In a curious twist, then, the laugh assists in adumbrating the unspeakable that testifies to the catastrophe. At the limits of comprehension and articulation, the sound of laughter signals the nervous energy and sense of vulnerability that attests to the magnitude of the event and how it exceeds verbal communication. The laughter in and at Beckett's work is therefore parallel to the way a stutter might physically react to the urge to speak and not speak. Far from the simple expression of pleasure, the laugh is associated with the spoken silence that connects Beckett's expressive obligation to testimony after the Holocaust.

Words and flesh in *Endgame*

Beckett's humorous textual performances offer a textual embodiment of the human subject's rational and linguistic failures. He degrades the representative powers of language to the visual, aural and formal impacts that evoke the physicality of a spectacle. As a part of this performance, laughter bursts forth as a vocal and physical expression that occurs at language's limits, and is related to the necessity and impossibility of bearing witness accentuated after the Holocaust by implication. It is possible to extend the way in which language is bound up with bodily issues, not in terms of Beckett's debased novelistic content or textual performances, but rather how words are part of the physical humour of creaturely suspension as it appears on stage. In Beckett's theatre, the dialogue ensures that characters' physical presences are maintained; while they are speaking they stay put. The restless verbal exchanges therefore underwrite the physical joke in Beckett's plays, namely that words prolong the creatures' physical incarceration. When language is uprooted from its human ability to make sense effectively and efficiently, it is transplanted into a more visceral, inhuman capacity. The words lose much of their semantic value and become the minimal stimulus required to continue the characters' fettered bodily conditions on stage.

In Maud Ellmann's essay 'Changing into an Animal', on what she perceives as the dehumanizing process of writing in Joyce's composition of the 'Circe' episode in *Ulysses*, she highlights language's connection to materiality in its ability to make the author a medium. Ellmann writes that '[r]eason, consciousness, free-will – those "wideawake" attributes supposed to elevate the human over the inhuman – give way to animal drives and mechanical compulsions, while language, rather than transcending those automatisms, dances to their epileptic rhythm' (2006: 75–6). Language appears to be subject to the convulsive energies associated with the nervous system, thereby framing words as involuntary reflexes originating in the unconscious. She goes on to say, '[l] anguage, far from transcending the body, is present as a form of discharge, comparable to the hallucinations of the Freudian dream, in which impulses discharge themselves as spectacles' (2006: 91). For Ellmann, this degradation of words to the body suggests a kind of anxious outflow that recalls both rejected animality and the automatism of the mind. Beckett stages similar verbal discharges, most famously in Lucky's 700-word tirade in *Waiting for Godot*, but also in more sustained forms, such as the 1964 stage piece *Play*, in which three figures in urns take turns to rapidly meditate on their triangular love affair, and the 1972 dramatic monologue *Not I*, in which a stream of words spew from an illuminated mouth. The effect is called *logorrhoea*, which describes an excessive outpouring of language and highlights the reduction of words to waste. The delivery of language in such a way can accentuate the materiality of the word as it is spoken over its symbolic meaning to develop more physicalized spectacles.

It is a relationship Eric Santner develops in relation to creaturely life in his study *The Royal Remains* (2011), which makes use of an eclectic range of complex sources in order to trace how 'the normative pressures injected into human life by way of one's inscription into a symbolic order are imagined to return as real bodily impingements and violations' (2011: xiv). Referring to the sovereign's duality as a divine icon and mortal being, as well as the modern biopolitical development from a single royal subject to the collective sovereign citizenship, Santner argues that representative value translates to the physical self. Broadly put, the significations housed in the mind and the word materialize through the workings of the brain and nerves. In his epilogue to the text, Santner refers to Beckett's theatre as 'a unique kind of convergence of *language* and *physical comedy*' (2011: 251). In an echo of the sovereign transition

from the symbolic order to a bodily incarnation, he claims that
Beckett's characters and settings are strangely abstract and concrete.
In terms of the creature, this existence as both idea and thing
pertains to the creaturely junction between the human constructed
world, invested with conceptual content, and the animal open, with
its carnal, corporal form. As such, 'in Beckett's theatre, the time of
creaturely life invades the space of the play, *Trauerspiel* is not so
much elevated to the dignity of tragedy as it is lowered to the
comedy of an *Endspiel*, in which, in a rather new sense, flesh
becomes words and words take on the agitations of the flesh'
(Santner 2011: 251). The psychosomatic relationship that Santner
develops suggests that the contingency of creaturely life contributes
to the humorous physical dimension of Beckett's drama.

Santner asks whether Beckett's Hamm and Clov, amongst others,
are 'figures in and through which the verbal and physical twitches of
creaturely life [. . .] take centre stage?' (2011: 251). It was noted earlier
that, on a figurative level, Beckett's *Endgame* depicts a 'skullscape'
occupied by two components of a single identity and, on a literal level,
depicts two characters in a room. In this way, the physical situation
and the psychological monodrama are blurred as Beckett's play
conveys both private and public spheres. In Santner's suggestion, this
type of convergence of body and mind applies to the action and words
of Beckett's creatures, particularly how the tensions of the endgame
are perpetuated through language to realize the physical joke of their
entrapment. Beckett's protagonists in *Endgame* are enclosed in a
shelter, with each other for company and nothing but the grey remains
of a world outside. The possibility of a swift release is the prevailing
comic tension in the play, as Hamm points out in one of his few
laughs: 'I imagined already that I wasn't much longer for this world.
(*He laughs. Pause*)' (*E*, 33). Life is agonizingly prolonged and, as
Hamm and Clov encounter new avenues of discussion to stretch out
their denouement, the language works to reveal their physical
situation. The more inconsequential the dialogue becomes, the more
the creatures develop a vacuous but neurotic quality that emphasizes
their bodily stasis. These digressions play a fundamental part in the
mutual obligation the pair have to one another, which grounds them
in the room. In effect, the irresolution of their language games marks
the amusing physical element of the play.

However, the convergence of language and physical comedy in
Endgame is not an easily exemplified idea since every instance of

speech is implicated in Hamm and Clov's on-going plight. When language is employed to say nothing in particular, but to dwell on the fact that things are still being said, the focus turns from the value of words to the act of speech. As with the pure existence of enunciation, the semantic level collapses into the *action* of language. Consequently, the entire speaking relationship between the pair reveals their need to talk in order to carry on together. The physicality of language is therefore intimated as soon as Hamm wakes up at the beginning of the play. He says, 'Enough, it's time it ended, in the shelter, too. (*Pause.*) And yet I hesitate, I hesitate to . . . to end. Yes, there it is, it's time it ended and yet I hesitate to—(*He yawns.*)—to end' (*E*, 6). The hesitation here forms a stutter, which magnifies the twitching action of the body through the words. The repetition of 'hesitate' reveals Hamm's convulsive reaction to the tension between the desire to end and the reluctance to end. In an echo of Hamlet's famous question 'to be, or not to be', Hamm's uncertainty shows his pressing existential dilemma 'to end, or not to end', which materializes in the faltering verbal expression. The body is appropriately present within this briefly disruptive hesitation that sees him clutching onto his bodily existence. Hamm's stuttering language performance demonstrates the agitations of his physical predicament.

At the same time, Hamm's entrapment is very much dependent on the vital stimulation and objectification that language provides. The ability to respond to his own words, evident in the 'Yes, there it is' cited above, helps to sustain his physical existence by allowing him to perform his hesitation again, this time with another telling involuntary action, the yawn. Since the focus is on the act of speaking, Hamm effectively confirms that he is hesitating in order to speak again, but a sign of fatigue invades his sentence the second time around to remind him of his bodily presence also. As with the stutter of hesitation, the yawn arises through language, as though the body tenants and responds to the uttered words. Since it is vital for Hamm to talk in order to induce these bodily actions, it is no surprise that he later associates the end of his entrapment with the absence of language: 'It's finished, we're finished. Nearly finished. There'll be no more speech' (*E*, 31). The repetition of 'finished' and the modifier 'nearly' shows how language is liable to postpone his physical end. The restless pulse of energy in this recurring and variable combination of words maintains Hamm's animated presence.

Hamm equates speech with his existence as a physical entity, but more important are his conversations with Clov, such as the one that keeps Hamm from returning to bed in the first place: 'I can't be getting you up and putting you to bed every five minutes, I have things to do' (*E*, 7). Once Hamm is awake, however, it is the master who refuses to let the servant leave. The dramatic tension of *Endgame* begins with Clov's threats to leave, but as his threats are repeatedly shown to be empty or easily ignored, this non-departure becomes a running gag. The physical comedy of not leaving is also bound up with the continuation of the words, so that what Clov actually *does* is speak with Hamm. On nine separate occasions, Clov says 'I'll leave you' and each time Hamm manages to distract him, often with questions, such as 'So you remember when you came here?' (*E*, 24), 'Is my dog ready?' (*E*, 25) and 'Have you had your visions?' (*E*, 26). This deflective tactic is employed to keep Clov talking and consequently keep them both there. Yet these are questions that require minimal mental activity for Clov to answer. He exclaims, 'All life long the same questions, the same answers' (*E*, 7) and 'You've asked me these questions millions of times' (*E*, 25). Since Clov is often reduced to stock responses, he is called upon as an active speaker and not so much as a thinking presence. Hamm engages Clov as a co-speaker in a way that incites an emotional response and emphasizes the delivery of the words as opposed to their conceptual meaning.

Towards the end of the play, Hamm makes his dependence on speech and the dialogues with Clov more explicit:

Clov I'll leave you.

Hamm It's time for my story. Do you want to listen to my story? (*E*, 30).

Clov I'll leave you.

Hamm No!

Clov What is there to keep me here?

Hamm The dialogue (*E*, 36).

Clov I'll leave you. (*He goes towards door.*)

Hamm Before you go ... (**Clov** *halts near door.*) ... say something (*E*, 47).

If the act of speaking helps to incarnate Hamm's life conditions, it is a listener to his stories and an addressee in dialogue that objectifies him. The physical anchor of language is most evident in the second example, although this time the weight of the word also applies to Clov's existence. The dialogue 'keeps them here', but at this juncture in the play it is rather strained and desperate. Hence Hamm abandons the prompts of his distracting questions and simply exclaims 'No'. It is now that the agitations of their conversations really reflect the frustrations of being trapped in the room, tethered to each other. Beckett's stage directions suggest that Hamm and Clov's exchanges get 'anxious', irritable, 'very agitated', angry and 'violent'. While the jerks of inner hesitation intimate nervous energy, it is the inane dialogue between Hamm and Clov that exhibits how the slight mental stimulation of their words gives primacy to their bodily conditions. Although the words are all but empty, venting them remains necessary. As with relief laughter, then, the pair channel their excess nervous energy, but they do so through charged words rather than bursts of laughter. These exchanges are certainly amusing for the viewing audience, yet Hamm and Clov rarely bridge silence with laughter unless an obvious joke arises. Instead, they resort to saying things that implore or oblige the other to reply. The tension in the language between master and servant therefore coincides with the suspended physical conditions that mark the comedy of *Endgame*. The postponed departure is invested into the fraught language of the play.

Hamm's blindness also contributes to the necessary physicality of the words. Since Hamm experiences a sensory detachment from the physical world, he relies on Clov's descriptions to make it known. The blind master can only imagine his environment and situate himself in it through the commentary that his servant provides. Clov's words act as Hamm's eyes and this arrangement injects a tangible quality into the language as it renders the place that Hamm inhabits. At the same time, this relationship agitates both Hamm and Clov, and again their physical frustration is highly apparent in their dialogue. It is worth quoting a longer passage of conversation to illustrate this correlation between their verbal tensions and bodily transfixion:

Hamm   Open the window.

Clov   What for?

Hamm   I want to hear the sea.

Clov   You wouldn't hear it.

Hamm   Even if you opened the window?

Clov   No.

Hamm   Then it's not worth while opening it?

Clov   No.

Hamm   (*violently*) Then open it! (**Clov** *gets up on the ladder, opens the window. Pause.*) Have you opened it?

Clov   Yes.

(*Pause.*)

Hamm   You swear you've opened it?

Clov   Yes.

(*Pause.*)

Hamm   Well …! (*Pause.*) It must be very calm. (*Pause. Violently.*) I'm asking you is it very calm! (*E*, 39).

This kind of double act is funny in the way they quarrel over trivial details and the fact that Clov was correct to begin with. It is notable that even though there is no purposeful reason to do things, these futile actions are all they have. Through the pointless opening of the window, Hamm and Clov can continue to bloviate, which emphasizes the very breath in speaking over the content of what is said. The whole comic dynamic of them being there is therefore entangled in their conversations, as they act out the words that constitute their stationary lives. Beckett's play is not exactly a case of words and action coexisting in a dual or even complementary layering of meaning. Rather, the action in *Endgame* is so intimately bound with language as to showcase the creaturely combination of words and flesh. The words become the senseless action that occupies the creatures.

As language and physical comedy merge in the stimulations of *Endgame*, it is possible to see how creaturely contingency applies to Hamm and Clov. These figures are subject to the pressures of performance as they cultivate or revisit opportunities for speech in anticipation of the end. They are dependent on words, and therefore afflicted with a particularly human property, but it is this language, the realm of the signifier, that translates into Hamm and Clov's physical state of becoming, or realm of the signified, that will not finally let them be. For Santner, this kind of discomfort emerges at an interstitial point, namely the tension of an endgame between idea and thing, which questions the possibility of ever sitting comfortably in the 'office' of the human. It can be inferred that to be human is to be caught in a state of vicissitude between words and flesh that cannot be accepted as human. In other words, the human is subject to the duality of Man and man, representation and actuality, which denies him a singular position. Santner goes on to refer to Herman Melville's *Bartleby, the Scrivener* (1853) and the inhuman declaration 'I prefer not to' to describe how the only way to endure, and perhaps even enjoy, this tension is to 'experience its pressures – its twitching – as a Lachkrampf, a paroxysm of laughter that simply cannot – and ought not – be held down. Bartleby could thus be seen as the harbinger of a new sort of "divine comedy" of creaturely life, one created out of the troubles that plague the office of the human' (2011: 247). In reacting to the tension between ideas and things with a convulsive outburst, the laugh refuses to resolve the pressures and instead strikes against them. In *Endgame*, this comic tension is apparent through the sustained co-dependence of Hamm and Clov. Their twitching materializes through the leases of language that keep them physically restrained. It is this intimacy between words and flesh that produces the comic dynamic that Santner sees in the dual pressures applied to the human. Hence, Santner deems comedy the 'genre par excellence of a *troubled monism*' (italics in original) (2011: 109). It is the art form that reveals the combination of symbolic and physical strains on the subject. Laughter and the humour in the convergence of language and the body in *Endgame* are products of such a disturbance of unity.

Metanarrative tragicomedy

Failure and degradation are sources of comic energy in Beckett, and the phosphorescence of decay spares his work from uniform darkness, but he does not anaesthetize the tragic suffering of his creatures. In the physical humour of the agitations and frustrations between Hamm and Clov, there is an undeniable unhappiness. Though it constitutes the humour of the play, the fact that Clov and Hamm are incarcerated is a sad state of affairs. Moreover, Beckett embroils the audience in a joke that is at the same time a miserable truth. The 'leaving' that underpins *Endgame*, for instance, captures the predicament and anticipates the reaction of a stultified audience, especially since Hamm concedes that the dialogue is the sole point of interest. As such, Beckett's audience is not detached from the poignant tragedy of the creatures' plight and, while the characters' melancholic immersion clearly contradicts the catharsis of Greek tragedy that Aristotle outlines in *Poetics*, there is room still for emotion and empathy. This hypothesis on Beckett's humour conflicts with one of Bergson's three tenets of laughter: 'Indifference is its natural environment, for laughter has no greater foe than emotion' ([1911] 1999: 10). Beckett's work complicates Bergson's argument, if only because his characters are familiar subjects with hopes and dreams. As John Orr notes, Beckett's 'heroes are at times pathetic creatures, but through aspirations which will not die they still achieve a genuine pathos we cannot take away from them' (1991: 6). Beckett manages to uphold the tension between pity and passivity, solidarity and superiority, as the audience can relate to and recoil from Beckett's creatures. It can be contended that Beckett's humour gains its full impact from the way both the characters and audience members feel.

The subtitle to *Waiting for Godot* offers a clue to Beckett's balance of the laughing Democritean and weeping Heraclitean dispositions. The play is set up as a 'tragicomedy', with the serious and the humorous as co-dependent as the play's two protagonists. The collocation of the solemn and the trivial is entrenched in the play to the extent that the characters have formal full names, Vladimir and Estragon, as well as the clownish nicknames Didi and Gogo. The audience witness tramp-like figures wearing ill-fitting shoes and hats but, like the clown, they are not altogether derelict. Beyond the façade of their comic interplay lies the vague suggestion of upstanding, intelligent men with past lives and relations. Vladimir says, 'You should have been a poet' to which Estragon replies, 'I was. (*Gesture towards his rags.*) Isn't that obvious' (*WFG*, 4). Although the reference to this particular vocation offers a metatheatrical joke that serves to withhold the idea of a real back story, it also comes after Estragon's recollection of the maps of the Holy Land and his plans for a honeymoon by the Dead Sea, which increases the possibility of him having a past. Admittedly, there is not a great deal of this kind of background in Beckett's play, and the repetition of events and the characters' defective memories nullify lineal temporality somewhat. The word 'again' appears four times on the very first page, but the past is hardly distinguishable from the present and the power of memory is not strong enough to recall details that would clearly differentiate then from now. Nevertheless, Beckett's woebegone creatures and their vaudeville routines are tinged with loss, and in their few references to the Eiffel Tower, to days when they were 'presentable' (*WFG*, 2), to the Macon country and River Rhône (*WFG*, 53, 47), there is a 'dead and buried' other world (*WFG*, 47), a sadness at having been dislodged from time and the hope that eventually there will be a release.

It is Pozzo, the privileged aristocratic figure of the play, who spells out the tragicomic balance: 'The tears of the world are a constant quantity. For each one who begins to weep, somewhere else another stops. The same is true of the laugh. (*He laughs*.)' (*WFG*, 26). When Pozzo laughs, Vladimir, Estragon and Lucky do not join him. All the others are members of the non-laughing population, which is necessary for Pozzo's own burst of joy. Beckett's play shows that the two genres, comedy and tragedy, do not simply meet and cohabit, but rather rely on one another to produce a new tonality, as Verna Foster recognizes: 'A tragicomedy is a play in which the tragic and the comic both exist but are formally and emotionally dependent on one another, each modifying and determining the nature of the other so as to pronounce a mixed, tragicomic response in the audience' (Foster 2004: 11). When the audience finds comic value in Beckett's play it is accompanied by the tragic, and vice versa. For example, when Pozzo says 'Can't you see he wants to rest? Basket!' (*WFG*, 19), what at first appears to be a defence of Lucky rouses empathy. Pozzo initially performs an uncharacteristic act of sensitivity that the audience can agree with. Yet the barked order 'Basket!' is the punch line that restores Pozzo's true colours and underscores Lucky's poor treatment. This glimpse of tenderness serves to confirm the persistent hardship Lucky suffers, but still the audience can laugh despite the pathos. In effect, Beckett orchestrates a divided reaction that exploits the ambiguity of tragicomedy. He encourages a chuckle at the irony and a shake of the head at Pozzo's hypocrisy.

As a result, Beckett is often described in mixed terms, as 'an alarming comedian' with a 'gloomy, humorous view' (Gurewitch 1982: 9). Essentially, the bisected mask of Thalia and Melpomene that depicts drama is shown to be part of the same countenance in Beckett.

The tragic undercurrent of the situation in Beckett's plays, as well as the pitiful and pathetic figures that populate them, cause a tragic aspect to occur within the laugh. The German reception theorist Wolfgang Iser builds upon this mixed reaction in his notion of the stifled laugh (2000: 201). In Iser's experience, Beckett's audience members are unsure when to laugh, laugh at different things and suppress their laughs depending on the collective response. Most audience members only acknowledge the tragedy after self-consciously reflecting on their initial outburst of laughter. As an inappropriate but entirely organic occurrence, the stifled laugh confronts natural reaction with social awareness. Iser clearly takes his impetus from the characters' situation:

> **Vladimir** *breaks into a hearty laugh which he immediately stifles, his hand pressed to his pubis, his face contorted.*
>
> **Vladimir** One daren't even laugh any more.
>
> **Estragon** Dreadful privation.
>
> **Vladimir** Merely smile (*WFG*, 3).

Vladimir curtails his laughter again moments later:

> *Laugh of* **Vladimir,** *stifled as before, less the smile.*
>
> **Vladimir** You'd make me laugh if it wasn't prohibited.
>
> **Estragon** We've lost our rights?
>
> **Vladimir** (*distinctly*) We got rid of them (*WFG*, 11).

The audience-response and communal aspects of Iser's reading are present within these two examples. Each instance implies that laughter is consciously restrained, not naturally absent. Terms such as 'privation', 'daren't', 'prohibited' and 'rights' all suggest obligations beyond that of the individual. These two exchanges between Vladimir and Estragon reveal the characters' awareness of social propriety and ethical codes, and nod to the incongruity of laughter in times of catastrophe, which waits in the wings in *Waiting for Godot*. In this way, Beckett evokes the totalitarian censure against the subversive power of laughter, such as the 1942 Nazi Germany propaganda posters directed at Roosevelt's administration and German Jews, which exclaim 'They Will Stop Laughing!!!' (*Das Lachen wird ihnen vergehen*) (Herf 2008). Beckett makes the audience laugh in tragic contexts where the very freedom of laughter is at stake.

For Foster, it is through tragicomedy that the tragic mode found an appropriate form of expression in post-war literature. As she points out, 'tragedy presupposes form and our world has none; tragedy presupposes individual guilt and responsibility, but these qualities have eroded; tragedy, finally is predicated on an audience that is already a community, and this, too, no longer exists' (Foster 2004: 31). The tragicomic mode, however, reinstates some of the qualities that the serious voice has lost. If the connection to community has been severed in the serious mode, the trivial still unites people, albeit negatively, and with recourse to Iser's observation, it is possible to see how the stifled laugh introduces a community of individuals. Normally, the audience might join in with laughter, as Robert Provine asserts in his study on the behaviour of laughter: 'When we hear laughter, we become beasts of the herd, mindlessly laughing in turn, producing a behavioural chain reaction that sweeps through our group, creating a crescendo of jocularity or ridicule' (2012: 40–1). In the spontaneous impulse to laugh at Beckett's work, however, the laughing spectator can be isolated and in order to return to the community the laugh must be suppressed, 'cut-off, so to speak in mid-guffaw' (Iser 2000: 203). In this moment, the guilt of laughing without the synchronicity of the audience leads to a tragic element. From the individual laugher's perspective, the other audience members are not only a non-laughing community, they are an anti-laughing community, condemning humour and bespeaking the tragedy within the laugh. The spectators are aware of the tragedy through the laugh, as Iser's reading implies, but they are also contributing to the tragedy by laughing.

Beckett achieves tragic undertones in his comedy, and yet he is also acutely aware of the comic potential of tragedy. If the purity of the comedy has been compromised, so too has the tragedy as it reveals its own brand of laughter. As Nell phrases it in *Endgame*: 'Nothing is funnier than unhappiness' (*E*, 14). It seems that misery propagates humour for Beckett. His comment on *Waiting for Godot* in a letter to Roger Blin offers a better insight into this dynamic than Nell. Beckett insists that in the scene where Estragon's trousers fall down, they must drop to his ankles. He explains: 'The spirit of the play, to the extent to which it has one, is that nothing is more grotesque than the tragic' (quoted in Bair 1990: 200). 'Grotesque' is not typically interchangeable with 'funny' despite the comic elements to its meaning, but the term does encapsulate the divided quality of Beckett's humour. In Bakhtin's work on the grotesque, he asserts that 'exaggeration, hyperbolism, excessiveness are generally considered fundamental attributes of the grotesque style' ([1965] 1984: 303). It is this sense of the familiar but alien in the grotesque that produces the simultaneous condition of relation and revulsion in humour. In the grotesqueness of tragedy, then, Beckett points out the relief experienced at the expense of others' misery, which recognizes tragedy as a human predicament but also detaches from and laughs at the particular situation. This type of humour brings together feelings of relief and unease, or as Vladimir puts it, 'Relieved and at the same time . . . appalled' (*WFG*, 3), before he utters the word 'funny' shortly thereafter. It engenders a state of compassion and self-centredness that recognizes tragedy as a general possibility and yet deflects its specificity. Therefore, Beckett's vision of the grotesque in tragedy realizes both the tragedy and the comedy; each aspect is found in the other to create the tragicomic tone that binds together conflicting feelings.

The laugh that unhappiness stimulates is the third type of laughter Beckett mentions in *Watt*:

> The bitter, the hollow and – Haw! Haw! – the mirthless. The bitter laugh laughs at that which is not good, it is the ethical laugh. The hollow laugh laughs at that which is not true, it is the intellectual laugh. Not good! Not true! Well well. But the mirthless laugh is the dianoetic laugh, down the snout – Haw! – so. It is the laugh of laughs, the *risus purus*, the laugh laughing at the laugh, the beholding, the saluting of the highest joke, in a word the laugh that laughs – silence please – at that which is unhappy (*W*, 40).

The mirthless type is a remote laugh that undermines and satirizes the action of laughing. Rather than counter sadness or tragedy, it finds fault in laughter's composition and alters the tenor. In one sense, this laughter devoid of cheer is akin to the howls and wails, or 'modes of ululation' (W, 39), that suggest a release of emotion or tension. Yet the dianoetic snort 'down the snout' is not intuitive, and this indicates a more deliberate and deliberated personal affair. In relation to Beckett's audience, the mirthless laugh favours the textual form, as the experience of humour in Beckett's novels and drama on the page is different from that on stage. Beckett's texts elicit the mirthless laugh more readily because they privatize the jokes, thus allowing the deriding smile to go unnoticed and the dianoetic laugh to resonate without fear of condemnation from the theatre audience. In other words, the reader can focus on the laugh at unhappiness as opposed to fellow spectators.

If, as Bergson notes, 'laughter is always the laughter of a group' ([1911] 1999: 11), it follows that the mirthless laugh deviates from conventional laughter in that it does not feed off the present community. Its pessimism is not contagious like a funny sight, sound or implanted thought. The laugh at the laugh prevails over and silences the Bergsonian communal type of humour, as the 'silence please' in Watt indicates, and works to reveal another side of laughter. To return to Nell's 'nothing is funnier than unhappiness' in Endgame, the less-quoted second part of her speech alludes to the silence in which mirthless laughter can also emerge: 'we laugh, with a will, in the beginning. But it's always the same thing. Yes, it's like the funny story we have heard too often, we still find it funny, but we don't laugh any more' (E, 14). When the unadulterated, hearty guffaw is no longer operative or appropriate, the mirthless laugh can replace it. In this respect, the mirthless laugh can reside in the aftermath of the stifled laugh; it still exists in the absence of the reflex laugh.

Beckett's humour probes the substance of laughter as it shifts instantaneously in tone. In one of Beckett's standout incongruity jokes, Clov looks in the trashcan at Nagg and announces 'He's crying' before Hamm replies 'Then he's living' (E, 38). The impulse is to laugh at the character in a detached way, and this initial phase contributes to the existential tragedy of Sisyphean 'hellish hope' (T, 133), or the 'joke of being' as Beckett describes it (quoted in Feldman 2006: 61). As the laugh matures or fades, it develops into a mirthless laugh as the spectator apprehends the shared nature of the characters' dilemma. Although this example might not provoke a laugh from the entire audience, those that do laugh respond to a personal realization of the parity between themselves and the character. Since each laugher does this, it can be described as a common laugh directed at individualization, which conveys a mutual understanding of conditions that are universal and at the same time must be felt as particular. To underline this complicity, Beckett has his characters poke fun at the reading and viewing audience's own dire situation. He does this through the waiting, repetition, endurance and boredom on page and stage that is the shared human condition. He also resorts to metatheatrical pointers, which embroil the audience in a joke that recognizes the style and duration of the prose and drama as a demonstration of the human condition. Consequently, Beckett's humour moves from the fictional level that laughs at the other, to that which is felt *in esse* and laughs as an other at the self.

Beckett's post-war prose displays his second phase of humour, according to Carla Locatelli, which she labels 'metanarrative'. In this period, Beckett creates 'an art whose shortcomings are amusing, enjoyable even if they are ridiculed' (Locatelli 2000: 239). Jonathan Greenberg goes a step further to argue that 'laughter is something the reader can cling to in the oceans of possibilities in which Beckett's prose immerses her' (2011: 180). As with Beckett's use of puns, the reader can identify instances of communicative incapacity and be entertained by the misuse and abuse of convention. Laughter is a welcome retreat from the overwhelming indecision of Beckett's narrators and the tedium of their narrative tasks. However, laughter also tricks the reader into drawing out the perpetuity, or humouring the narrator's weakness. The reader's privileged position of knowledge outside of the text could be enjoyed if the story progressed regularly and the momentum stalled only intermittently but, on the contrary, Beckett's humour derives chiefly from a realization of the irony that 'literary production grows on the shortfalls of literary self-reflection' (Locatelli 2000: 239). The humour of narrative failure is effectively locked into the monotony of its own downfall. Since the narrators identify narrative and expressive weaknesses, seen clearly in Malone's ironically repetitive 'What tedium' (*T*, 187, 189, 216, 219, 254) as well as 'Mortal tedium' (*T*, 218) and 'This is awful' (*T*, 191), the awareness of a fumbling artistry, or mastery of failure, means the reader is no longer distanced from the joke but ensnared by it. The metanarrative joke of Beckett's post-war prose is that the reader is cast as an object of humour.

Sianne Ngai proposes that such an incessant torrent of inanity in literature produces a shocking or boring effect, or both, that amounts to a stupor. In *Ugly Feelings* (2005), Ngai coins the portmanteau 'stuplimity' to capture the essence of this awesome tedium, or the 'simultaneously astonishing and deliberately fatiguing' that Beckett demonstrates (2005: 260). The double bind of Ngai's 'stuplimity' grasps the wider joke in Beckett, in which the overwhelming commitment to failure is woven into the textual fabric of the work and, as such, is without a punch line. Beckett's readers are made to endure the stupidity and stupor that do not frequently offer the impact of a revelation. Hence, the aesthetic accentuates the mutual struggle to progress – in the mould of Beckett's own experience of reading Franz Kafka's *The Castle*, 'I must say it was difficult to get to the end' (quoted in Adelman 2004: 147) – although it is a struggle fragmented by intermission for the reader who can choose if and when to consume the text and for how long.

The real-time of theatre, on the other hand, exacerbates Beckett's drawn-out humour and his metatheatrical techniques actualize an experiential joke, as opposed to the illusion of synchronicity between character and reader in the textual equivalent. The auditorium doubles as a cage as Beckett forces the observer to undergo inaction and participate in boredom. In a staging of *Waiting for Godot* at the Criterion Theatre in London, an audience member responded to the line 'What shall we do now, now that we are happy?' (*WFG*, 51) with 'I'm not happy, I've never been so bored in my life.' The actor Hugh Burden, playing Vladimir, released the tension of this heckle, which is itself a common feature of stand-up comedy, with 'I think that was Godot' (Bradby 2001: 78). Inadvertently, the actor replicates a technique that Beckett himself employs to subtly pierce the barrier of performance between stage and audience. Beckett has his characters seemingly reflect on the situation and allude to the audience to relieve the bind of 'stuplimity' on several occasions in *Waiting for Godot*. Vladimir's assessment 'This is becoming really insignificant' (*WFG*, 60) and the refrain 'We're waiting for Godot' show an awareness of the situation for character and audience alike. Similarly, the audience is invoked when Estragon faces the auditorium and surmises 'Inspiring prospects' (*WFG*, 6), and later as Vladimir gestures to the front announcing 'There! Not a soul in sight' (*WFG*, 66). The moments when Beckett's figures threaten to break out of the façade of performance combine to remind the audience they are implicitly connected to the characters and cast as extras, subject to the protagonists' plight. Yet the recognition of this kinship lightens the tedium momentarily, shifting the emphasis towards a cognizant and playful tone, tantamount to an authorial wink, rather than an outright bore owing to artistic incompetence. The audience can appreciate Beckett's hand in constructing a play that captures the audience but purposely does not engross. Although there is no punch line, then, there is comic relief that punctuates the extended joke of failure.

The tedium that Beckett's aesthetic inflicts moves his work into creaturely territory. As Santner understands the concept, by way of Agamben, boredom paves the way to the realm of the creaturely as it recognizes humanity's proximity with animal captivity in 'the open' (2006: 10–12). For Agamben in particular, human existence constitutes a paradoxical state of enlightened consciousness that delivers humanity from, and realigns it with, an animalistic being: '*Dasein* is simply an animal that has learned to become bored: it has awakened *from* its own captivation *to* its own captivation' (2003: 70). The cleft that boredom precipitates between the human and animal conjures the creaturely for Santner, as the boundaries of classification are destabilized and inclined to overlap. Beckett's characters, readers and viewing audience are subject to a similar profound boredom that is made noticeable by humour's ability to throw one out of a stupor, to shock one into consciousness. Yet the initially amusing and ultimately paralysing aesthetic of Beckett's work underpins these humorous jolts, offering only a short relief from the context of enduring failure. As incessant failures and humorous interjections numb and enliven the reading and viewing audience, the effect is to draw the audience into the characters' creaturely suspension. Faced with the degraded cerebral sphere and the grotesque investment in language and reason, Beckett's audiences are encouraged to reflect on the fabrication of art through humorous metanarrative techniques. The creaturely shift from dull captivation to conscious captivation replicates the reading and viewing audience's participation in and distance from the narrative goings-on, whereby the audience is in and out of proceedings, facilitating the old joke of being and alienated by the artistic recognition of artifice. Beckett's humour captures the audience in the physical joke of entrapment and then intermittently pierces this incarceration with humorous metanarrative asides that reveal the tragicomic creaturely captivation.

'Turd waiting for the flush':
Gallows humour

The foregrounding of failure and degradation in Beckett takes the unpleasant or unwelcome negatives in life and turns them into an absurd joke. This experience of living through the joke and at the same time being aware of the joke forms another bifurcated tension indicative of the 'sovereign as creature', or (in)sovereign, dimension. In the same way that Beckett's creatures reconstitute testimony by articulating the inability to speak and are co-dependent in their master–servant relationships, humour fashions a convergence of potency and impotence as the subject recognizes a hopeless situation but attempts to reign over it through an ironic assessment. Steve Lipman describes how laughter 'kept countless persons from taking their own lives or slipping into the zombie-like state of the "Muselmanner"' (1991: 12). Those that could reflect on their dire situation and laugh had the capacity to endure it better. In extreme cases of destitution the Holocaust victims used humour as a tool to persevere but, in the aftermath, when the human has revealed its capacity for such devaluation and the sanctity of human life is in pieces, humour appears to act as a measure to survive in a vacuum of meaning. A sense of humour is a vital resource for deflecting incomprehensible and destabilizing events. Last-ditch bouts of laughter attest to the affront to reason that such an event produced and respond to the threat facing the idea of the human. In this way, humour and laughter can appear as ways of moving on, of negotiating the fragments of meaning and ruins of culture left in the wake. Indeed, Des Pres proposes that certain works on the Holocaust that include humour might break out of the impasse facing attempts to find meaning from the catastrophe. In such texts, 'what survives is the integrity of an imagined world that is similar to, but deliberately different from, the actual world of the Holocaust. Our knowledge of history is not denied but displaced, and we discover the capacity to go forward with, so to speak, a foot in both worlds' (Des Pres 1988: 220–1). However, humour is not a lasting solution to the human predicament, but rather a complicit fixture in the enduring struggle with the hardships of life. Suzanne Dow asserts that 'Beckettian comedy does not allow us to laugh off the negativity of senescence, decrepitude, death, finitude, nothingness etc. that intrudes or impinges upon life; it invites us to laugh at this egregious excess, this *in*finitude, that sallies forth or seeps, and which refuses to be shaken off or staunched' (2011: 133). To take this persuasive argument a step further, it is possible to assert that Beckett's humour is a necessary component in the perpetuation of negativity as it contributes to the cycle of release and restoration that sustains failure and degradation.

For Sigmund Freud, the different levels of the psyche allow consciousness to protect itself from the full weight of the stark realities it must confront. In his essay 'Humour' ([1927] 2001), Freud finds a particularly impressive example of this defence mechanism in the levity of gallows humour, a type of humour that posits self as both subject and object in the joke, thus taking ownership of a situation but diminishing its severity. 'The grandeur in it', Freud writes,

> clearly lies in the triumph of narcissism, the victorious assertion of the ego's invulnerability. The ego refuses to be distressed by the provocations of reality, to let itself be compelled to suffer. It insists that it cannot be affected by the traumas of the external world; it shows, in fact, that such traumas are no more than occasions for it to gain pleasure ([1927] 2001: 162).

In this instance, the pleasure in gallows humour derives from an apprehension of one's reality admixed with a detached perspective on that reality. Unusually, this humour on the edge of annihilation renders its subject both victim and victor, since it comes from and is directed towards a single party. Gallows humour revels in the self-centredness of narcissism, at once cognizant and dismissive of reality, responding with the authority of wit to one's grave situation. The example to which Freud refers reads: 'a criminal who was being led out to the gallows on a Monday remarked: "Well, the week's beginning nicely"' ([1927] 2001: 161). This gallows humour is ironic and can only feign its distance from reality, as the joke relies on the context and betrays its position of knowledge. Indeed, '[t]hese jokes may be a form of bravado, a kind of necessary defence mechanism, designed to articulate genuine fears and at the same time partly allay terror through humor' (Dundes and Hauschild 1983: 249). This bravado is a projection of superiority and an outward performance of immunity. In its self-possession, gallows humour anaesthetizes the reflex action and rationalizes an alternative perspective.

However, the original self-awareness at the centre of gallows humour is not completely detached from the situational context since the triumph of narcissism stems from seeing oneself in the world. In its incongruity, gallows humour is clearly a manifestation of the fear and anxiety that befits imminent death. As such, the liberation that gallows humour offers is questionable. Paul Lewis observes that the subject 'experiences a moment of detachment from his fear or anxiety, but as Freud notes, since this humor works by denying or evading reality, by definition the joke can do nothing to change the reality it evades' (1993: 49). In fact, the escape from reality helps to deliver the victim to the fate of reality. The tragicomic element of Freudian gallows humour, then, is that it is packaged as a rebellion but displays docile acceptance. This is evident in self-abasing Jewish humour, such as the compliant Jew before the firing squad who says to his fellow detainee, 'Take a blindfold. Don't make trouble' (Lewis 1993: 47). This coping mechanism replaces the furniture of distress with that of pleasure, but it is a counterfeit pleasure, since humour's 'release' is into inevitability. It steps obediently into physical captivity under the pretence of psychological ascendency.

It is clear that humour in Beckett's prose and drama does not strictly adhere to the gallows variety. Within the texts, his characters do not make light of imminent death and their circumstances are not as pressing or clear-cut as the gallows. However, in Antonin Obrdlik's study of Nazi oppression and the resultant humour in Czechoslovakia, he uses the term gallows 'in a more general sense as referring to humor which arises in connection with a precarious or dangerous situation' (1942: 709). Beckett's work is more consistent with this view as his characters endure bodily afflictions and mental duress. Many are in purgatorial states, subject to goading lives that dangle death over them. Gurewitch suggests that gallows humour, as 'the kind of humor that transforms into joke material both the fact of catastrophe and the threat of death – resonates in the repeated self-derogations of Beckett's disaster-ridden voyagers and immobilized inmates of calamity' (1982: 95). The difference is that life is the source of suffering and misery in Beckett; life is a slow demise on death row. The result of this is that Beckett's creatures have incongruous views and inverted valuations of life and death that are bountiful sources of black humour.

Like the descending incongruity of the relief laugh, black humour distorts the typical view of things. Andre Breton describes this dark sense of humour in his 1938 *Anthology of Black Humour*, drawing on a fellow soldier named Jacques Vache, who was active in the First World War: 'In Vache's person, in utmost secrecy, a principle of total insubordination was undermining the world, reducing everything that then seemed all-important to a petty scale, desecrating everything in its path' (1997: vii). Beckett's pessimism is also humorous in its sheer devaluation of life. Molloy's take on life as 'air in a water-pipe' (*T*, 53) and especially Moran's aphorism on existence as 'that of the turd waiting for the flush' (*T*, 163) are comic in the way they relegate human being and conflict with the common inclination to appreciate life. Beckett treats death with the same inverted principle for comic effect and, as opposed to ignoring impending death as gallows humour does, Beckett's characters embrace it as a merciful release. In *Malone Dies*, for example, Malone says, 'The end of a life is always vivifying' (*T*, 212) and, in a more graphic image, 'The feet are clear, already, of the great cunt of existence. Favourable representation I trust' (*T*, 285). The reflection at the end of this second example recognizes the misogyny of this representation, but it also relates to the transposed values of life and death. Beckett's aberrant and vulgar depiction of death introduces a note of levity on profound issues and this kind of surprising oxymoronic approach is ludicrously humorous.

Nevertheless, Beckett's black humour in the disdain for life and morbid fixation on death is also saddening in that it reinforces his creatures' incarceration. In terms of gallows humour's enlightened superiority over grave situations, Beckett's characters are mindful of their destitute conditions and helpless to actually alter them, but they are also unable to mitigate them through witty humour, and are therefore not typical gallows victims. Although they understand life as a grave situation, that apprehension does not allow them to alleviate it. Beckett's dark humour is rooted in their risible existence, the fact that they are still trapped in moribund lives with the hope against hope and cannot manage a perceptive, wry twist on serious circumstances in the way that the gallows victim can liberatingly ignore foreknowledge. Martin Esslin makes the point that '[t]he *dianoia*, the insight of the classical tragic hero, is denied to these paradigmatic figures who clearly stand as metaphors for humanity itself, enmeshed, as we all are, in a web of self-deception, illusion, and deliberate repression from our consciousness, of the harsh realities of the human predicament' (1986: 18). Esslin alludes to the melancholy immersion that fixates on a preferable state in order to distract from the bitter existential truth, as seen in Vladimir's melancholic subscription to Godot. It is true that Beckett's creatures are not released from their plights through tragic realization, but it is not simply the case that Beckett's creatures allay their suffering through self-deception. They certainly do not combat misery with the protective irony associated with conventional gallows humour. In fact, their dire predicaments are often rooted in their commitment to quests bound to failure, in which they realize the futility but must carry on regardless. Beckett's creatures simultaneously acknowledge their failures and continue to submit to their imperatives, which might be construed as self-deception, but actually reveals that they perceive no other choice. This mixture of awareness and necessity leads Beckett's creatures to articulate miserably distorted perspectives on life that are humorous, albeit inadvertently, and at the same time carry out the physical tragicomedy of their incarceration.

Beckett's characters are amusingly pessimistic not simply because they mock states of being and finitude, but because they are clearly suspended in the conditions of life, experiencing the hardships of mortal existence as subjects in the lifelong gallows. In *Waiting for Godot*, Estragon and Vladimir consider hanging themselves to end it all, yet even this morbid exchange is wrapped up in practical considerations that trivialize the scene. Estragon explains the problem: 'Gogo light – bough not break – Gogo dead. Didi heavy – bough break – Didi alone' (*WFG*, 10). Vladimir soon asks, 'Well? What do we do?' and Estragon replies, 'Don't let's do anything. It's safer' (*WFG*, 10). As with the well-known gallows joke in which an inmate steps up to the electric chair and asks his executioner 'Are you sure this is safe?', Beckett plays on the word 'safe', not to joke about the risk of death but the risk of loneliness. Similarly, as Estragon wonders if they should 'strike before the iron freezes' (*WFG*, 10), his negative philosophy towards life is a mirror image of the quasi-positivity in gallows humour prior to death. Death is a possibility before it ceases in Estragon's case, as opposed to an opportune moment to seize. This configuration of the aspirational idiom is so pessimistic as to inspire laughter while at the same time retaining the sad remnants of the original rallying cry. Beckett's characters do not use humour that discerns or escapes from reality, then, because every funny moment is bound up with their adversity. They demonstrate a kind of gallows humour that comes not in spite of life or in flight from life, but in the grim conditions of living. That is, humour is contained in the horror; it is not seen from afar, but always an integral part of the tragic experience.

However, the audience does benefit in part from a kind of universal gallows humour as it is played out and endured before them, with Beckett repeatedly embroiling and releasing the audience from the existential joke through bouts of tedium and humour. His characters do not knowingly compose gallows jokes, and are therefore riveted to their predicament. Nevertheless, they are naively humorous and convey humour in a way that their lives actually condition, that ridicules and is ridiculous in the sustained experience of suffering. Towards the end of *Molloy*, in the final scene before Moran makes his way back home, Gaber relays Youdi's words 'life is a thing of beauty, Gaber, and a joy forever'. Moran is sceptical and asks, 'Do you think he meant human life?' (*T*, 165). Moran clearly fails to equate human life with beauty and joy. This is not apparently meant as a joke since there is no laughter from either character. Despite this, the reading audience can at least appreciate the insinuation that the human lives they lead are miserable, thereby transforming it into a source of pleasure. When Beckett jokes about human life, then, it allows the reader to either enjoy the surprisingly sacrilegious devaluation or simply laugh in agreement with the truth of his assessment.

In his essay on Beckett's stifled laugh, Wolfgang Iser recognizes that humour can help to distance anguish as the laugh confronts pain. Iser initially suggests that humour can 'face up to unhappiness, which in being faced is no longer exclusively itself but appears in the perspective of its being perceived' (2000: 222). The laugh gives the impression of observing unhappiness rather than feeling it. However, he questions the longevity of this once-removed position, asking 'are we really able to free ourselves from unhappiness by facing up to it?' (2000: 225). It is doubtful for Iser, as he suggests that the subject has an urge to cultivate or revert to states of captivation in order to continue the possibility of liberation, without entering into the actual bewildering state of freedom. It is the tension between the alleviating effect of laughter and the resumption of unhappiness that comes closest to describing the joke of entrapment in Beckett's work. Beckett's humour feeds on negativity and this ensures that his work does not perish in the depths of arrant despair. Yet it is clear that humour does not convert or remedy suffering, but rather sustains suffering as the source of its own existence. Humour and suffering are therefore self-perpetuating; the laugh is the sadistic knot of perseverance that forms a loop of pain.

The laugh at gallows humour is never simply defensive, particularly when it pokes fun at the life one must endure and not the oblivion one must ignore. As noted above in the discussion of Freud, gallows humour is also damning in its concession to the horror of reality. Lisa Colletta touches on this fact in her reassessment of humour in modernism. She writes: 'In dark comedy, rooted as it is in gallows humor, change – even survival – is beside the point. The point is to wrest from pain a momentary victory in laughter; it makes no other claims' (Colletta 2003: 11). Similarly, in Beckett, the bitter truth contaminates the fantasy and evasion of gallows humour. Laughter is less about protecting the self and escaping reality, and more to do with the diminishing space of untruth to hide in. Therefore, it is no surprise that Beckett's characters rarely laugh in a purely joyous spirit and that laughter is increasingly curtailed, ambivalent and silent. In a more obvious example of gallows humour, Moran contemplates his failure to find Molloy and comments that 'at the thought of the punishments Youdi might inflict upon me I was seized by such a mighty fit of laughter that I shook, with mighty silent laughter and my features composed in their wonted sadness and calm' (T, 163). Moran experiences the convulsive nature of laughter as it silently dominates his body and leaves a pensive countenance. Humour is still present, but the laughter is contradictory, at once hysterical and reposed, dramatic and muted. This is a composite outburst that reveals its miserable origins and coping strategy in equal measures.

If conventional gallows humour releases the subject, with the ego under the protection of the superego, Beckett's gallows humour focuses on the actual possibility of deriving humour from the worst, not in conciliatory or tendentious tones, but as part of the engagement with and experience of struggle. Freud works to separate the psychological levels of gallows humour and trace their interaction, whereas Beckett takes up the idea of division that Freudian psychoanalysis advances but channels out the mental sense of liberation. Beckett brings the poles of joy and sorrow into contact, whereby relief from pain betrays further pain, every interlude to suffering renews suffering and each end marks a point of survival. These repeated imperious gestures of victory, the next last laugh, give way to the persistent toil of reality, which actually refreshes unhappiness, dressing wounds only to open them again. Beckett dissociates humour from superiority, and instead utilizes it as part of an amusing and depressing phenomenon that effects a convergence of mind and body, Man and man, comedy and tragedy, potency and impotence, to offer different levels of light and shade to the general gloom.

4

Survival:

Incompleteness and continuation

The animation of contingent creatures, subject to the immediacy of creation and the vulnerability of meaning and matter, occurs through the obligation to testify, the insoluble tensions between co-dependent masters and servants, and the awakening to captivation through humour. The shared characteristic of these creaturely elements is survival, which Beckett inscribes in his work through a sense of continuity in deadlock, as the creatures appear to be encumbered and yet manage to live on. Gary Adelman argues that the spirit of survival marks a watershed in Beckett's literary development. In *Naming Beckett's Unnamable* (2004) Adelman avers that 'Beckett's Unnamable narrator merged in his mind with the idea of the Jew survivor of the Holocaust, giving him a powerful analogy for exploring the plight of the artist' (2004: 79). Beckett's artistic approach, according to Adelman, is itself evidence of an engagement with the extreme figures of survival who endured the horrors of the camps. Beckett produces an aesthetic of survival whereby his creatures manage to keep speaking through figments, attachments to real and projected others, and the supplement of humour, despite their narrative failures and identities in ruins, which not only parallels the real survival of the context but also appears to recognize the status of art after Auschwitz. The obligation to speak despite the inability to speak in Beckett is the artistic predicament after, and artistic equivalent to, the historical climate of survival.

Adelman continues to assert that the voice in the final text of the trilogy 'is the interior life of the *Muselmann*, who is neither living nor dead, refusing, resisting both life and death' (2004: 81). It is in the context of this suspension between life and death, and knowledge of the possibility of such a survival, that Beckett addresses the extent to which survival is burdensome. The fact of the matter is that Beckett's creatures are 'festooned with lifebelts, praying for rack and ruin' (*T*, 342). They are possessed of an existence of sorts, as though an authority, creative or otherwise, has issued survival. This vision of the Beckettian creature sees it going on and not going on, *doing* nothing when there is nothing to be done. The theme of survival in Beckett, then, conveys a dimension of being that evokes the suspended existence of the *Muselmann* and yet also appears to bespeak humanity's endurance during a period of great destabilization after the Holocaust.

This chapter traces how Beckett's post-war texts bear out a kind of straightened artistic vitality, which, I argue, evokes the idea of survival as an affliction experienced by beings whose meaningful lives have evaporated. In particular, the perseverance at the point of impasse, or 'stirrings still' as Beckett expressed it late in his life, relates to Eric Santner's notion of 'undeadness', a term that plays an integral part in Santner's theorization of creaturely life. Whether survival is desired or not, the creature is consigned to a performative being that conveys the inhuman potential to experience a symbolic death in the absence of recognized value and subsist as raw matter beyond meaningful life. The chapter culminates in an extended reading of *Molloy*, Beckett's most substantial output from his turn to an art of failure during his intensely productive post-war period. After elucidating the incomplete narrative structures and aesthetics of continuation in Beckett's novel, I examine how the creaturely author-narrators in this text reveal the excess spirit of the human, whereby religious, political and social systems are remote, and yet the creature remains subject to the power of their absence. This exclusionary dynamic governs Beckett's abandoned creatures as they repeatedly attempt to adhere to networks of meaning that fail to acknowledge them as ideologically valuable or redeemable. Beckett's creatures are not exactly dissidents, then, but rather inadvertent eccentrics owing to their ignorance of the governing system's essence. They are unconventional by nature of their exclusion from the logic behind these conventions, as opposed to being purposely aberrant. Thus, Beckett's creatures exist in an endless spiral of nonfulfilment in their actual detachment from and psychological reprisal of the idea of sovereign order.

'Oh all to end': Beckettian stirrings still

Survival means that life goes on, that finality has not arrived, but it does not obviate the possibility of experiencing a type of death. Jean-François Lyotard contends that 'the word "survivor" implies that a being who is dead or should have died is still living' (1993: 144). This survival after death, or cheating death having accepted it, illustrates how survival transgresses the divide between life and death. Similarly, in Beckett's work, his creatures subsist despite their profound inertia; they continue in deadlock, living out peri-mortem lives. The end, whether silence or death, is not something that finally occurs in Beckett but is rather endured.

Throughout his career, Beckett repeatedly expresses the ideas of incompleteness and continuity that constitute the spirit of survival in his writing. His work after 1945 up until his last texts in 1989 finds various ways of refiguring aporia to extend the exploration of stasis and evoke the capacity to persist. In his dialogues with Georges Duthuit in the late 1940s, Beckett offers a prescient point: 'There are many ways in which the thing I am trying in vain to say may be tried in vain to be said' (1983: 144). Around the same time, however, Beckett also shows his awareness of the diminishing creative opportunities for his writing in the reflective 'Where now? Who now? When now?' (*T*, 293) that begins his text *The Unnamable*. These questions depict the narrating voice at a loose end, without a specific place, subject or time. Indeed, the following word of this opening line 'unquestioning' suggests the narrator has abandoned an earnest pursuit of these narrative foundations. As discussed in the first chapter on (in)sovereign testimony, Beckett's work reflects on expressive dilemmas as a means of speaking without necessarily having anything to speak about: 'Yes, in my life, since we must call it so, there were three things, the inability to speak, the inability to be silent, and solitude, that's what I've had to make the best of' (*T*, 400). As Beckett distils his art of failure, the narrators negotiate the shrinking creative forum as well as they can.

In the 1956 interview with Israel Shenker, Beckett claims that this approach is at its limit: 'For some authors writing gets easier the more they write. For me it gets more and more difficult. [. . .] In the last book – "L'Innommable" – there's complete disintegration. No "I," no "have," no "being." No nominative, no accusative, no verb. There's no way to go on' (quoted in Shenker 1979: 162). Beckett's dismantling of the text has seemingly ushered him to a grammatical dead end. Yet *The Unnamable* itself suggests otherwise in the last line 'I can't go on, I'll go on' (*T*, 418). The narrative voice vows to continue, although it does not happen in this text, as the last full stop leads into the desolation of the blank white page. The affirmation 'I'll go on' appears to be false, yet the metafictional value of this line implies that it is Beckett who will go on and, of course, Beckett does continue to write. In the same interview with Shenker, Beckett describes *Texts for Nothing* as 'an attempt to get out of the attitude of disintegration' (1979: 162). Beckett clearly seeks ways of progressing beyond a tapering form, but, he concedes that this series of thirteen false starts ultimately 'failed'. Pacing '[l]ike a hunted animal' (1979: 163), Beckett himself recognizes that he must continue with a process of disintegration that was thought complete after *The Unnamable*, which indicates that there is further creative substance to decompose. His assault on the pretence of narrative lacks the absolute degree zero as it entails reduction but not extinction.

As much as Beckett attenuates, he is unable to produce silence to get beyond the language that allows surviving figures a lifeline. Indeed, in Christopher Devenney's essay 'What Remains?' on Beckett's departure from an atomizing literary approach, he argues that 'the path of escape is continually obscured by the images, the voices, the figures, the characters and identities, the endless proliferation of shapes, narratives, and narrations, that suggest the outline of a legible and identifiable presence' (2001: 144). In the pursuit of less, Beckett's testimony of fiction conjures material that refuses to be totally lifeless. As *Texts for Nothing* shows, Beckett is inclined to reiterate the questions: 'Where would I go, if I could go, who would I be, if I could be, what would I say, if I had a voice, who says this, saying it's me?' (*TN*, 17). Beckett employs a hypothetical register here that is always available and, as Eric Levy recognizes, 'hypotheses enable not understanding, but continuation of the "perplexity" from which they spring' (2006: 103). Therefore, these texts in favour of nothing are not exactly nothing themselves since writing fosters irrepressible activity even as Beckett minimizes the extent of this textual sustenance.

In kind, Beckett's eponymous characters make cameo appearances in other texts, as though their survival is not limited to a prescribed sphere. In *Malone Dies*, for instance, Beckett's prophetic title appears to confirm that Malone's dwindling account of Lemuel on the last page represents the narrator's own demise: 'never there he will never / never anything / there / any more' (*T*, 298). But this is predominantly a novel about the process of dying and the present tense of the title connotes that Malone's death is continuous or prospective. When Malone appears in the following text, *The Unnamable*, it is clear that the names are transferable, that Beckett's characters can transcend their texts and survive beyond their ostensible deaths. This kind of overlapping contributes to a sense of continuity across Beckett's body of work as it assimilates the individual survivors in each text into a broader *oeuvre* of survival.

Beckett repeatedly returns to the degree to which creative forms entail a level of survival but, as his work gets shorter and more abstract, his already relatively sparse characterization recedes further to leave only obscure voices and stark presences. Although there is a distinct absence of the protagonists' appearances, backgrounds, occupations, nationalities, motivations and aspirations, the tendency to subtract in Beckett's later texts still reveals the survival spirit. The three-page text *Imagination Dead Imagine*, written in French and translated into English in 1965, exemplifies Beckett's engagement with residual life in otherwise sterile environs.[1] As light and heat rise and fall, two bodies lie murmuring on the ground. The scene begins with 'No trace of life anywhere, you say, pah, no difficulty there, imagination not dead yet, yes, dead, good, imagination dead imagine' (*TN*, 86). The phrase 'imagination dead imagine' contains a directive to envision the death of creative powers, but as with Beckett's use of language to interrogate language, the death of imagination can only be imagined, thereby ensuring its own survival. Thus speech and imagination soon populate the lifeless space with a presence that observes. This kind of unavoidable attendance has a particularly Freudian resonance, relating to a psychoanalytical view of morbid thoughts. In his 'Timely Reflections on War and Death', Freud asserts that '[o]ur own death is indeed unimaginable, and however often we try to imagine it, we realize that we are actually still present as onlookers. Thus, the psychoanalytic school could venture to say: fundamentally no one believes in his own death or, which comes to the same thing: in the unconscious each of us is convinced of his immortality' (2005: 183). As with the spectator witnessing the death of a projected self, the implicit point of view that comes with thought and speech continues to accompany Beckett's etiolated works. In a textual sphere that conspires to reduce the presence of beings, Beckett's creatures abide as they observe and express their deterioration.

Incompleteness and continuation occupy Beckett right up until *Stirrings Still*, his last expression of activity and inertia. Written between 1983 and 1987 in English and French, this final prose piece is nine pages in length, divided into three parts, and attests to Beckett's propensity for less. However, as the title suggests, Beckett never stopped writing and his minimalism never arrived at naught. 'Stirrings still' makes it known that an impassioned level remains, that stirrings occur 'even now'. While there continue to be stirrings, the pun on 'still' as adjective, intensifier and verb also implies that the stirrings cease. As an oxymoron, Beckett's phrase indicates that the work 'provokes' stillness, in terms of conjuring and disturbing it, and that stirrings occur despite or through stillness. Such variation on a similar theme has been the basis of a whole body of writing for Beckett. Since it occurs at the very end of Beckett's career, the phrase 'stirrings still' is significant in the way it connects his artistic revision with the thematic concern of survival. Beckett's corpus has circled the idea of death without becoming entirely 'corpsed' itself (*E*, 20).

In *Stirrings Still*, a familiarly hatted and coated protagonist exists in a strange elevated place, 'high above the earth' (*C*, 107) but unable to look down and 'seeking the way out' (*C*, 108). Trapped within his four walls, the narrator ceases to listen and look, despite hearing and seeing. In this passive sensory condition, he decides to seek sanctuary in thought. The protagonist's desire to escape means that existence appears as an imposed condition. As he observes himself rising and leaving, his attitude is one of 'half hoping when he disappeared again that he would not reappear again and half fearing that he would not' (*C*, 108). This split self clearly repeats the Freudian spectacle of imagined death as the figure remains as an onlooker, but the remaining figure is split again between the desire for his other self both to depart and return. The result is the confluence of destruction and creation, as Beckett's creatures exist in a suspended predicament in which survival is intractable as it exceeds powerlessness and the unity of self. Without finishing or progressing, disappearing or returning, the creatures endure in the equilibrium of competing inabilities and hopes.

The majority of *Stirrings Still* meditates on a handful of recognizably Beckettian motifs: light and dark, cries and silence, waiting, time, memory, and reason. Yet the text practises the title's interplay between torpor and stimulation, as Beckett writes: 'soon weary of vainly delving in those remains he moved on. [. . .] So on unknowing and no end in sight' (C, 113). Although he contemplates recurrent images and themes, the protagonist is also restless, which inscribes a sense of motion into the text. It is his weariness that moves him on, so that he exhausts things and searches for something else. As with the bouts of tedium and vigour that cause a creaturely state of suspension in Beckett's humour, this fluctuation between enervation and invigoration frustrates completion to make the 'stirrings still' dynamic an excruciating continuation:

> Perhaps thus the end. Unless no more than a mere lull. Then all as before. The strokes and cries as before and he as before now there now gone now there again now gone again. Then the lull again. Then all as before again. So again and again. And patience till the one true end to time and grief and self and second self his own (C, 110).

Every encounter with what seems like finality is actually an interval that can restore activity. This passage is suffused with the repetition of 'again' and 'before', which focuses attention on going back to life to resume past conditions but in the present. Beckett accentuates this present vitality with the frequent use of 'now' to highlight the being-in-the-moment that survival encompasses. The survivor must struggle through each moment, but does so in anticipation of a better future, whether that is 'the one true end to time' as suggested here, or an alternative experience of living without the intense pressures that survival implies. This desire for an end effectively confirms that survival can be undesired. As the temporary somnolence of the words 'lull' gives way to agitations that return the protagonist to the pressing 'strokes and cries' of survival, the provisional 'perhaps thus the end' gives way to the wishful exclamation 'oh all to end' (C, 115) in the final line of *Stirrings Still*.

Since each supposed limit is illusory, the abiding experience for Beckett's figures appears to be perseverance in spite of themselves; they consciously pursue an end while subject to a conflicting will to continue. In *Remnants of Auschwitz*, Agamben also questions whether the capacity for survival is desirable. Agamben discusses Xavier Bichat's distinction between the 'animal', the aspect of being engaged with the world environment, and 'organic', the biological substance of being (Bichat 1986: 200–6). Bichat suggests that the animal can perish while the organic survives, as in the comatose patient. However, Bichat also imagines an organic death while the animal survives, in a type of immaterial consciousness from the excess of human spirit. Agamben's conclusion is that '[w]hether what survives is the human or the inhuman, the animal or the organic, it seems that life bears within itself the dream – or the nightmare – of survival' (2002: 155). Bichat's division asserts that a being can survive without its animal or organic aspect and, for Agamben, this means life contains the hopeful or horrific potential for survival.

Agamben goes on to place this type of fragmented continuation in the context of modern biopolitics and its exemplum the Nazi concentration camps, which aim to rive the inhuman from the human to activate pure survival. The dream of survival appears to apply to world-conscious beings 'surviving' under the wing of the state, complete with military protection and the insurance of medical science. The nightmare of survival sees continued life forced upon ostracized creatures denuded of all human value and subjected to a state worse than death. It is this desensitization, demoralization and negation of all human value that reveals the biological level of bare life that is pure survival. In other words, the Nazis extinguish the human to expose the inhuman survival of the *Muselmann*. Theodor Adorno had already expressed his horror at this ontological dimension exposed in the camps. In his 'Notes on Kafka', Adorno writes: 'In the concentration camps, the boundary between life and death was eradicated. A middle ground was created, inhabited by living skeletons and putrefying bodies, victims unable to take their own lives, Satan's laughter at the hope of abolishing death' (2003b: 227). Modern biopolitics therefore declares the 'survival' of the included citizen as the justification for the real biological survival that follows the exclusion of others. The supposed 'survival' of the insider is more like a will to power and progress, or an excess of resources that ensure life, whereas the desperate survival of the degraded outsider actually traverses the edge of death. It is this latter nightmare of survival that induces the plea for an end to life in the camps, which chimes eerily with the last line of *Stirrings Still*:

'[In Auschwitz] only death could bring deliverance, the final rest, oh rest' (Stabholz quoted in Neumann 2002: 129).

Both Agamben and Beckett refute the idea that survival is desirable, and instead suggest that it can be a *pensum* – a task set as a punishment. In Agamben, this survival punishment is the biopolitical consequence of Nazi ideology. In Beckett, the literary beings who appeal for an end to their suffering clearly resonate with the imposed survival conditions that Agamben relates to Auschwitz. But survival in Beckett also extends to an oppressive thanatology that sees mortal subjects born into death, as the prospect of the end overshadows life and renders human existence an agonizing meantime. Life already contains the survival dynamic that finds its most odious form in the concentration and extermination camps as the Nazis turn the will to life against their victims. Survival is therefore a nightmare, devoid of the desirable human values and meaning of a good life, and exposed to a state of incompleteness that denies life or death.

Yet, in one remarkable case, Beckett implores that one of his creatures be given the right to a completion of sorts, in order to avoid going on indefinitely in a state of abandonment. In 1946, Beckett learned that a truncated version of the story 'Suite', the French version of the short story *The End*, was to be printed in the magazine *Le Temps Modernes*, thus leaving his character unfinished. Beckett's acting literary agent submitted half of the story to editor Simone de Beauvoir who published it under the impression it was an entire text. Beckett reacted angrily, writing a candid letter expressing the gravity of the situation as he saw it:

> I am thinking of the character in 'Suite', denied his rest. [. . .] [I]t is quite impossible for me to evade the duty I feel towards a creature of mine. Forgive these grand words. If I were afraid of ridicule I would keep quiet. [. . .] You are immobilising an existence at the very moment at which it is about to take its definitive form. There is something nightmarish about that (2011: 41–2).

The voice of a writer determined to protect his work is distinct here and it is no exaggeration for Beckett to regard his creatures as living beings in the making. The publication process has clearly interfered with the form of a life, leaving this stifled being a formless nightmare.

It forces an open end upon him, but as something curtailed and therefore always *in potentia*.

However, it is striking that Beckett posits 'denied rest' alongside 'immobilisation' in the letter, which brings to mind a survival dynamic analogous to the activity and paralysis in his own conclusion to the short story. Beckett's 'end' in *The End* is to contemplate the other stories the narrator might have told, which could have related the conditions that resemble his life more accurately, namely an existence 'without the courage to end, or the strength to go on' (*FN*, 57). Beckett depicts a type of being not altogether finished or developing in this line. The creature lacks certain heroic attributes that would grant him an end or a means of progression. It is notable, then, that Beckett's sense of duty to his beings involves enabling them to survive finally, to be fully incomplete, in a manner that would properly sustain the creatures and grant them their stirrings still.

Creaturely 'undeadness'

Beckett's ability to rejuvenate limited themes shows that a contradictory mix of vitality and inertia pervades his work. This meeting conjures a creaturely dimension, linked to the boundless potential and vulnerability of human subjectivity that dovetails with human animality and the exposed bodily life that is manacled to death. Santner's notion of 'undeadness' theorizes this kind of life–death amalgam demonstrated in Beckett's 'stirrings still'. Santner's term refers to a tenacious revenant that shares the proximity with death but resistance against finality that characterizes survival in Beckett. Santner derives the term from Walter Benjamin's 'petrified unrest' and it is therefore worth glossing Benjamin's idiosyncratic views of allegory and natural history in order to elucidate Santner's concept sufficiently. In the 'Central Park' drafts on Baudelaire, Benjamin borrows the phrase 'petrified unrest' from Gottfried Keller's poem 'Lost Right, Lost Happiness'. Benjamin uses the phrase twice, noting firstly that '[a]llegory holds fast to the ruins. It offers the image of petrified unrest' (2003: 169) and later that '[p]etrified unrest is also the formula for Baudelaire's life history, which knows no development' (2003: 171). The idea of petrified unrest is part of Benjamin's complex writings in *The Origin of German Tragic Drama* on the temporal differences between the symbol and allegory. The symbol accesses the 'mystical instant', achieving a momentary glimpse of totality, whereas Benjamin claims that allegory produces a series of moments in the friction between religious, literal meaning and secular, other meaning (1977: 165). As with Benjamin's famous 'dialectics at a standstill' (1999: 10), the idealist project of synthetic progress is halted. Instead, the clash of signification in allegory between denotation and connotation dislodges transcendent value and produces artefacts that continue to exist but outside of their meaningful place.

Benjamin's dissection of allegory has wider implications in terms of human life and an understanding of historical time. Through the antisystematic imprint of allegory, he poses a melancholic subject that is thrown out of the hegemonic thought space and into the creaturely expanse of 'natural history'. Santner notes that the word *Naturgeschichte* in Benjamin's work means that 'the artefacts of human history tend to acquire an aspect of mute, natural being at the point where they begin to lose their place in a viable form of life' (2006: 16). In this sphere, the 'creaturely life' that Santner develops from Benjamin's 'creature' survives as an anachronism, hence the paradoxical state of suspended animation that is 'petrified unrest'.

In Benjamin's study, allegory is a key element of *Trauerspiel*, the mourning play. Like architectural ruins, in which the structure is both shattered and preserved, the melancholic disposition of the mourning play sets up an alternative history that bears witness to a kind of 'still life' that transfixes the dialectical abrasion between types of meaning. Beatrice Hanssen suggests that, in Benjamin's view, 'the mourning play no longer pointed to a "higher life" or realm of transcendence. Instead it was caught in an infernal game of reflections destined to display the empty mirror image of transcendence, which it infinitely reflected and deflected' (2000: 58). Unlike the messianic fulfilment of time that Benjamin later formulated, the inauthentic time of allegory and the mourning play demonstrate a repetitive turning about that finds no real progress or closure.

The expression 'still life' suggested in the 'petrified unrest' of Benjamin's interpretation of *Trauerspiel* grasps the peculiar concomitance of motion and stasis in Beckett's work. It encompasses the same mixture of cessation and continuation that Beckett implies in 'stirrings still'. While the visual art genre 'still life' depicts inanimate subject matter, Beckett's use of the term in *Ill Seen Ill Said* injects activity into this inertia. In this 1981 text, an old woman resides in a cabin surrounded by twelve sentinels that stand in the pastures. The narrator imagines lambs on a moor, and briefly describes their behaviour: 'Still. Then a moment straying. Then still again. To think there is still life in this age' (C, 48). Stillness and liveliness oscillate here to form this Beckettian 'still life' that indicates both a halted existence and a remaining existence. In Mary Bryden's discussion of Beckett's relationship with the 'dynamic still' of painterly art, she remarks that the expression 'still life'

> draws into collocation two tendencies which, though *potentially* mutually exclusive, are in fact part of an uncomfortable continuum in Beckett's scenic world. As well as being an adjective, 'still' can be a noun. A 'still' denotes an image which, while not being cinematographic, may be applied to a frame, or series of frames, from an ongoing reel of pictures (1994: 182).

Bryden argues that the contradiction in still life is not simply equal to stagnancy, but to a sense of movement within confines that works to intensify the image. This is evident in the brief tableaux that begin and end *Endgame*, which draw on the traditions of the *tableau vivant*, or 'living picture', to capture the life present in a single moment. In Beckett's play, this captivation in a moment is entirely relevant to the characters' experiences of life, and the tableaux serve to magnify the paralysing tensions of their lingering existence.

However, there is a specific type of survival intimated in 'still life' that I want to stress, which evokes the ruins and lack of development evident in Benjamin's 'petrified unrest'. Still life suggests both suspension, as in the frozen single frame, and continuation, as in the implied series of frames. Hence, Bryden surmises that '[i]mplicit in the mobility is the immobility and *vice versa*' (1994: 182). The result of this dialectic is that life is always in tension with stillness, and it is this dynamic in Beckett that relates to Benjamin's notion of historical time. There is movement but no progression, as all activity is tethered to virtually static points. This sense of excess energy that revolves around past things and unviable meanings marks the suspended animation of Beckett's creatures. For example, Moran embodies the concomitance of motion and stasis in *Molloy* during young Jacques' trip to buy a bicycle in Hole. Moran waits restlessly at the shelter, occasionally exploring the near surroundings: 'But each time I had to retrace my steps, the way I had come, to the shelter, and make sure all was in order, before I sallied forth again. And I consumed the greater part of this second day in these vain comings and goings, these vigils and imaginations' (*T*, 148). Moran is moving to and fro, but from a wider perspective he is actually static. His movements are restricted to the shelter and the process of 'retracing' shows him literally going over old ground. Since Moran reviews what has already been done, he effectively consumes time with his vacillations rather than using it productively. This physical motion between the shelter and the wilderness reflects an attachment to the past, fixated on the shelter of the old, even as he attempts to venture forth into the unknown future. In this way, Moran is simultaneously continuing and suspended, as he survives to demonstrate there is still life, but is caught in what is essentially a still life.

As much as the restricted movement intensifies the survival conditions of Beckett's creatures, it nevertheless incorporates a deadening activity. The exposure to a life stuck in a rut, subject to the competing forces of activity and inertia, implies the kind of purgatorial state seen in Benjamin's inauthentic time. In the tensions of allegory and pensiveness of mourning, the artefacts of history fall into perpetual destruction, as Howard Caygill notes: 'The events of historical time are inauthentic, repeats and copies of earlier repetitions. There is no possibility of an authentic "source"; historical time drains its events of any significance. There is no moment or place where the "passing over" of tradition can be gathered; its sole issue is ruination and dispersal' (Caygill 1994: 11). Benjamin compares this irresistible decay to a sign of death in life and the spiritual plane of the undead. He asserts firstly that 'in allegory the observer is confronted with the *facies hippocratica* of history as a petrified, primordial landscape' (Benjamin 1977: 166). Allegory is the 'death face' of the past, a countenance that stands for the throes of historical meaning. Benjamin takes this a stage further, noting that '[g]hosts, like the profoundly significant allegories, are manifestations from the realm of mourning; they have an affinity for mourners, for those who ponder over signs and over the future' (1977: 193). These agitated spectres from the past drag their histories with them, unable to rest in peace. In the same way that the obligation to testify, melancholy immersion and perseverance through humour noted in previous chapters all contribute to Beckett's 'hell of stories' (*T*, 383), the sepulchral monuments of allegory and the mourning play present a vision of enduring death.

The unfinished business of allegory and *Trauerspiel* leads Santner to propose the term 'undeadness' as a description for the aesthetic, but also historical and political movements, that Benjamin describes. In Santner's reading, petrified unrest is a mesmeric combination of excitation and numbness as a result of the repetitive motions of modern capitalism's production culture. He refers to the alienation and fetishization outlined in Marxist and Freudian discourse to explain humankind's entry into natural history. In turn, the term 'undeadness' refers to the state of living that remains in the overflow of manic activity. Santner connects this lingering being to an extra capacity within the human: 'Man's subordination to the course of natural history is a consequence of a spiritual supplement that separates man from animal while in some sense making him more animal than animal, this "more" being the very seal of his "creatureliness"' (2006: 105). The human slips into the contingent level of natural history by virtue of a subsisting drive, more habit than instinct. This detachment from the human constructed world, which stops short of the animal open, suggests a 'sur-vival' in the etymological sense of additional life, a substrate of human existence levied by the accretion of the human repetition compulsion.

The work of German writer W.G. Sebald acts as Santner's paradigm for tracing the creaturely void found in Benjamin's notion of natural history. The presence of historical remains in Sebald's images of decay and spectres of memory, and particularly his focus on dust, ash and sand, captures the inexorable spirit of undeadness. Santner writes that 'for both Benjamin and Sebald creatureliness signifies a materiality dense with "deposits" of unredeemed suffering' (2006: 114). Benjamin and Sebald refer to this process of 'deposition', or the layering of sediment, to evoke the logic of disintegration and perpetuation in simultaneously transient and persistent historical artefacts. This type of engagement with the past is also highly apparent in the disintegrated material substances with which Beckett depicts perpetuating denouements. As Clov announces unconvincingly that it is 'nearly finished' at the very beginning of *Endgame*, he realizes that the near end will continue indefinitely as a series of moments that will never constitute a whole but always form a 'heap' of single particles. He says 'Grain upon grain, one by one, and one day, suddenly, there's a heap, a little heap, the impossible heap' (*E*, 6). Hamm recognizes the same problem late on in the play, noting, 'Moment upon moment, pattering down, like the millet grains of . . . (*he hesitates*) . . . that old Greek, and all life long you wait for that to mount up to a life' (*E*, 42). Clov and Hamm continually anticipate the wholeness of a life, as if they could survey the cairns of their complete existences.

Despite this elusive finality, there is the impression that dying pastimes envelop Clov and Hamm. In an echo of T. S. Eliot's 'heap of broken images' in *The Waste Land* (2005: 58), Beckett's impossible heap suggests his characters are subject to a fragmented experience of life, forced to draw on and add to a mound of dilapidated ideas in an 'Old endgame, lost of old' (*E*, 48). In this respect, the heap also evinces an intertextual legacy, a history of literary traditions and their products that resurface in subsequent generations. Beckett engages with a particularly modernist idea as he draws attention to these nostalgic and allusive aspects of the present in his image of positive entropy. But as the past comes to occupy the present as memory, the irresistible flow of time means the past is infinitely transposed into new contexts and perceived from fresh perspectives. The past is always being reshaped by the present, so there is always more material for Clov and Hamm to pile on the heap, thereby forestalling totality. As the chess term of the title suggests, *Endgame* stretches out and is locked into a final stage so that life has seemingly passed but death itself remains a formality, allowing the characters to continue playing.

Beckett employs the image of layering in both of his other major dramas after *Endgame* to describe the bearing of past experiences on the present. In *Krapp's Last Tape* (1958), Krapp listens to and reflects on annual tape recordings that capture his past thoughts on earlier recordings in a process that adds layers of commentary to his life in a growing archive of spools. On tape, a 39-year-old Krapp refers to the composition or editing of his writing as 'separating the grain from the husks' and says: 'The grain, now what do I mean by that, I mean. . . (*hesitates*) . . . I suppose I mean those things worth having when all the dust has – when all *my* dust has settled' (*K*, 5). Krapp implies that he wishes to leave the kernel of his writing as a legacy, free from all superfluous paraphernalia, but his autobiographical project on tape does not settle on the past, but rather disturbs the memories and appends the archive. The present is simply an interpretation of the recorded past, meaning he lives through the cannibalization of his memoirs. As Krapp's name indicates, he is immersed in material he has already digested once. Most notably, in *Happy Days* (*HD* [1961] 2006c), Winnie is embedded up to her neck in a mound that signifies her imprisonment in a 'world without end' (*HD*, 35) complete with the existential pressure to be stoic, but also, more specifically, the societal expectations of women, hence the daily cosmetic and sartorial routine. As she brushes her teeth and applies lipstick, Winnie's monologues are peppered with references to Shakespeare and Milton, so that she effectively recites the 'exquisite lines' of the 'classics' to subsist (*HD*, 35). Winnie is therefore stuck in the repetitive patterns of life and an inherited stockpile of quotes from literary history.

This brief sketch of the temporal deposits in Beckett serves to show that the past continues to impact his creatures in the present, but not in a perspicuous way that catalogues memory from a superposition. As with Benjamin and Sebald, the movements of time and history disobey linear chronology for Beckett. In a metaphorical sense, these heaps and mounds are not simply accumulations of experience, thought and memory, as if the characters behold their pasts as a panorama from the summit of their lived lives. These sediments are transient moments, stirring in the memory but decaying with the subject; they symbolize the attachments to traces of life that bury his creatures alive. Clov, Hamm, Krapp and Winnie cannot sift through their life material and extract specific grains of experience at will. Instead, the heap of history is all around Beckett's creatures. They are inhabitants not curators of their time, at once estranged from the past but haunted by revisiting images. In effect, their past lives are both irretrievable and engrossing as they submit to autobiographical and fictional projects, attempt to relate the story of their lives and the lives of figments, but revolve around the empty spaces of lost experiences and absent selves. Immersed in the temporal deposits of creaturely life, the characters themselves stand as ruins of their pasts, evoking history and enacting their survival as they struggle to account for the detritus of their being.

The creative process of memory and the habitual re-enactment of the past is key to the survival of Beckett's creatures. In one of the most explicit comments on memory in Beckett's work, the narrator in *The Expelled* underlines how recalling the past can be deadly but how frequent remembering can also make the past so unrecognizable as to bury the truth. After the narrator is thrown out of his place of residence, down a flight of stairs and into the vestibule, he tries to remember the number of steps to the staircase, before stating:

> Memories are killing. So you must not think of certain things, of those that are dear to you, or rather you must think of them, for if you don't there is the danger of finding them, in your mind, little by little. That is to say that you must think of them for a good while, every day several times a day, until they sink forever in the mud (*FN*, 3).

First, these killing memories suggest that a melancholic absorption in the past is an enervating existence. A disproportionate indulgence in memory stagnates life through the repetitive engagement with the bygone. Second, the narrator suggests that in actively pursuing memories, the past experience is distorted and the essence remains elusive. This particularly Proustian conception of intentional recollection accesses a selective or censored version of the past, complete with the interpretative embellishments of the subject. When the actual memory is lost, then, it is the loss of memory that is not forgotten. Beckett's characters remember *that* they have forgotten, but not always *what* has been forgotten. Hence, the ad hoc memory unravels the past and can thwart any possibility of gleaning its essence, thus making the past irretrievable but also, crucially, allowing 'the long sonata of the dead' (*T*, 32) to play on. Beckett's characters engage with the infinite lacunae of the past, which occupies them in the present and encourages their continuation. In this way, they reveal the survival in undeadness as they are absorbed in senescent personal histories and sustained by the missing essence of the misremembered past.

Repetition and performance

The repetitive nature of undeadness means that existence persists in the restless fixation with the past. The survivor is largely detached from the original meaning of a formerly authentic life that he tries to recuperate, so that survival is composed of an obsession with bygone things. As such, the survivor effectively endures a symbolic death as the repetition compulsion is affixed to a meaningful life that has died. While Santner's undeadness presents survival as a state additional to meaningful life and beyond a symbolic death, Derrida develops a contrasting line of thought in which survival is immanent to life. In a 2004 interview with *Le Monde*, conducted while Derrida was terminally ill with pancreatic cancer, he asserts: 'I have always been interested in this theme of survival, the meaning of which is *not to be added on* to living or dying. It is originary: life *is* living on, life *is* survival' (2005b: 25). At the end of the interview, Derrida reaffirms that

> survival is an originary concept that constitutes the very structure of what we call existence, *Dasein*, if you will. We are structurally survivors, marked by this structure of the trace and of the testament. [. . .] Surviving is life beyond life, life more than life, and my discourse is not a discourse of death, but, on the contrary, is the affirmation of a living being who prefers living and thus surviving to death, because survival is not simply that which remains but the most intense life possible (2005b: 52).

In no uncertain terms, Derrida asserts that survival is intrinsic to the structure of life. It does not derive from life, nor is it an excess of life. Instead Derrida argues for an intensity of life in all forms of survival, as though even the repetition compulsion could still constitute a powerful vitality. In contrast to Benjamin's 'petrified unrest' and Santner's subsequent 'undeadness', Derrida's survival is always unsettled and does not simply enact an unsettled past. As such, he does not consider surviving as the remnants of what was before, as if there could be an index of life force. According to Derrida, anything that survives is alive as the greatest manifestation of life possible in the present.

Santner's term 'undeadness' is a particular mode of survival that is activated with the loss of settled meaning, whereby viable life forms are nullified to produce the suspended animation of a repetition compulsion. Since undeadness is triggered, it follows that there is still an alternative form of life existing beyond the realm of this agitated survival. On the other hand, in Derrida, unsettlement is fundamental so that survival is a ubiquitous condition of being. Although more sweeping than Santner in his discussion of survival in general, the implication of Derrida's view is that there is no alternative to survival – life can never be relieved from the urgent pressures of 'living on'. If survival is not a remnant or leftover as it is in undeadness, the conditions of life appear all the more pressing since survival is not a substrate of human existence but an ontological necessity.

In his post-war drama, Beckett sustains the tension between the possibility of achieving a viable form of life that Santner's undeadness contains, and the unconditional survival described by Derrida. Beckett prefigures both views of survival in *Waiting for Godot* and *Endgame* as he negotiates the benumbing monotony and revitalizing presence of repetition. Through the respective waiting for a non-attendee and exposure to the abiding end, Beckett's two plays navigate the restricted conditions of undeadness and call upon deconstruction's infinite play of difference. As such, phases of vigour temper the inertia, as Vladimir exemplifies: 'We were beginning to weaken, now we're sure to see the evening out' (*WFG*, 86). A comparable perseverance drives *Endgame*, as when Hamm says, 'This is deadly' and Clov replies 'Things are livening up' (*E*, 20). As Beckett's characters get caught in the bottleneck of repetition, they begin to lack the affirmation of life that Derrida sees in survival and verge instead on the still life of undeadness. Yet, as iteration discloses contrast, an indefatigable life force resurfaces so that while undeadness appears petrified, the type of volatility that Derrida traces underwrites its unrest.

The verbal sparring that occupies Beckett's characters exacerbates the sense of deferred resolution in both plays. As Vladimir and Estragon anticipate Godot's arrival, and Hamm and Clov await the resolution of the end times, they rely on discursive crosstalk with one another to distract themselves. Each word bears witness to Beckett's characters going on while simultaneously revealing stasis through the repetitive phrases that emerge. The line 'waiting for Godot' appears nine times over the course of Beckett's play, serving as a catchphrase to remind the characters of their default position and restart their fatuous chatter. Nevertheless, each repeated utterance contains a negligible difference. Although the repeat is identical to the previous version, it is displaced from the original site and subsequently acknowledged as a reproduction. Derrida finds this transference of the same expression to different contexts intrinsic to communication in 'Signature Event Context' (1972). He

names this possibility 'iteration', noting that *iter* comes from the
Sanskrit for other and that his entire essay 'may be read as the
exploitation of the logic which links repetition to alterity' (Derrida
1977: 7). Derrida elaborates on iterability in 'Limited Inc a b c . . .'
(1977) to explain that 'the structure of iteration [. . .] implies *both*
identity *and* difference. Iteration in its "purest" form – and it is
always impure – contains *in itself* the discrepancy of a difference
that constitutes it as iteration. The iterability of an element divides
its own identity a priori' (1977: 53). This iteration applies in
Beckett's play to make the same phrase 'waiting for Godot' include
a difference with each appearance. Every recurrence identifies with
its namesakes but is at the same time other. These minor incongruities
between repeated utterances convey transit, but they also serve to
accentuate the essentially unchanging circumstances. Words are
duplicated yet the context only alters superficially so that linear
time is obscured owing to the general lack of change.

Likewise, in *Endgame*, Beckett introduces the elderly Nagg and
Nell endeavouring but failing to kiss, after which Nell says, 'Why
this farce, day after day?' (*E*, 12). Clov repeats Nell's question
halfway through the play only for Hamm to reply 'Routine' (*E*, 21).
The question itself includes the idea of imitation in the word 'farce'
and emphasizes monotony in the repeated element 'day'.
Furthermore, the two references to this question during the play
indicate the repetitive structure of their activities to underline both
similarity and difference. The overall situation remains the same,
which precludes the end, and yet Beckett's characters are subject to
time, represented by their physical decay and the dimming light,
which implies procession. The difficulty with labelling Beckett's
work either dynamic or static is that the reliving of the past is a
process that occurs in the present, thus making the repeat a current
view of the past that is never fully identical to what went before.
This rendition of the past injects a level of liveliness into repetition
that contradicts the idea of a static immersion in the past. The
iteration of the words betrays the movement of difference as well as
stagnancy of similarity. Beckett's use of repetition and refrain
effectively produces the inertia and activity of 'still life'.

While Beckett marries tedium with renewal through his repetitive
techniques, he also manages to balance habit and spontaneity in
these plays to create the metatheatrical blurring of performance and
reality. Indeed, Beckett is already eradicating the distinction between

action and acting in the repetitive elements noted above. In their catchphrase, Vladimir and Estragon appear to insist that they are waiting for Godot and *Waiting for Godot*; the pair seemingly accept that they are subject to an imperative and constitute the play itself. Equally, Hamm the ham-actor recognizes his situation as a 'routine', thus indicating the repeat performances of theatre productions. These kinds of references are numerous and serve to underline the fact that the characters' 'lives' are perilously close to exhibitions. The characters appear to speak from habit at times, particularly in the use of stichomythia, which suggests scripted and rehearsed lines. These exchanges are often delivered with unnatural rapidity that presumably bypasses thought. However, the characters are lost for words on occasion too, as if defective memories call for improvisation. For example, after a swift passage of dialogue, Estragon says 'That wasn't such a bad little canter' before Vladimir replies 'Yes, but now we'll have to find something else' (*WFG*, 56). These hiatuses in conversation call for impromptu shows to fill the meantime, but the emphasis remains on performance.

In *Waiting for Godot*, as the pair guess what period of day it is, Vladimir says 'it is not for nothing I have lived through this long day and I can assure you it is very near the end of its repertory' (*WFG*, 78). Each day is thus an act made up of several stock pieces, and although Vladimir suggests he is at the end of his repertoire, the rendition is likely to return tomorrow. Similarly, as Clov removes the sheet to reveal Hamm in his chair, like a second curtain rising from the stage, Hamm's first yawning words are 'Me ... to play' (*E*, 6). His life is framed as a tiresome performance since there is minimal variety to his existence. Each day is a recapitulation of the well-worn routine or, as Clov puts it, 'All life long the same questions, the same answers' (*E*, 7). As this reference to the futility of their actions shows, the authenticity of the characters' everyday existences is contaminated by issues of performance, which suggests they are going through the motions as opposed to actually living through completely new events. Therefore, the idea of continuation through reiteration that occurs within the two plays is a microcosm of the play itself continuing through multiple performances.

Taking these metatheatrical links to performance into consideration, it is notable that survival for Beckett's characters involves echoing their own existence, with the repeated awareness of the waiting and unending mimicking an actual experience. As they reflect on their predicaments and operate within a trite range of actions, Beckett's creatures continue in a state of replication. Godot and the end appear as postures as the characters recite previous utterances and imitate the suspense of an impending release from banality. In fact, Beckett implies that Vladimir has already met Godot, that Hamm has experienced the end, and that existence continues in a state of nostalgia for these past junctures. Before the audience is introduced to the boy messenger, Vladimir indicates that Godot himself arranged to meet them 'by the tree' on 'Saturday' (*WFG*, 6, 7), which differs notably from the infinitely renewable 'tomorrow' the boy later uses (*WFG*, 44). Likewise, in *Endgame*, Hamm refuses to call their existence 'life', labelling it 'this . . . thing' (*E*, 28) before he laments 'The end is in the beginning and yet you go on' (*E*, 41). Beckett keeps open the possibility that the desired moment has gone and is being replayed. Therefore, he supports both the deferral of the desired event and the idea that desire actually transcends the experienced event in a retrospective yearning for the past. The creatures' onward momentum shows that survival can occur as an excess of life after the end of the ideal life, which compels the subject to perform a rendition of the possibility now passed.

In terms of survival, the pertinent issue from this simulation of self is the degree to which Beckett's characters lose their fictional bearings to become hollow interlocutors. The focus on repetition distorts the causal chain of events of realist narratives that represent human life. Rather than depicting 'realistic' personal experiences, Beckett's texts are concerned with their status as constructed performances, or what Hamm calls the 'prolonged creative effort' (*E*, 37). According to Beckett, this kind of self-awareness is crucial for the staging of his plays. When directing the 1975 production of *Waiting for Godot* at the Schiller Theatre in Berlin, he explained: 'It is a game, everything is a game. When all four of them are lying on the ground, that cannot be handled naturalistically. That has got to be done artificially, balletically. Otherwise everything becomes an imitation, an imitation of reality. [. . .] It should become clear and transparent, not dry. It is a game in order to survive' (quoted in Knowlson 1997: 607). Beckett is obviously intent on minimizing the naturalistic elements of his plays, but what it is that actually survives remains ambiguous. Although Beckett might refer to the spectacle of the play itself, 'survival' inevitably evokes organic life.

Beckett insists that the figures are precisely choreographed but the games resist total impersonality, as they appear to have continuation in mind. Hence, the slapstick pile-up in *Waiting for Godot* is not a natural coincidence, but Vladimir and Estragon must still perform these diversions to busy themselves. Despite yearning to be 'saved' (*WFG*, 87), the characters are nevertheless impelled to survive in the meantime, which lends each new playful game an existential weight. It is difficult for survival to escape its ontological resonance, even if that being is alienated distinctly from a recognizable reality.

In Steven Connor's discussion of Beckett's metatheatrical techniques, he argues that '[a]ll these features induce consciousness not of the stage simply itself, but of the stage as representation – even if it is the minimal representation of itself. No matter what is stripped away from character, plot and setting on the stage, there always persists, within the most reduced performance, a residual self-doubling – the stage representing itself *as* stage, *as* performance' (1988: 124). Connor makes the point that in acknowledging the medium, the plays reflect on the dramaturgy and come to represent dramatic performance. The plays are therefore about performance, making use of *mise en abyme* to return to the contract of performance as depiction, if only as a representation of itself. The characters even appear to realize this tendency to satisfy a mimetic function and acquire meaning. Vladimir observes 'This is becoming really insignificant' and Estragon replies 'Not enough' before adding 'We always give ourselves the impression we exist' (*WFG*, 60, 61). Likewise, Hamm queries 'We're not beginning to . . . to . . . mean something?' (*E*, 22). As much as Beckett leans towards metatheatre to eliminate representation, the performance and performers rebel against their vacancy to retain the semblance of life.

As with *The Unnamable*, Beckett includes non-endings in *Waiting for Godot* and *Endgame* in the respective 'Let's go. (*They do not move*)' (*WFG*, 87) and 'You . . . remain' (*E*, 50) to encourage a sense of continuity and sustain the promise of resolution. Although the expectations of these eventualities diminish, it is patent that the creatures have 'resumed the struggle' (*WFG*, 1) and that 'life goes on' (*E*, 40). With this possibility in tow, the implication is that despite the repetitive nature of the plays, Beckett's creatures survive as the hypothetical interruption of the repetition process. As Beckett himself notes, '[t]he key word in my plays is "perhaps"' (quoted in

Driver 1961: 23), and it is this uncertainty that nurtures the possibility of real life aside from the surface play of repetition. In other words, they are passengers in a performed life but can potentially disembark, at least according to the models provided by 'Godot' as a validating figure and the 'end' as a liberating event.[2] This potential means that Beckett's creatures are beings in waiting, as yet unformed and thus continuous. Nevertheless, they require the active performance of the suspended self to sustain the hope of an authentic life.[3] The possibility of achieving a non-survival state, such as authentic living or termination, actually drives their continuation; they are stuck in survival due to their hope for a more meaningful life. The repetitive survival is therefore peculiar in Beckett in that the desired condition that will emancipate the creatures from survival is also the aspiration that binds them to it.

Forms of activity and stasis in *Molloy*

The animated impasse of undeadness is a creaturely dimension integral to the aesthetic, subjective and testimonial significance of Beckett's post-war work. It is indigenous to his writing after the war years and runs deep in the stylistic, structural and thematic levels of both the prose and plays. Beckett's first major publication in the immediate post-war years, *Molloy*, is an appropriate example with which to conduct a sustained examination of the creaturely survival that his work evokes, since the text is contemporaneous to his realization that the future of his writing was in 'incompleteness'. On Beckett's return from Saint-Lô after the war, he recalls seeing his mother, May, when she was stricken with Parkinson's disease. Beckett remarks:

> Her face was a mask, completely unrecognizable. Looking at her, I had a sudden realization that all the work I'd done before was on the wrong track. I guess you'd have to call it a revelation. Strong word, I know, but so it was. I simply understood that there was no sense adding to the store of information, gathering knowledge. The whole attempt at knowledge, it seemed to me, had come to nothing. It was all haywire. What I had to do was investigate not-knowing, not-perceiving, the whole world of incompleteness (quoted in Shainberg 1987: 106).

The deterioration of such an influential maternal figure could only add to the general sense of passing and provisionality that Beckett felt in the post-war years, as expressed in 'The Capital of the Ruins' and in his conversations with Charles Juliet. More acutely, May's impending death appears to act as the final nail in the coffin for a sincere, rich, urbane and capable literary form that must have seemed perversely imperious after 1945. As a result of this 'revelation', *Molloy* features ignorant and incognizant protagonists stuck in expressive and epistemological graves. 'Not-knowing' and 'not-perceiving' echo the 'non-knower' and 'non-can-er' whose (in) sovereign testimonies exhibit the creaturely indecisiveness that results from attempts to adhere to the human way of prioritizing and ordering meaning. As such, Beckett exemplifies the 'sovereign as creature' dynamic that relegates his creatures from a position of narrative power to a predominantly impotent narrative condition. This culminates in the 'incompleteness' that pervades *Molloy* on a narrative level, and induces the creaturely modes of continuation seen in melancholy immersion and humour, which evoke the excess being of natural history that Santner identifies. As Molloy and Moran try to follow the bewildering social and expressive conventions that isolate them, they appear as artefacts removed from a meaningful sphere but persist as creaturely life in the void.

The remainder of this chapter is dedicated to a close analysis of the aesthetic and ontological levels of survival embedded in *Molloy*, particularly the first part on Molloy. Beckett develops several narrative techniques ranging from the internal dialogues of uncertainty to the cyclic structure of the text in order to enact both activity and stasis. The inability to speak together with the obligation to speak sustains his author-narrators, but these same conditions mean they persist in unproductive, enervating tasks. Beckett's creatures are therefore exposed to the '*excitations*' noted in Santner's concept of undeadness (2006: 24), which result in a rechargeable deadening process that allows them to survive without really living. Although confined to a footnote, Santner suggests that this type of creaturely existence finds a parallel in the *Muselmann*. He writes:

> The *Muselmann* is, it seems, the figure whose being has been fully reduced to the substance of a 'cringe,' whose existence has been reduced to its pure, 'protocosmic' being, who is there yet no

longer 'in the world.' What remains, that is, at this zero degree of social existence, in this zone between symbolic and real death, is not pure biological (animal or vegetable) life but rather something like the direct embodiment of creaturely life. We might say that the *Muselmann* is the human in the neighborhood of zero (Santner 2006: 25).

The structural and existential modes of survival analysed in Beckett's *Molloy* are evocative of the *Muselmann* as the 'direct embodiment of creaturely life'. Locked into repeating stories and drifting into psychical worlds, Beckett's creaturely forms and beings enact the peculiar type of lingering life that relates to the *Muselmann*. Yet, these repetitive narrative structures and moribund lives also intimate the precarious state of the human after Auschwitz. As Slade recognizes, the 'survivor ethos is the effect of material losses related to traumatic historical events, and the effect of the loss of an idea, the idea of the human' (2007: 4). With the symbolic value of the human in ruins after the Holocaust, the human category is shown to be a hollow construction made evident by the very performance of the now defunct model of humanity.

Although *Molloy* did not appear in print until 1951, the year after his mother's death, Beckett wrote the novel in French between May and November 1947 during a concentrated period of creativity after the war that he called the 'siege in the room' (Bair 1990: 367). He translated the novel into English, in collaboration with Patrick Bowles initially and then alone, before receiving some final assistance from Maria Perón. It is divided into two monologues, capturing the confused perspectives of the increasingly decrepit narrators Molloy and Moran as they move from town to countryside and back. In part one of *Molloy*, there is a cyclic pattern to Molloy's odyssey that involves different motivational intensities ranging from purposeful imperatives to idle stopgaps. Although generally preoccupied with his mother, Molloy notes that 'these were ancient cares and the mind cannot always brood on the same cares, but needs fresh cares from time to time, so as to revert with renewed vigour, when the time comes to ancient cares' (*T*, 64). As such, the cycle in Beckett's novel lurches onwards:

the buckled wheel that carried me, in unforeseeable jerks, from fatigue to rest, and inversely for example. But now I do not wander any more, anywhere any more, and indeed I scarcely stir at all, and yet nothing is changed. And the confines of my room, of my bed, of my body, are as remote from me as were those of my region, in the days of my splendour. And the cycle continues, joltingly, of flight and bivouac, in an Egypt without bounds, without infant, without mother (*T*, 66).

This example encompasses both the narrative rhythm of Beckett's *Molloy* and the sense of survival in the absence of a governing system. The reference to Egypt, according to Knowlson, evokes the many 'Rest on the Flight to Egypt' paintings that Beckett viewed in European galleries (Knowlson 1997: 375). For example, Caravaggio's baroque version depicts an angel in a violin recital, Joseph holding the musical score, the mother Mary cradling the infant Jesus and an inconspicuous donkey in the background. In contrast, the 'without infant, without mother' line in Beckett's evocation suggests that the relationship between the 'infant' Molloy and his mother is elided while the rest and flight routine goes on. Beckett removes the maternal care present in many of the paintings that depict the escape from Herod the Great, and instead retains an impression of the journeying, the burdensome 'donkeywork' in the patterns of 'flight and bivouac'. On a greater scale, though, the whole religious iconography of the Madonna and Christ-child images is absent. Considering that this iconography conveys divinity on earth in human form, its absence leaves only the boundless struggles of a secular world. The consolation of religious meaning is gone, and yet life continues nonetheless. Embedded in this case in point is a glimpse of the larger implication of survival in Beckett: through the intermittent narrative movement, which suggests a mode of continuation, it is possible to discern creatures surviving in the aftermath of or exclusion from established ideological systems.

The spirit of living on in Beckett includes contextualizing intervals that revitalize the impetus and consequently highlight the tedium of the enduring imperative. The Beckettian predicament is not a single monotonous activity or, to invoke Benjamin, a mystical instant capturing eternity. Rather, it is a dialogue between phases that serves to emphasize the repetitive nature of the cycle. This contrast means that Beckett's creatures are perpetually worn down as each new lease of life eventually dwindles only to be resuscitated and so on *ad infinitum*. Beckett's prose style pays testament to this renewable energy, deploying the logic of alternatives to take detours away from each creative cul-de-sac. The idiosyncratic Beckettian collocation 'don't know' occurs 46 times and the adverb 'perhaps' 192 times in the 78,000 words of *Molloy*. In James Joyce's slightly longer text, *A Portrait of the Artist as a Young Man* (1916), at around 85,000 words, these examples appear 7 and 38 times respectively. Beckett clearly intensifies ignorance and possibility, yet he combats complete stagnancy through his repeated use of 'but', particularly to begin new sentences, and 'not', which he employs approximately twice as frequently as does Joyce.[4] This ability to keep talking in contrasting and negative registers allows the narrators to say double without doubling the amount of meaning. On the contrary, Beckett effectively reduces the text to ruins when exercising this contradictory mode; his narrators sabotage any claim to verisimilitude, professing their unreliability and cancelling out statements. Despite the restrictive position of ineptitude, Beckett's writing reveals ways of reflecting on and responding to itself as the author-narrators accentuate their uncertainty to juggle different possibilities and proffer new suggestions that counter, modify or converse with old ones.

Beckett cultivates an aesthetic of ignorance to leave trains of thought open and posit his creatures in a world of incompleteness. Molloy, for example, is partial to internal dialogues that encourage further speech. At the end of the A and C episode, in which Molloy observes two passing strangers, he describes an ambiguous meeting with one of the two men. It is unclear whether this is an imaginary or actual meeting, but after the man has left, Molloy returns to thinking of himself:

> And once again I am I will not say alone, no, that's not like me, but, how shall I say, I don't know, restored to myself, no, I never left myself, free, yes, I don't know what that means but it's the word I mean to use, free to do what, to do nothing, to know, but what, the laws of the mind perhaps, of my mind (*T*, 13).

Molloy's thinking is plagued with digression here as he suggests ideas that he either denies or accepts and poses questions to himself. This type of dithering narration makes Molloy an unreliable narrator. His meditation is reduced to fragments of thought as he fumbles around for the right idea. Although the meaning is all but submerged in cognitive waste, it is this inconclusive expressive and mental practice that sustains Molloy's narrative. The internal dialogue of doubt in Molloy allows him to perpetuate his account as he negotiates different formulations in pursuit of the precise expression.

The ability to continue despite the incapacity for positive statements extends to Molloy's analyses of self. Beckett's creatures manage to reflect on their conditions despite recognizing the limits of self-analysis. While in the Lousse house, Molloy recalls having tried to find a meaning for the human condition in the disciplines of astronomy, geology, anthropology, psychiatry and magic. This last school of supernatural phenomena and mysterious trickery is the final straw for Molloy; his absorption in magic has the 'honour' of his ruins, consigning him to a confused shambles of being (*T*, 39). This deteriorated self

> is not the kind of place where you go, but where you find yourself, sometimes, not knowing how, and which you cannot leave at will, and where you find yourself without any pleasure, but with more perhaps than in those places you can escape from, by making an effort, places full of mystery, full of the familiar mysteries. I listen and the voice is full of a world collapsing endlessly, a frozen world, under a faint untroubled sky, enough to see by, yes, and frozen too. And I hear it murmur that all wilts and yields, as if loaded down, but here there are no loads, and the light too, down towards an end it seems can never come. For what possible ends to these wastes where true light never was, nor any upright thing, nor any true foundation, but only these leaning things, forever lapsing and crumbling away, beneath a sky without memory of morning and hope of night (*T*, 40).

The broken subjectivity that Molloy sketches is a result of the lack of meaning or explanation for existence and an inability to discover the truth of the human experience. In contrast to the other science-based disciplines, the magic that brings about this condition is synonymous with alchemy, the occult transformation of matter. Alchemy includes the *nigredo phase*, a darkening chemical process that reduces substances to black *prima materia*. Jungian analytical psychology adopts the *nigredo phase* to discuss the mind as it confronts the chaos of its inner shadows (Jung 1970: 497). This initial stage in a process of individuation, or wholeness, is associated with the self-examination of melancholy. Similarly, Molloy associates the obscurity of magic with his exposure to the welter of the human condition. His engagement with the perplexing illusions of magic and the self only direct him to the abyss of being, riddled with echoing voices, lost memories and unexplainable impressions. But the result is not totally distasteful since, unlike the 'familiar mysteries' of the human self and metaphysical truth, there is no prospect of escape when resigned to this formless being. His study of magic enters him into a state of ruin, or 'the indestructible chaos of timeless things' (*T*, 40), in which there is no longer magic or mystery. If '[a] final overcoming of melancholy is not possible', in Beckett, and 'the *nigredo phase* is endless' (Birnbaum and Olsson 2008: 81), the ability to surrender to this chaos would at least exempt Molloy from the alternative pursuit of positive knowledge.

Self-examination is a Platonic exercise to remove ignorance, as Ernst Cassirer asserts: 'Man is declared to be that creature who is constantly in search of himself – a creature who in every moment of his existence must examine and scrutinize the conditions of his existence. In this scrutiny, in this critical attitude towards human life, consists the real value of human life' (1972: 6). Molloy and Moran exemplify the scrutinizing part of this attitude through their questioning inclinations. Moran, the more meticulous of the two narrators, produces three fifths of the questioning material in *Molloy*.[5] He says: 'to kill time I asked myself a certain number of questions and tried to answer them' (*T*, 154). In one passage, Moran even includes a list of thirty-three questions, which is a technique that keeps him thinking as the answers elude him or generate more questions (*T*, 167–9). Molloy on the other hand employs the question mark for a series of suggestions: 'For otherwise how could I have reached the enormous age I have reached. Thanks to moral qualities? Hygienic habits? Fresh air? Starvation? Lack of sleep? Solitude? Persecution? The long silent screams (dangerous to scream)? The daily longing for the earth to swallow me up?' (*T*, 80–1). Molloy's approach, like Moran, fails to identify information, but nevertheless manages to maintain activity through deliberation. Through their inquiries, Beckett's creatures can adopt a probing attitude that avoids the certain knowledge that would pacify contemplation. For Beckett also, the question mark fills the text with doubt, which resists the quietus of totality but essentially revolves around the same enigmas.

In contrast with Cassirer, however, Beckett's work does not sustain the exaltation of self-examination nor accept it as a defining human property. The scrutiny of human existence and subjectivity in Beckett only proliferates ignorance, foregrounding the incompleteness of the self. It is unable to transcend the infinite mirroring of self-reflection to perceive such practice as a veritable human value. Thus, the 'place' that Molloy discovers is, in part, the prison of self-reflection and the cage of the *cogito*. Indeed, this constant search is precisely the creaturely condition of incompleteness, which is a fact that Molloy appears to accept as the lesser of two evils – the inescapable, ruined self over the familiar mystery of the meaning of the human. This is not to say that Molloy finishes with self-examination, but that he is open to the logic of disintegration and the 'endlessly collapsing world' that ensues. In fact, he is unusually lucid about his entropic condition, diagnosing 'leaning things, forever lapsing and crumbling away' from a place 'where true light never was'. Although Molloy often insists upon his fallaciousness, noting 'I express without sinking to the level of oratio recta, but by means of other figures quite as deceitful, as for example, It seemed to me that, etc., or, I had the impression that, etc.' (*T*, 88), he actually recognizes his tentative approach and is surprisingly eloquent when describing his ruination. Consequently, Molloy is in a frozen world with an equally frozen sky, the 'frozen' suggesting a particularly melancholic self-examination. His exploration of the ruins of self keep him at a standstill, yet this condition is nevertheless fuelled by the half-light of comprehension represented by the pale sky, which preserves the subject in the very process of obliteration, immanent in its effacement. It is this kind of reflection on his state of ruin that reveals traces of a subject privy to its own desubjectification. Although Eric Levy argues that 'the admission of futility ultimately becomes an affirmation of purpose' (2006: 108), this aporetic activity, 'without memory of morning and hope of night' (*T*, 40), clearly lacks an origin and terminus, *arche* and *telos*, meaning that Molloy is suspended in the limbo of narrative scepticism.

Beckett's image of the buckled wheel captures the disrupted revolutions around a fixed point experienced in Molloy's search for his mother and Moran's search for Molloy. The overall structures of both parts of *Molloy* also convey a more complex helical shape to the narrative movement. Molloy's account ends with him in a ditch, 'Molloy could stay where he happened to be' (*T*, 91), but presumably he is then transported to his mother's room, 'perhaps in an ambulance' (*T*, 7), since this is where he writes his account. In the chronological *fabula* (the elemental materials of the story) of Molloy's journey, the initial framing paragraph is the last event to take place, with Molloy the author-narrator in his mother's room discussing the writing process.[6] The second paragraph and indeed the remainder of Molloy's tale are retrospective, representing the events leading up to the scene in the first paragraph. Beckett advertises the fact that this is the *syuzhet* (the concrete representation used to convey the story) and that Molloy lives in the text twice, or rather is twice removed, first in the confused experience of events and second in the unreliable account. In effect, the story loops, yet in a way that allows the repeated cycles to worm forward in a parallel real time. In other words, the account is repeated, but there is the sense that time is not simply repeated but wasted as the old eats up the new. Molloy is therefore perpetually searching for the object of his narrative, his mother, which sustains his own demise. As Molloy replays his quest, he effectively languishes in a past event.

In the second part, Moran's final words are: 'Then I went back into the house and wrote, It is midnight. The rain is beating on the windows. It was not midnight. It was not raining' (*T*, 176). The penultimate lines declaring the rain at midnight repeat the opening lines of part two, which insinuates that the account the reader has read is Moran's submitted report. However, in conjunction with the last eight words, asserting that it is no longer midnight or raining, the reiteration of the first sentences reminds the reader of the previously narrated events and encourages one to see Moran writing the rest of his report again, similar to the account just read but with the added knowledge of a parallel present forming a subtext to the narrated past events. Accordingly, there would be an eventual return to the writing of the report at the 'end' again, where the evocation of the beginning would occur again. The implication is an ever-increasing series of loops progressing on a forward-moving timeline, projecting the same story or memory into the future, which would mean the target Molloy is preserved in thought and yet always elusive. In this way, Moran's report anticipates the paradox of simultaneously not going on and going on explored in *The Unnamable*.

In the Beckettian helix, the composition process undercuts the related account and intimates the teller behind the tale. As with the tradition of the oral narrative, Molloy and Moran's stories are reiterated and repositioned, but the same absence is invested into each new generation of the text. Like a zoetrope in which still images appear animated when glimpsed through the apertures of the rotating wheel, the performative quality of *Molloy*, the sense of *doing*, gives the impression of the active hand behind the writing. As the stories revolve, the written subjects Molloy and Moran are reprised, appearing repeatedly in the narrative loops, while Beckett's narrators appear as vague figures trapped behind on a single coiled path that insinuates a perpetually destructive activity. The compositional real time is effectively swallowed in the literary other time; both past and present are lost and lost again in the writing. This is the loophole of Beckett's iteration process, in which the explicit foreground and implicit background work in tandem to produce cyclic repetition on a degrading trajectory.

Retelling the moment he sets off for Molloy country, Moran recognizes the truly Sisyphean aspect of his duty to report the past as though present: 'For it is one of the features of this penance that I may not pass over what is over and straightaway come to the heart of the matter. But that must be again unknown to me which is no longer so and that again fondly believed which then I fondly believed, at my setting out' (*T*, 133). Moran's account means the past has not passed, but is reanimated. In Benjaminian terms, temporality in *Molloy* is inauthentic as the fulfilment of historical progression is emptied to reveal duration, or evanescent moments that spin out into a melancholic frozen time. Beckett, like Benjamin, 'replaces the agent – the one who, as we say "makes history" – with the creature overtaken by or lost in history' (Pick 2011: 73–4). For Beckett's creatures, then, the past is not an accessible archive of distant experiences. It is an overflow of time that saturates the present with anachronisms to give rise to the suspended animation of undeadness.

'Finish dying': Death without death in *Molloy*

While Benjamin's conceptions of time and history have Marxist-inflected preoccupations with materiality at the root, he is sensitive to the psychological implications of ruins that Beckett's novel incorporates. As Santner notes, 'what Benjamin refers to as petrified unrest pertains to the dynamics of the *repetition compulsion*, the psychic aspect of the eternal recurrence of the same that for Benjamin defined the world of commodity production and consumption' (italics in original) (2006: 81). Beckett's 'stirrings still' also threaten the very idea of the originary or unique aura as Molloy's and Moran's narratives mime the process of reproduction, stuck in a making and breaking oscillation. These creatures survive in an annular pattern that poses as life, as Molloy expresses: 'If I go on long enough calling that my life I'll end up by believing it. It's the principle of advertising' (*T*, 53). Yet, as both Steven Connor and James O'Hara note, the repetition compulsion evident in the sceptical imperative of Beckett's work is indicative of the Freudian death-drive – the thanatological urge towards the inorganic material form (Connor 1988: 9–11; O'Hara 1997: 133). In 'Beyond the Pleasure Principle' (1922), Freud theorizes that 'all instincts tend towards the restoration of an earlier state of things' but, owing to the convergence of the preservative instinct and the death-drive, he adds that each 'organism wishes to die only in its own fashion' (1989: 612, 614). As Beckett's characters recommence their quests and repeat their stories compulsively, they display this magnetism towards a singular death and enter into a drawn-out negotiation between the pleasure principle and the death drive that delineates the very precise death immanent to the subject.

The obsessive repetition of stories in *Molloy* causes a slow physical and psychological decay that sees the protagonists ailed and addled. The combination of a diminishing and enduring will translates to the body, which is subject to the atrophy caused by psychological absorption. The lame Molloy crawls on his front, 'racked by a kind of chronic arthritis' (*T*, 89), whereas Moran is diseased with a 'sick leg' and 'failing flesh' (*T*, 165, 166). Such physical afflictions are apparent in Agamben's sketch of the associations and physiological consequences of melancholy, which, given its parity with decline in Beckett, is worth quoting in full: 'The physiological syndrome of *abundantia melancholie* (abundance of melancholy humor) includes darkening of the skin, blood, and urine, hardening of the pulse, burning in the gut, flatulence, acid burping, whistling in the left ear, constipation or excess of feces, and gloomy dreams; among the diseases it can induce are hysteria, dementia, epilepsy, leprosy, hemorrhoids, scabies, and suicidal mania' (1993: 11). Beckett's infirm tramps are riddled with similar symptoms; they are senile cripples with palpitating hearts, oozing body fluids and bristling with skin conditions. Their bodies deteriorate while the mind is gripped in the saturnine state. More than this, however, the grotesque physical symptoms that Agamben notes serve to offer an outward representation of the purely psychological self-evaluation that dominates Freud's definition of melancholy. In 'Mourning and Melancholia' (1917), Freud writes, '[i]n mourning, the world has become poor and empty, in melancholia it is the ego that has become less so. The patient describes his ego to us as being worthless, incapable of functioning and morally reprehensible, he is filled with self-reproach, he levels insults against himself and expects ostracism and punishment' (2005: 205–6). For Freud, melancholy is based on an assessment of personal inferiority, not physical infirmity. Yet, when read together, Freud's psychoanalysis and Agamben's overview suggest a psychosomatic melancholy that harvests self-hatred and shows on the body. Certainly, in Beckett's case, the melancholy that begins internally is manifest as an external deterioration in *Molloy*. The material self is a casualty of the cyclic repetition of Molloy and Moran's imperatives as they externalize the inner emptiness and disappointments that pervade their doomed but dogged quests. Freud concludes his view of melancholic self-deprecation with the thought that '[t]he image of this – predominantly moral – sense of inferiority is complemented by sleeplessness, rejection of food, and an overcoming of the drive – most curious from the psychological point of view – which compels everything that lives to cling to life' (2005: 206). He identifies a disregard for life, and yet a lack of self-preservation does not necessarily mean that death automatically ensues. Although Freud's melancholia relinquishes the preservative life force and precipitates an existence open to the death-drive, the ruined body evokes a kind of living death. This is not quite an absolute lack of will at every level of the psyche or a determined pursuit of death, but rather an organic existence after life that is snagged on the retrogressive slide towards death; it is the enduring being of the worthless life divested of the Eros principle.

Beckett also engages with this idea of an apathetic living death in the second part of *Molloy*. As a mirror image of 'libido', the Obidil figure suggests a reversal of desire and the antithesis of the life instinct. The lack of an actual meeting with Obidil, however, implies that Moran never achieves or fully subscribes to the death-drive towards non-will. After his son abandons him, Moran reflects, 'And with regard to Obidil, of whom I have refrained from speaking until now, and whom I so longed to see face to face, all I can say with regard to him is this, that I never saw him, either face to face or darkly, perhaps there is no such person, that would not greatly surprise me' (*T*, 162). With wry self-consciousness, Beckett pokes fun at the fact that Obidil fails to materialize. He plays with fiction's capacity to incarnate a psychological drive and jettison this embodiment at the same time. If Obidil is a personification of the death-drive, it seems that Moran questions the very existence, or at least his acquaintance with, this particular Freudian phenomenon. The absent Obidil, the figure representing the radical absence of desire, exists on the edge of Moran's consciousness, held in check by a lingering life force. As such, Moran is consigned to a level of survival and not to the inorganic state that his material deterioration forecasts.

At times, both Molloy and Moran speak as though they have already endured a death and survive beyond it. As Moran departs his house having introduced the region of Ballyba, he takes a short walk from his living quarters, 'twenty-paces from my wicket-gate', to visit the graveyard (*T*, 135). Moran says:

> Sometimes I went and looked at my grave. The stone was up already. It was a simple Latin cross, white. I wanted to have my name put on it, with the here lies and the date of my birth. Then all it would have wanted was the date of my death. They would not let me. Sometimes I smiled, as if I were dead already (*T*, 135).

It is significant that Moran's house is close to his grave as it indicates the space between life and death in Beckett's work, ranging from a narrow margin to a distorting crossover. The fact that Moran's headstone has already been erected confirms the grip that mortality has on Beckett's creatures. It invades Moran's consciousness and commands his prospective view. Adorno asserts that this fixation on death is characteristic of Beckett's *Endgame* too, in which '[a]ll existence is levelled to a life that is itself death, abstract domination' (1982: 145–6). The oppressive shadow of death is also evident in Moran's fascination with the graveyard, especially his own resting place, as if the thought of dying suffocates his life. However, the cross is anonymous and undated, which suggests that Moran cannot prepare for death or take control of it. While death waits on the horizon as a potential, his demise nevertheless remains deferred. Yet, more disconcertingly, Moran's date of birth is also refused, as though life is only determined on expiry. In one sense, Moran has not lived until he has died, but equally, if he does not have a birth and is not living, he cannot truly die. Furthermore, through the strange smile 'as if I were already dead' at the end of this excerpt, Beckett gives the impression of rictus, which is a fixed grimace associated with the countenance of death. Moran's corpse-like expression confuses the appearances of vitality and inanition so that he effectively endures death but is unable to finally die. Moran is clearly a creature susceptible to the obfuscated boundaries of life and death.

Similarly, on the opening page of part one, Molloy aims to 'finish dying', which implies that he has died partially already but, like his mother, wants to die 'enough to be buried' (T, 7). For Molloy, this mode of existence is a mystery:

> My life, my life, now I speak of it as of something over, now as of a joke which still goes on, and it is neither, for at the same time it is over and it goes on, and is there any tense for that? Watch wound and buried by the watchmaker, before he died, whose ruined works will one day speak of God, to the worms (T, 36).

First, Molloy refers to the expressive and temporal difficulties of his existence as his undeadness confounds both the logic of grammatical tenses and time frames. He must necessarily speak of his past life as though it is total, which seems to imply that his death is present in every living moment. If Molloy cannot talk about what life is and chronicle it, he is destined to perform as a middle voice, shuttling indifferently between death and life, between the refusing 'no' and the insistent 'on'. Since Molloy is over in one sense but goes on in another, he evinces an ontological status of survival that exists between different types of life and death. The autobiographical tense wants to address life as a complete experience but every reflection on that life exposes the fact that his life is incomplete. Molloy is therefore subject to a survival that sees many 'deaths' as each new word extends and replaces his life.

Molloy is also subject to a symbolic death that sees the collapse or removal of a meaningful mode of being and entails the suspended,

anachronistic existence of creaturely life. In Beckett, the parameters
of life and death are not only determined by the physical limits of
the human body, they are also a question of existential value and
identification with worldly worth. If a person cannot find a sense of
meaning for their life, they endure the death of their valuable
existence, which places emphasis on the human as a bare,
melancholic entity. Beckett's reference to the watchmaker analogy
implies that Molloy is on the edge of such an existential crisis. In
Treatise on Man ([1664] 1972), Descartes offers a mechanistic
conception of the living body, arguing that internal 'functions
(including passion, memory, and imagination) follow from the mere
arrangement of the machine's organs every bit as naturally as the
movements of a clock or other automaton follow from the
arrangement of its counter-weights and wheels' ([1664] 1972: 113).
The components of the living body interact like a machine, with the
implication that, like a timepiece, the human machine is evidence of
a maker. The English theologian William Paley employs the
watchmaker analogy in *Natural Theology* ([1802] 2006) in his
argument for the divine design of the universe. He infers that since
the intricacies of a watch imply that 'there must have existed, at
some time, and at some place or other, an artificer or artificers who
formed it for the purpose which we find it' (Paley [1802] 2006: 8),
the same principle applies to the intricacies of nature. In *Molloy*, the
presence of a watchmaker would guarantee Molloy an origin and
purpose as part of a pre-determined mechanism fashioned by
intelligent design.

   However, Molloy points out that the authorial presence is dead
and therefore his own function is forever unknown. Since the
creator figure is not with him now, Molloy is an abandoned creature,
charged with life and left to survive. As with Beckett's elision of the
religious elements in his allusion to Mary and Jesus's 'flight and
bivouac', the validation offered by a totalizing system of thought
is absent for Molloy, leaving only a terrestrial existence devoid
of higher meaning. He is as much evidence of divinity, or the
absence of divinity, as other primitive earthbound creatures. The
transcendental meaning of being is therefore stripped, and yet
Molloy subsists undeniably as a vulnerable, rootless life. As a buried
ruin in a secular world with only the memory of an origin story, he
demonstrates that 'life can persist beyond the symbolic forms that
gave it meaning' (Paley [1802] 2006: 17). Molloy has died according

to the idea of the human as a meaningful part of a divine plan, which moves him closer to the raw matter of mere existence.

Although the loss of a divine governing figure suggests a rather commonplace existential reading of Beckett, this sense of alienation is enacted on a more local level in the vacuum of biopolitical care that takes place for Beckett's creatures. In Chapter 2 on master–servant relationships, I argued that a process of territorial sovereignty excludes Beckett's creatures from a state of biopolitical protection. This kind of segregation and devaluation took place at an unprecedented level during the Third Reich and ultimately led to designated spaces of exclusion, the concentration and extermination camps, in which the detached *Muselmann* was forced into being. Molloy describes such an experience of exclusion:

> But I entered the first shelter I came to and stayed there till dawn, for I knew I was bound to be stopped by the first policeman and asked what I was doing, a question to which I have never been able to find the correct reply. But it cannot have been a real shelter and I did not stay till dawn, for a man came in soon after me and drove me out. And yet there was room for two (*T*, 60).

Molloy appears as a misfit when he comes into contact with other people in society. Although Lousse takes him in, Molloy is subjugated and pauperized by her charity and, given that the policemen treat him as a second-rate citizen, Molloy lacks the value of respected subjects. The policemen in particular, as representatives of the state, reveal the official policy on these subaltern creatures. Clearly this exclusion pertains to a survival mode for Beckett's creatures as they exist on the periphery of state welfare, but there is another sense of survival that occurs as they try to adhere to social and legal structures. Alongside a bodily survival that attempts to secure a less vulnerable position by achieving the immunity and respect granted to other citizens, Beckett's creatures also attempt to comply with the ideas and ideals of a civilized world to gain a sense of ideological belonging. Considering that this status is denied to them in various ways, their enduring attachment to the template of meaning precipitates their creaturely suspension, or what could be described as the survival of undeadness.

After Molloy's first encounter with the police in which he is briefly detained for violating public decency, threatened with a cylindrical ruler and impudently interrogated, he insists: 'I have only to be told what good behaviour is and I am well-behaved, within the limits of my physical possibilities' (*T*, 25). As far as his bodily limits go, Molloy exemplifies the Latin maxim *necessitas non habet legem* (necessity has no law). He is governed by physical necessity at times and incapable of abiding by certain rules, particularly 'no loitering'. However, it is not only Molloy's physical infirmity that makes him transgressive. His need to understand the underlying principles that produce the intricacies of public order is also problematic. Molloy is not apprised of the nature of these statutory laws, and therefore exists in an inapprehensible snare he is bound to trigger. He argues: 'if I have always behaved like a pig, the fault lies not with me but with my superiors, who corrected me only on points of detail instead of showing me the essence of the system' (*T*, 25). Molloy requires the founding reasons of the structure in order to extrapolate the correct action in any given situation. In stark contrast, he is subject to the mechanics of authority that preclude his ability to conform and integrate. As such, he subscribes to the rules but is unable to abide by them fully as he is refused access to their logic. The point to stress is that Molloy is at least willing to conduct himself according to propriety in order to fit in and is therefore not purposely rebellious. The idea of conforming is still active for Molloy even though the system of thought rejects him or no longer applies to him. Consequently, Beckett's creatures exemplify the survival of undeadness as they repeatedly appeal to a mode of living that is untenable for them and subsist as a surplus nostalgic energy.

Santner alludes to the collapse of a viable worldview in *The Royal Remains* when he notes that creaturely life is an exposure, not 'simply to the elements or to the fragility and precariousness of our mortal, finite lives, but rather to an ultimate lack of foundation for the historical forms of life that distinguish human community' (Santner 2011: 5). Beckett's creatures are subject to the fragility of biological life, but in their inadvertent perversity they also threaten to expose the entire system as an absurd contrivance. The civilized construct appears unable to accommodate a creature like Molloy and, while he endeavours to be assimilated into the order, he ends up revealing the limitations of this form of life. As he is released from the police station, Molloy recognizes his transgressive quality: 'Were they of the opinion that it was useless to prosecute me? To apply the letter of the law to a creature like me is not an easy matter. It can be done, but reason is against it' (*T*, 24). Such peculiar creatures seem to upset the system not because they are especially fractious, but because they are ignorant subjects, without the vigorous body or docile mind courted by the state. Crucially, Molloy's thoughts on the destabilization of propriety come as a result of his proximity with a kind of death: 'I was in the dark, most of the time, and all the more completely as a lifetime of observations had left me doubting the possibility of systematic decorum, even within a limited area. But it is only since I have ceased to live that I think of these things and the other thing' (*T*, 25). Although Molloy ceases to live as a subject in this ideological domain, he nevertheless tries to reengage with it, and in his confrontations with order, Molloy ultimately serves to unsettle the status quo. He survives in a 'raglimp stasis' (*T*, 26) as a dehumanized pariah after his viable life in the civilized world.

Molloy's mode of being intimates a symbolic death and invokes the additional capacity for existence noted in Santner's undeadness. Survival in Beckett does not completely avoid death, then, but rather distends the last relics of vitality in an otherwise moribund life bereft of import. Nevertheless, the fact is that Molloy treks through the wilderness of the forest and lapses into a ditch, at which point he hears that 'help' is coming and says that 'other scenes of my life came back to me' (*T*, 91). As noted above, he subsequently finds himself in his mother's room, which is where his account begins. Therefore, Molloy's investment in a former mode of life occurs in the mind, through habitual narratives, memories and imaginings. He does not simply cultivate a physical attachment to a particular way of life, as though he obstinately hangs around the town, hoping to learn from his encounters with the police, make himself a less indigent figure and acquire a meaningful sense of being. Instead, the helical structures of the novel explain how Molloy repeatedly traces his engagements with lost ideological models through virtual recitals. He replays the possibility of finding his mother and restoring her as a figure in his life. At the same time, Molloy relives the memory of his past endeavours to comprehend the governing structures of the biopolitical domain that would offer him a life worth living. It is through the idea of undeadness that Beckett's aesthetics of continuation and the incompleteness of the narrative structure convey a psychological state, in which Molloy survives as still life by repeating his pursuits of now dead figures of meaning.

Molloy is estranged from meaningful domestic, social and political worlds, and descends into the abyss of thought. He persists in this mental space through the ruined performance of past meaning structures, such as the guarantee of a source in his mother and the value of a dignified social existence. Despite being disconnected from the structure of a governed realm and resembling biopolitically worthless material, Molloy survives in a spiralling narrative that finds him absorbed in the act of bearing witness to the past, complete with a projected alterity figure and a platform for humour. All of these creaturely modes contribute to this survival that subscribes to the possibility of stable meaning even while it is shown to be elusive. They maintain the creature's contact with previous ideals and, although this continuation sustains the present possibility of restoring the past, it also suggests that creaturely life is composed of a moribund rendition. In this way, the natural historical artefact outside of viable life emerges as a psychological repetition compulsion fixed on lost sources and past structures. Beckett's creatures are disposed to inaccessible but nonetheless aspirational models of meaning that leave them surviving with the remnants of history and showing that there are stirrings still beyond the values attributed to a life worth living.

EPILOGUE

In a letter to Georges Duthuit dated 12 August 1948 Beckett apologizes for the 'unbelievably silly letter' he had sent previously in which he offers some near inscrutable thoughts on art, before noting that: 'One must shout, murmur, exult madly, until one can find the no doubt calm language of the no, unqualified, or as little qualified as possible' (2011: 102, 98). As Beckett picks up momentum in this earlier letter he stops himself, saying: 'But I'm starting to write' (2011: 98). Beckett's correspondence drifts into his current creative direction, which suggests some parity between his fiction and the request for pardon in the next letter: 'Forgive me now and always for all my stupidities and blanknesses, I am only a tiny little part of a creature, self-hating vestiges, remains of an old longing, when I was little, for rounding out, even on a small radius. That shuts you in your whole life long. And one drives in vain towards figurelessness' (2011: 102).

This short extract covers several of the creaturely dimensions raised over the course of *Beckett's Creatures*. The 'stupidities and blanknesses' to which Beckett refers parallel the ignorant and incompetent testimonies of his author-narrators. He appears to recognize the same asininity and lacunae in his letters that constitute his art of failure and attest to the impossibility of bearing witness. The idea of being 'part of a creature' itself recalls the creaturely subjectivity that emerges when the subject is present at its own desubjectification. Beckett describes himself as a fragmented being in the way Beckett's creatures are sundered as they articulate their own disordered identities. 'Self-hating vestiges' and 'remains of an old longing' offer a striking depiction of a melancholic figure, particularly the ruined result of a sustained saturnine disposition. Similarly, Beckett's creatures are the disintegrated subjects of the unfulfilled desire for resolution and subscription to previous templates of meaning. The fact that Beckett's longing is for 'rounding out' evokes the manner in which humour helps to persevere with failure and contribute to a perpetual cycle of relief and suffering. As the laugh relieves the pressures at the limits of language and the tolerance of monotony, the creature is granted a reprieve that allows further misery to ensue. More than this, the idea of rounding out 'on a small radius' betrays the kind of exacting economy that characterizes the aesthetic trajectory of Beckett's *oeuvre* but maintains the creaturely spirit of survival. These small spaces of vitality precipitate the futile drive 'towards figurelessness' that renders Beckett's characters enervated and etiolated creatures, but resists complete liquidation.

The complex shape of creaturely life in Beckett is dominated by what I have repeatedly called 'suspension' and 'survival'. A number of tensions give rise to the suspended lives of Beckett's creatures: the incapacity to speak together with the obligation to speak; the urge towards distinction and ascendancy together with the reliance on a necessary other; the pursuit of an end to words together with the laugh that signals and forestalls conclusion; and the inability to go on together with the act of going on. These contradictions create figures subject to open-ended processes, often repeating the same in the hope of change and subsequently surviving on the small differences of iteration that prevent the creatures' completions. Beckett depicts subjects engaging a past they cannot fully comprehend or express, burdened with the search to make sense of and validate their lives, and driven by the prospect that a resolution will come. The creature is therefore carrying a past it cannot quite grasp and a future it cannot quite realize. Beckett's creatures live on encircling the loss, or worse, the absence, of a meaningful life.

This reading is significant in the way it deploys a particular trope, the creature, as a means of accessing the historical and biopolitical relevance of Beckett's work. The creature traverses the borderline between aesthetic and extra-literary levels to show how Beckett's art of failure is attentive to the way models of expression and epistemology are destabilized in the wake of catastrophe. Adorno describes the artist's predicament in *Aesthetic Theory*, asserting that 'externally art appears impossible whilst immanently it must be pursued' (1997: 320). For Adorno, the Holocaust has a profound impact on the very validity of art, philosophy, language and knowledge. This kind of enlightened culture effectively pulls the rug from under its own feet to appear barbaric in light of recent history. Thinking through

Beckett's work in terms of the suspended but surviving creature encompasses the contradiction of this creative impasse in which art is undermined but must endure all the same. The stirrings still of Beckett's creatures implies a process of persevering under these difficult conditions, in which the success of a final product is denied and whereby the creature emerges as a persistent figure of failure. Yet this failure is itself an ethical and empathic response to the catastrophe. Beckett's writing enacts 'a writing of terrorized disempowerment as close as possible to the experience of traumatized victims without presuming to be identical to it' (La Capra 2001: 105–6). He confronts the impossibility in the challenge facing art after Auschwitz and conveys the fact that speaking will always be *instead*, as a powerless secondary witness.

The creature is particularly related to the biopolitical nature of the Holocaust. The creaturely aesthetic based on ignorance and impotence in Beckett's work offers an oblique response to the contemporaneous climate in which the value of the human was the focus of a political ideology that interfered with the bodily conditions of its subjects. In terms of the narrative obligation itself, Beckett's creatures are bound to a necessity that sees their very existence dominated by their negotiations with the complete overhaul of the idea of a valuable human life. As Agamben writes: 'One of the essential characteristics of modern politics [. . .] is its constant need to redefine the threshold in life that distinguishes and separates what is inside from what is outside' (1995: 131). This effort to decide upon a new criterion for life worthy of political significance relates to Beckett's aesthetic first, as his creatures pursue a field of meaning that is perennially denied to them. As they employ language and reason in their accounts, their narrative endeavours clearly lack the human ability to master positive meaning and the author-narrators are instead stranded in the creaturely world of insistent creation. On the level of words, then, Beckett's creatures offer an implicit critique of certain key humanist assumptions.

Beckett's creatures are also subjected to more explicit biopolitical exclusions on a social level, which I have discussed in previous chapters. In Santner's brief mention of Beckett in the epilogue of his book *The Royal Remains*, he refers to the phrase 'merely human' to describe Beckett's subaltern characters. He writes: 'Recalling Arendt's account of the stateless, one could say that Beckett's characters acquire their particular strangeness by being rendered merely human'

(Santner 2011: 251). In the footnote, he adds that 'Arendt's great insight was that being rendered "merely human" results in becoming something *less than human and yet not simply animal*' (2011: 251). Santner refers here to the exclusion from viable forms of life that engenders debased creaturely life, 'a dimension *created*, in a word, by a process of destitution' (2011: 57). Though Beckett's creatures are refused human belonging in the biopolitical sense, they are not united with the natural world in the way the animal is with the open. Rather the creature is estranged from the world through consciousness and alienated from socio-political value as a result of biopolitical order. With an awareness of their exclusion from both spheres, Beckett's creatures drift in between, closer to the raw matter of a biological entity but with awareness of the potential for human meaning. This 'merely human' state is the uncanny proximity of the creature to the progressive human and autotelic animal.

On the edge of these human and animal modes of being, the creature subsists in negotiating the remains of the former frameworks of value and meaning. The biopolitical interference in classifying types of people ruptures the idea of humanity founded on civilized standards, universal rights and the sacrosanctity of human life. In this way, the creature offers a rather global perspective in which '[m]aking sense of the senseless remains the essential element in recovering the idea of humanity after the holocaust' (Fine 2000: 23). This process of refiguring the human in a post-human era discloses the human's creaturely potential. As we have seen in Beckett, human components are distorted: language is inadequate, reason is defective, power is dependent, laughter is tragic and life is a death. These properties do not have the same authorial efficacy or organic quality, and can appear to be antithetical to themselves. Thus, as the creature seeks to be readmitted from its double poverty in world, it acts out a human template subject to reconfirmation, which, to use Beckett's phrase, shows that 'Humans are truly strange' (*FN*, 65). In adhering to the human after the model has been undermined and made incongruous, the survivor unveils the creaturely dimension of the human.

However, as Beckett wrote in the 1946 Radio Éireann broadcast 'The Capital of the Ruins', to which I refer in the Introduction: '"Provisional" is not the term it was in this universe become provisional' (1986: 75). Since Enlightenment humanism has been destabilized, in its place is a strange performance of that ideal. Evidently, Beckett recognizes that everything is subject to a continual meantime, that systems of thought can be revised or refuted and that the human condition effectively becomes the conditional human. In offering a kind of grotesque simulation of the human, then, Beckett's creatures convey the *pro tem* conditions between the outmoded stability of the past and the unforthcoming solution to the crisis. This creaturely life is suspended in transition after the fall and before any satisfactory replacement. It is effectively an afterlife of waiting for life to come, as Beckett shows in *Endgame* when Clov asks 'Do you believe in the life to come?' and Hamm replies 'Mine was always that' (*E*, 30–1).

Although Hamm has the last word in this exchange, Clov's more anticipatory question pervades Beckett's work. If the mid-twentieth century saw the perversion of the human cosmos, it is not necessarily the absolute end to these former systems. Beckett's work indicates that the spectre of the human goes on in the habitual repetition of its own ruined model. It still attends the creaturely life of trying to reconstitute a viable sense of meaning. In the final passage of 'The Capital of the Ruins', Beckett's ambivalence towards this salvaging process surfaces:

[S]ome of those who were in Saint-Lô will come home realizing that they got at least as good as they gave, that they got indeed what they could hardly give, a vision and a sense of a time-honoured conception of humanity in ruins, and perhaps even an inkling of the terms in which our condition is to be thought again. These will have been in France (1986: 76).

The idea of humanity is one that is repeatedly destroyed and what survives is a re-conception of a broken image. In a kind of token of humanism, however, Beckett suggests that the lesson for humanity appears to be within its own ruins, which might offer the opportunity for the human condition to be reconsidered. As Andrew Slade notes, '[t]he ruins of St. Lô are not just in St. Lô, they will be the material with which thought must grapple if it is to re-think its condition without falling into the amnesia of repetition or the conscious repetition of remembrance' (2007: 58). Despite this, the phrase 'thought again' is itself deeply equivocal as it envelops both perpetuation and transformation. The creaturely disposition would indicate a relapse into the habitual performance of the disaster-bound human. Equally, the creature is dissatisfied with perpetual reversion. It awaits a better future, holding on to the possibility of change and an implied otherwise: 'The fact is, it seems, that the most you can hope is to be a little less, in the end, the creature you were in the beginning, and the middle' (*T*, 32). In the melancholic fixation on past models of meaning, then, Beckett's characters are not completely bare, but creaturely, surviving as a haunting echo of meaning, a remnant of the past and a hope for the future. Indeed, it is this progressive desire without the means of progression that engenders a creaturely state of suspension. The Beckettian creature is an anti-humanist figure that emerges from a ruined humanist ideal, but retains, even if only negatively, an element of humanism that cannot be expunged.

NOTES

Introduction

1 All definitions are taken from *OED online*. Available at: www.oed.com

2 Dirk Van Hulle draws on these connections between creation and Romanticism in Beckett in '"Accursed Creator": Beckett, Romanticism, Modern Prometheus', *Samuel Beckett Today/Aujourd'hui*, Vol. 18, All Sturm and No Drang, Beckett and Romanticism, ed. by Dirk Van Hulle and Mark Nixon (Amsterdam: Rodopi, 2007), 115–29.

3 Concepts of creaturely life could have significance for understanding Beckett's writing in Irish colonial and postcolonial contexts, in the way Matthew Brian Nicholas, for example, uses creatureliness to examine Irish identity in relation to James Joyce: 'For nineteenth and twentieth-century Irish citizens, [. . .] creaturely life helps put into focus the political effectiveness of the dehumanised bestial imagery used to degrade the Irish', Matthew Brian Nicholas, '"Scrupulous Sympathy": James Joyce's "Ulysses" and the Ethics of Modern Sentimentality', Doctoral dissertation, May 2008, Washington University Press (Proquest, 2011), p. 197.

4 Although Theodor Adorno and Max Horkheimer do not address the political state of exception, my reading is informed by ideas described in their co-authored book *Dialectic of Enlightenment* (1947): 'With the spread of the bourgeois commodity economy the dark horizon of myth is illuminated by the sun of calculating reason, beneath whose icy rays the seeds of new barbarism are germinating' (Adorno and Horkheimer 2002: 25).

Chapter 1

1 See Matthew Feldman, *Beckett's Books: A Cultural History of the Interwar Notes* (London: Continuum, 2006).

2 For convenience, I refer to the narrator of *The Unnamable* as 'he' in this book, but strictly speaking the voice is without gender.

3 James Joyce also felt his authorial grip on *Ulysses* slipping at times, particularly in the 'Circe' episode. Maud Ellmann writes: 'Joyce's complaints about the episode suggest that writing is dehumanizing in a double sense, first because it goes on writing regardless of the writer, like the robotic music of the player piano, and second because it animalizes its creator, reducing the author to a beast in the machine' (Ellmann 2006: 75). Joyce's struggle with his 'monster-novel' in these instances is closer to the expressive dilemmas that Beckett explores with his author-narrators.

4 The description 'sovereign as creature' appears on the content page of Benjamin's *The Origin of German Tragic Drama* (1977).

5 Beckett illustrates the ambivalence of 'cleave' in *Malone Dies*. Two lovers form a unity, 'cleave so fast together that they seem a single body', and are then distinctly separate beings, 'each enclosed within its own frontiers' (*T*, 238).

Chapter 2

1 Beckett also highlights Watt's inability to self-reflectively determine himself: 'prevented him from saying [. . .] of the creature that still in spite of everything presented a large number of exclusively human characteristics, that is was a man' (*W*, 68). In this passage, Watt also makes reference to inorganic material: 'he made the distressing discovery that of himself too he could no longer affirm anything that did not seem as false as if he had affirmed it of a stone' (*W*, 68).

2 The narrator Sam explicitly refers to Watt's likeness to a representation of Christ: 'His face was bloody, his hands also, and thorns were in his scalp. (His resemblance, at that moment, to the Christ believed by Bosch, then hanging in Trafalgar Square, was so striking, that I remarked it)' (*W*, 136). Several critics expand on the parallels between Watt and Christ. See Hesla 1971: 62 and Parrott 2001: 425–33.

3 The act of duly maintaining absent powers is exemplified and tested in the *Shoah*. Etty Hillesum wrote in a concentration camp shortly before her death: 'You God cannot be God unless we create a dwelling place for you in our hearts' (Hillesum quoted in Kearney 2011: 53).

4 For example, Charles Patterson, *Eternal Treblinka: Our Treatment of Animals and the Holocaust* (New York: Lantern, 2002); and Boria Sax, *Animals in the Third Reich – Pets, Scapegoats, and the Holocaust*

(New York: Continuum, 2000). For a discussion of the differences and similarities between Jews and animals as 'figures', see Andrew Benjamin, *Of Jews and Animals* (Edinburgh: Edinburgh University Press, 2010).

5 Patterson outlines Haeckel's view: 'Ernst Haeckel, whose ideas had a strong influence on Nazi ideology, maintained that since non-European races are "psychologically" nearer to the mammals (apes and dogs) than to civilized Europeans, we must, therefore, *assign a totally different value to their lives*' (2002: 25–6).

Chapter 3

1 For example, see Manfred Pfister, 'Beckett, Barker, and Other Grim Laughter', in *A History of English Laughter – Laughter from Beowulf to Beckett and Beyond*, ed. by Manfred Pfister (New York: Rodopi, 2002), pp. 175–89; and Laura Salisbury, *Samuel Beckett: Laughing Matters, Comic Timing* (Edinburgh: Edinburgh University Press, 2012), pp. 77–112.

2 See also David Houston Jones, *The Body Abject: Self and Text in Jean Genet and Samuel Beckett* (New York: Peter Lang, 2000).

3 Beckett refers to Democritus' aphorism in *Murphy*, 'the Nothing, than which in the guffaw of the Abderite naught is more real' (*M*, 154) and in *Malone Dies*, '*Nothing is more real than nothing*' (*T*, 193).

Chapter 4

1 According to Beckett, this text is the 'residue precipitate' of the abandoned work *All Strange Away*, which itself suggests that unfinished ideas have a tendency to re-emerge (*TN*, xiv).

2 As Steven Connor notes, in terms of subjectivity, the extrication from repetition into an authentic life means '[t]he self will pursued as though it were a locatable essence, or presence, even though that pursuit is to reveal the self as difference' (1988: 49).

3 In response to a world of mechanical reproduction that Benjamin identified, Beckett's creatures are afflicted by what Jean Baudrillard calls 'the nostalgia for origins and obsession with authenticity' (2005: 80).

4 'But' appears 749 times and 'not' appears 865 times in *Molloy*. The words appear 355 and 448 times respectively in *A Portrait of the Artist as a Young Man*.

5 Question marks appear 385 times in *Molloy*: 140 times in Molloy's part and 245 times in Moran's part.

6 Definitions of Russian formalism narrative terminology are taken from M. H. Abrams, *A Glossary of Literary Terms* (London: Thomas Wadsworth, 2005), p. 181.

BIBLIOGRAPHY

Abbott, H. Porter, *Beckett Writing Beckett: The Author in the Autograph* (Ithaca: Cornell University Press, 1996)

Abrams, M. H., *A Glossary of Literary Terms* (London: Thomas Wadsworth, 2005)

Ackerley, C. J. and Gontarski, S. E., *The Grove Companion to Beckett* (New York: Grove, 2004)

Adelman, Gary, *Naming Beckett's Unnamable* (Lewisburg: Bucknell University Press, 2004)

Adorno, Theodor, 'Trying to Understand Endgame', *New German Critique*, Critical Theory and Modernity, No. 26 (1982), trans. by Michael T. Jones, 119–50

Adorno, Theodor, *Notes to Literature*, Vol. 2, trans. by S. W. Nicholsen (New York: Columbia University Press, 1992)

Adorno, Theodor, *Aesthetic Theory* (London: Athlone, 1997)

Adorno, Theodor, 'Commitment', in *Can One Live After Auschwitz?: A Philosophical Reader*, ed. by Rolf Tiedemann (Stanford, CA: Stanford University Press, 2003a), pp. 240–58

Adorno, Theodor, 'Notes on Kafka', in *Can One Live After Auschwitz?: A Philosophical Reader*, ed. by Rolf Tiedemann (Stanford, CA: Stanford University Press, 2003b), pp. 211–39

Adorno, Theodor, 'Dossier: Adorno's Notes on Beckett', *Journal of Beckett Studies*, 19.2 (2010), trans. by Dirk Van Hulle and Shane Weller, 157–78

Adorno, Theodor and Horkheimer, Max, *Dialectic of Enlightenment: Philosophical Fragments*, ed. by Gunzelin Schmid Noerr (Stanford, CA: Stanford University Press, 2002)

Agamben, Giorgio, *Stanzas: Word and Phantasm in Western Culture*, trans. by Ronald L. Martinez (Minneapolis: University of Minnesota Press, 1993)

Agamben, Giorgio, *Homo Sacer – Sovereign Power and Bare Life*, trans. by Daniel Heller-Roazen (Stanford, CA: Stanford University Press, 1995)

Agamben, Giorgio, *Remnants of Auschwitz – The Witness and the Archive*, trans. by Daniel Heller-Roazen (New York: Zone Books, 2002)

Agamben, Giorgio, *Open: Man and Animal*, trans. by Kevin Attell (Stanford, CA: Stanford University Press, 2003)

Arendt, Hannah *The Origins of Totalitarianism* (San Diego, CA: Harcourt, 1973)

Aristotle, *Poetics*, trans. by S. H. Butler (New York: Dover Thrift, 1997)

Aristotle, *On the Parts of Animals*, trans. by James G. Lennox (Oxford: Oxford University Press, 2001)

Aristotle, *Politics*, trans. by Ernest Barker (Oxford: Oxford University Press, 2009)

Armstrong, Philip, *What Animals Mean in the Fiction of Modernity* (Oxford: Routledge, 2008)

Badiou, Alain, *Metapolitics* (London: Verso, 2005)

Bain, Alexander, *The Emotions and the Will* (London: Longmans, Green, and Co., [1859] 1899)

Bair, Deidre, *Samuel Beckett: A Biography* (London: Vintage, 1990)

Bakhtin, Mikhail, *Rabelais and His World*, trans. by Hélène Iswolsky (Bloomington: Indiana University Press, [1965] 1984)

Barkai, Avraham, 'The Fateful Year 1938: The Continuation and Acceleration of Plunder', in *November 1938: From 'Reichskristallnacht' to Genocide*, ed. by Walter H. Pehle (Oxford: Berg, 1991 [1988]), pp. 95–122

Barry, Peter, *Beginning Theory* (Manchester: Manchester University Press, 2002)

Baudrillard, Jean, *The System of Objects* (London: Verso, 2005)

Beckett, Samuel, *Company / Ill Seen Ill Said / Worstward Ho / Stirrings Still* (London: Faber and Faber, 2009a)

Beckett, Samuel, *Murphy* (London: Faber and Faber, [1938] 2009b)

Beckett, Samuel, *The Expelled / The Calmative / The End / First Love* (London: Faber and Faber, 2009c)

Beckett, Samuel, *Watt* (London: Faber and Faber, [1953] 2009d)

Beckett, Samuel, *The Letters of Samuel Beckett, 1929–1940*, Vol. 1, ed. by Martha Dow Fehsenfeld and Lois More Overbeck (Cambridge: Cambridge University Press, 2009e)

Beckett, Samuel, *Krapp's Last Tape and Other Shorter Plays* (London: Faber and Faber, 2009f)

Beckett, Samuel, *How It Is* (London: Faber and Faber, 2009g)

Beckett, Samuel, *All That Fall and Other Plays for Radio and Screen* (London: Faber and Faber, 2009h)

Beckett, Samuel, *More Pricks than Kicks* (London: Faber and Faber, [1934] 2010a)

Beckett, Samuel, *Texts for Nothing and Other Shorter Prose, 1950–1976* (London: Faber and Faber, 2010b)

Beckett, Samuel, *Mercier and Camier* (London: Faber and Faber, 2010c)

Beckett, Samuel, *The Letters of Samuel Beckett, 1941–1956*, Vol. 2, ed. by
George Craig, Martha Dow Fehsenfeld, Dan Gunn and Lois More
Overbeck (Cambridge: Cambridge University Press, 2011)
Begam, Richard, *Samuel Beckett and the End of Modernity* (Stanford,
CA: Stanford University Press, 1996)
Benjamin, Andrew, *Of Jews and Animals* (Edinburgh: Edinburgh
University Press, 2010)
Benjamin, Walter, *The Origin of German Tragic Drama*, trans. by John
Osborne (London: NLB, 1977)
Benjamin, Walter, *The Arcades Project*, trans. by Howard Eiland and
Kevin McLaughlin (Cambridge, MA: Harvard University Press, 1999)
Benjamin, Walter, 'Central Park', in *Selected Writings, Vol. 4, 1938–1940*,
ed. by Howard Eiland and Michael W. Jennings (Cambridge, MA:
Belknap, 2003), pp. 161–99
Bennett, Andrew, *'The' Author* (London: Routledge, 2005)
Ben-Zvi, Linda, 'Samuel Beckett, Fritz Mauthner, and the Limits of
Language', *PMLA*, 95.2 (Mar, 1980), 183–200
Ben-Zvi, Linda, *Samuel Beckett* (Boston: Twayne, 1986)
Bergen, Doris L., *War and Genocide: A Concise History of the Holocaust*
(Plymouth: Rowman and Littlefield, 2003)
Bergson, Henri, *Laughter: An Essay on the Meaning of the Comic*
(Kobenhavn and Los Angeles: Green Integer, [1911] 1999)
Berkeley, George, *Principles of Human Knowledge and Three Dialogues*
(Oxford: Oxford University Press, 1999)
Bernini, Marco 'Crawling Creating Creatures: On Beckett's liminal
minds', *European Journal of English Studies* (2015), 19.1, 39–54
Bichat, Xavier *Recherches physiologiques sur la vie et la mort* (Paris:
Flammarion, 1986)
Birnbaum, Daniel and Olsson, Anders, *As a Weasel Sucks Eggs – As Essay
on Melancholy and Cannibalism* (New York: Sternberg, 2008)
Blackman, Jackie, 'Beckett Judaizing Beckett: "a Jew from Greenland" in
Paris', *Samuel Beckett Today/Aujourd'hui*, All Sturm and No Drang,
Beckett and Romanticism, ed. by Dirk Van Hulle and Mark Nixon
(Amsterdam: Rodopi, 2007), 325–40
Blackman, Jackie, 'Beckett's Theatre "After Auschwitz"', in *Samuel
Beckett: History, Memory, Archive*, ed. by Sean Kennedy and Katherine
Weiss (Basingstoke: Palgrave Macmillan, 2010), pp. 71–87
Blanchot, Maurice, *The Writing of the Disaster*, trans. by Ann Smock
(Lincoln: University of Nebraska Press, 1986)
Blanchot, Maurice, *The Instant of My Death* (New York: Stanford
University Press, [1994] 2000)
Boxall, Peter, *Since Beckett: Contemporary Writing in the Wake of
Modernism* (London: Continuum, 2009)

Bradby, David, *Beckett: Waiting for Godot* (Cambridge: Cambridge University Press, 2001)

Breton, Andre, *Anthology of Black Humour*, trans. by Mark Polizzotti (San Francisco: City Lights, 1997)

Bryden, Mary, 'Beckett and the Dynamic Still', *Samuel Beckett Today/ Aujourd'hui*, After Beckett, ed. by Anthony Uhlmann, Sjef Houppermans, Bruno Clément (Amsterdam: Rodopi, 1994), 179–92

Bryden, Mary, 'Sounds and Silence: Beckett's Music', *Samuel Beckett Today/Aujourd'hui*, Crossroads and Borderlines, ed. by Marius Buning, Sjef Houppermans, Danièle de Ruyter (Amsterdam: Rodopi, 1997), 279–88

Butler, Judith, *Precarious Life: The Powers of Mourning and Violence* (London and New York: Verso, 2004)

Bytwerk, Randall L., *Landmark Speeches of National Socialism* (College Station, TX: A&M University Press, 2008)

Calarco, Matthew, *Zoographies* (New York: Columbia University Press, 2008)

Cassirer, Ernst, *An Essay on Man: An Introduction to a Philosophy of Human Culture* (New Haven: Yale University Press, 1972)

Caygill, Howard, 'Benjamin, Heidegger and the Destruction of Tradition', in *Walter Benjamin's Philosophy: Destruction and Experience*, ed. by Andrew Benjamin and Peter Osborne (London: Routledge, 1994), pp. 1–31

Cixous, Hélène, *Portrait of Jacques Derrida as a Young Jewish Saint* (New York: Columbia University Press, 2004)

Coetzee, J. M., *The Lives of Animals* (Princeton: Princeton University Press, 1999)

Cohn, Ruby, *Samuel Beckett: The Comic Gamut* (New Brunswick, NJ: Rutgers University Press, 1962)

Cohn, Ruby, *Back to Beckett* (Princeton, NJ: Princeton University Press, 1973)

Cohn, Ruby, *A Beckett Canon* (Michigan: University of Michigan Press, 2001)

Colletta, Lisa, *Dark Humor and Social Satire in the Modern British Novel* (Gordonsville, VA: Palgrave Macmillan, 2003)

Connor, Steven, *Samuel Beckett – Repetition, Theory and Text* (Oxford: Basil Blackwell, 1988)

Counsell, Chris, *Signs of Performance: An Introduction to Twentieth Century Theatre* (London: Routledge, 1996)

Crangle, Sara, *Prosaic Desires – Modernist Knowledge, Boredom, Laughter and Anticipation* (Edinburgh: Edinburgh University Press, 2010)

Critchley, Simon, *Very Little . . . Almost Nothing: Death, Philosophy, Literature* (Oxford: Routledge, 1997)

Critchley, Simon, *On Humour* (London: Routledge, 2002)

Cronin, Anthony, *Samuel Beckett: The Last Modernist* (New York: Da Capo, 1997)

Cunningham, David, 'Trying (Not) to Understand: Adorno and the Work of Beckett', in *Beckett and Philosophy*, ed. by Richard Lane (Basingstoke: Palgrave Macmillan, 2002), pp. 125–39

Darwin, Charles, *Darwin – Evolutionary Writings*, ed. by James A. Secord (Oxford: Oxford University Press, 2008)

Deleuze, Gilles, *Francis Bacon – The Logic of Sensation*, trans. by Daniel S. Smith (London: Continuum, 2003)

Deleuze, Giles and Guattari, Félix, *A Thousand Plateaus*, trans. by Brian Massumi (London: Athlone Press, 1988)

Derrida, Jacques, *Limited Inc.* (Evanston, IL: Northwestern University Press, 1977)

Derrida, Jacques, *Writing and Difference*, trans. by Alan Bass (London: Routledge, 1978)

Derrida, Jacques, '"Eating Well", or the Calculation of the Subject: An Interview with Jacques Derrida', in *Who Comes After The Subject?*, ed. by Eduardo Cadava, Peter Connor and Jean-Luc Nancy (London: Routledge, 1991), pp. 96–119

Derrida, Jacques, *Memoirs of the Blind – The Self-Portrait and Other Ruins*, trans. by Pascale-Anne Brault and Michael Naas (Chicago: University of Chicago Press, 1993)

Derrida, Jacques, 'Maddening the Subjectile', *Yale French Studies*, 84 (1994), 154–71

Derrida, Jacques, *Demeure: Fiction and Testimony*, published with *The Instant of My Death*, by Maurice Blanchot, both trans. by Elizabeth Rottenberg (Stanford, CA: Stanford University Press, 2000)

Derrida, Jacques, 'Poetics and Politics of Witnessing', in *Sovereignties in Question – The Poetics of Paul Celan* (New York: Fordham University Press, 2005a), pp. 65–96

Derrida, Jacques, *Learn to Live Finally – The Last Interview*, trans. by Pascale-Anne Brault and Michael Naas (Basingstoke: Palgrave Macmillan, 2005b)

Derrida, Jacques, *The Beast and the Sovereign*, Vol. 1, trans. by Geoffrey Bennington (Chicago: University of Chicago Press, 2009)

Descartes, Rene, *Treatise on Man* (Cambridge, MA: Harvard University Press, [1664] 1972)

Descartes, Rene, *Meditations on First Philosophy: With Selections from the Objections and Replies*, trans. by Michael Moriarty (Oxford: Oxford University Press, 2008)

Des Pres, Terrence 'Holocaust Laughter?', in *Writing and the Holocaust*, ed. by Berel Lang (New York: Holmes & Meier, 1988), 216–33

Devenney, Christopher, 'What Remains', in *Engagement and Indifference: Beckett and the Political*, ed. by Henry Sussman and Christopher Devenney (Albany: State University of New York Press, 2001), pp. 139–60

Dow, Suzanne, 'Ethics of Finitude to an Ethics of the Real', *Paragraph*, 34.1 (2011), 121–36

Driver, Tom F., 'Beckett by the Madeleine', *Columbia University Forum*, 4 (1961), 21–5

Dundes, Alan and Hauschild, Thomas, 'Auschwitz Jokes', *Western Folklore*, 42.4 (1983), 249–60

Eagleton, Terry, 'Political Beckett?', *New Left Review*, 40 (July/Aug 2006), 67–74

Eliot, T. S., *The Annotated Waste Land with Eliot's Contemporary Prose*, ed. by Lawrence Rainey (New Haven: Yale University Press, 2005)

Ellmann, Maud, 'Changing into an Animal', *Field Day Review*, 2 (2006), 75–93

Ellmann, Richard, *James Joyce* (New York: Oxford University Press, 1982)

Esposito, Roberto, *Terms of the Political: Community, Immunity, Biopolitics* (Bronx, NY: Fordham University Press, 2012)

Esslin, Martin, *The Theatre of the Absurd* (Harmondsworth: Penguin, 1961)

Esslin, Martin, 'Dionysus' Dianoetic Laugh', in *As No Other Dare Fail: For Samuel Beckett on His 80th Birthday*, ed. by John Calder (London: Calder, 1986), pp. 15–23

Esslin, Martin, *The Theatre of the Absurd*, 3rd edn (London: Methuen, 2001)

Feldman, Matthew, *Beckett's Books: A Culture History of Samuel Beckett's 'Interwar Notes'* (London: Continuum, 2006)

Felman, Shoshana and Laub, Dori, *Testimony – Crises of Witnessing in Literature, Psychoanalysis and History* (Oxford: Routledge, 1992)

Fine, Robert, 'Hannah Arendt: Politics and Understanding after the Holocaust', in *Social Theory after the Holocaust*, ed. by Robert Fine and Charles Turner (Liverpool: Liverpool University Press, 2000), pp. 19–46

Fogg, Shannon L., *The Politics of Everyday Life in Vichy France: Foreigners, Undesirables, and Strangers* (Cambridge: Cambridge University Press, 2009)

Foster, Verna, *The Name and Nature of Tragicomedy* (Aldershot: Ashgate, 2004)

Foucault, Michel, *The History of Sexuality: The Will to Knowledge*, Vol. 1, trans. by Robert Hurley (New York: Vintage, [1978] 1990)

Foucault, Michel, *Discipline and Punish – The Birth of the Prison* (London: Penguin, 1991)

Foucault, Michel, 'What is an Author?', in *Aesthetics, Method, and Epistemology*, ed. by James D. Faubion (New York: The New Press, 1999), pp. 205–22

Foucault, Michel, *Madness and Civilisation* (Oxford: Routledge, 2001)

Foucault, Michel, 'The Subject and Power', in *Power: Essential Works of Foucault 1954–1984*, Vol. 3, ed. by James D. Faubion (London: Penguin, 2002), pp. 326–48

Freud, Sigmund, *Jokes and their Relation to the Unconscious*, trans. by James Strachey (London: Penguin, 1976)

Freud, Sigmund, 'Beyond the Pleasure Principle', in *The Freud Reader*, ed. by Peter Gay (New York: W. W Norton, 1989), pp. 594–625

Freud, Sigmund, 'Humour', in *The Standard Edition of the Complete Psychological Works of Sigmund Freud, Vol. 21 (1927–1931): The Future of an Illusion, Civilization and its Discontents, and Other Works* (London: Vintage, [1927] 2001), pp. 159–66

Freud, Sigmund, *On Murder, Mourning and Melancholia*, trans. by Shaun Whiteside (London: Penguin, 2005)

Garrison, Alysia E., '"Faintly Struggling Things": Trauma, Testimony, and Inscrutable Life in Beckett's *The Unnamable*', *Samuel Beckett: History, Memory, Archive*, ed. by Seán Kennedy and Katherine Weiss (New York: Palgrave Macmillan, 2009) pp. 89–106

Gibson, Andrew, 'Comedy of Narrative: Nabokov, Beckett, Robbe-Grillet', *Comparative Literature*, 37.2 (1985), 114–39

Gontarski, S. E., *The Intent of Undoing in Beckett's Dramatic Texts* (Bloomington: Indiana University Press, 1985)

Gordon, Lois, *The World of Samuel Beckett 1906–1946* (New Haven: Yale University Press, 1998)

Gordon, Lois, 'France: World War Two' in *Samuel Beckett in Context*, ed. by Anthony Uhlmann (Cambridge: Cambridge University Press, 2013), pp. 109–25

Greenberg, Jonathan, *Modernism, Satire and the Novel* (London: Cambridge University Press, 2011)

Gurewitch, Morton, 'The Comedy of Decomposition', *Chicago Review*, 33.2 (1982), 93–9

Hanssen, Beatrice, *Benjamin's Other History: of Stones, Animals, Human Beings, and Angels* (Berkeley: University of California Press, 2000)

Harmon, Maurice, ed., *No Author Better Served: The Correspondence of Samuel Beckett and Alan Schneider* (Cambridge, MA: Harvard University Press, 1998)

Harrington, John P., *The Irish Beckett* (Syracuse, NY: Syracuse University Press 1991)

Harvey, Lawrence, *Samuel Beckett: Poet and Critic* (Princeton: Princeton University Press, 1970)

Hegel, G. W. F., *The Hegel Reader*, ed. by Stephen Houlgate (Oxford: Blackwell, 1998)

Herf, Jeffrey, *The Jewish Enemy: Nazi Propaganda During World War II and the Holocaust* (Cambridge, MA: Belknap, 2008)

Hesla, David, *The Shape of Chaos* (Minneapolis: University of Minnesota Press, 1971)

Hilberg, Raul, 'I Was Not There', in *Writing and the Holocaust*, ed. by Berel Lang (New York: Holmes & Meier, 1988), pp. 17–25

Hobbes, Thomas, *The Elements of Law, Natural and Politic* (New York: Oxford University Press, [1640] 1999)

Iser, Wolfgang, 'The Art of Failure: The Stifled Laugh in Beckett's Theatre', in *Samuel Beckett*, ed. by Jennifer Birkett and Kate Ince (London: Pearson, 2000), pp. 201–29

Jones, David Houston, *The Body Abject: Self and Text in Jean Genet and Samuel Beckett* (New York: Peter Lang, 2000)

Jones, David Houston, *Beckett and Testimony* (London: Palgrave Macmillan, 2011)

Joyce, James, *A Portrait of the Artist as a Young Man* (London: Penguin, 1996)

Joyce, James, *Ulysses* (Oxford: Oxford University Press, 2008)

Judt, Tony, *Postwar: A History of Europe since 1945* (London: Pimlico, 2007)

Juliet, Charles, *Conversations with Samuel Beckett and Bram van Velde*, trans. by Janey Tucker (Leiden: Academic Press, 1995)

Juliet, Charles, *Conversations with Samuel Beckett and Bram van Velde*, trans. by Tracy Cooke and Axel Nesme (London: Dalkey, 2009)

Jung, C. G., *The Collected Works of C. G. Jung*, Vol. 13, trans. by R. F. C. Hull (London: Routledge & Kegan Paul, 1968)

Jung, C. G., *The Collected Works of C. G. Jung*, Vol. 14, 2nd edn, trans. by R. F. C. Hull (London: Routledge & Kegan Paul, 1970)

Kalb, Jonathan, *Beckett in Performance* (Cambridge: Cambridge University Press, 1989)

Kant, Immanuel, *Critique of Judgement* (Oxford: Oxford University Press, [1790] 2007)

Katz, Daniel, *Saying I No More: Subjectivity and Consciousness in the Prose of Samuel Beckett* (Evanston, IL: Northwestern University Press, 1999)

Katz, Daniel, 'What Remains of Beckett: Evasion and History', in *Beckett and Phenomenology*, ed. by Ulrika Maude and Matthew Feldman (London: Continuum, 2009), pp. 144–57

Kearney, Richard, *Strangers, Gods, and Monsters* (Oxford: Routledge, 2003)

Kearney, Richard, *Anatheism: Returning to God After God* (New York: Columbia University Press, 2011)

Klemperer, Victor, *To the Bitter End: The Diaries of Victor Klemperer, 1942–1945*, trans. by Martin Chalmers (London: Weidenfeld & Nicolson, 1999)

Knowlson, James, *Damned to Fame: The Life of Samuel Beckett* (London: Bloomsbury, 1997)

Knowlson, James, and Knowlson, Elizabeth, *Beckett Remembering, Remembering Beckett* (New York: Arcade, 2006)

La Capra, Dominick, *History in Transit: Experience, Identity, Critical Theory* (Ithaca and London: Cornell University Press, 2004)

Lake, Carlton, *No Symbols Where None Intended: A Catalogue of Books, Manuscripts, and Other Material Relating to Samuel Beckett in the Collection of the Humanities Research Center* (Austin, TX: The Center, 1984)

Lamont, Rosette C., 'Samuel Beckett's Wandering Jew', in *Reflections of the Holocaust in Art and Literature*, ed. by Randolph L. Braham (Boulder: Social Science Monographs, 1990), pp. 35–53

Lamont, Rosette C., 'Fast-forward: Lucky's *Pnigos*', *Samuel Beckett Today/Aujourd'hui*, Endlessness in the Year 2000, ed. by Angela Moorjani and Carola Veit (Amsterdam: Rodopi, 2001), 132–39

Lawrence, D. H., *Kangaroo* (Cambridge: Cambridge University Press, 2002)

Levi, Primo, *If This Is A Man/The Truce*, trans. by Stuart Woolf (London: Abacus, 1979)

Levy, Eric P., *Trapped in Thought: A Study of Beckettian Mentality* (Syracuse, NY: Syracuse University, 2006)

Lewis, Paul, 'Three Jews and a Blindfold: The Politics of Gallows Humor', in *Semites and Stereotypes: Characteristics of Jewish Humor*, ed. by Avner Ziv and Anat Zajdman (Connecticut: Greenwood, 1993), pp. 47–58

Lingis, Alphonso, 'Nietzsche and Animals', in *Animal Philosophy – Ethics and Identity*, ed. by Peter Atterton and Matthew Calarco (London: Continuum, 2004), pp. 7–14

Lipman, Steve, *Laughter in Hell: The Use of Humor during the Holocaust* (Northvale, NJ: Jason, 1991)

Locatelli, Carla, 'Comic Strategies in Beckett's Narratives', in *Samuel Beckett*, ed. by Jennifer Birkett and Kate Ince (London: Pearson, 2000), pp. 233–44

Lukács, Georg, *The Meaning of Contemporary Realism*, trans. by John and Necke Mander (London: Merlin, 1963)

Lund, Jacob, 'Biopolitical Beckett: Self-desubjectification as Resistance', *Nordic Irish Studies*, 8.1 (2009), 67–77

Lupton, Julia Reinhard, 'Creature Caliban', *Shakespeare Quarterly*, 51.1 (2000), 1–23

Lyotard, Jean-François, 'The Survivor' in *Toward the Postmodern*, ed. by
    Robert Harvey and Mark S. Roberts (Atlantic Highlands, NJ:
    Humanities, 1993), pp. 144–63
Matzner, David, *The Muselmann* (New Jersey: KTAV, 1994)
McDonald, Ronan, *Tragedy and Irish Literature: Synge, O'Casey, Beckett*
    (New York: Palgrave Macmillan, 2002)
McNaughton, James, 'Beckett, German Fascism, and History: The Futility
    of Protest', *Samuel Beckett Today/Aujourd'hui*, Historicising Beckett/
    Issues of Performance, ed. by Marius Buning et al. (Amsterdam:
    Rodopi, 2005), 101–16
Milchman, Alan and Rosenberg, Alan, eds., *Postmodernism and the
    Holocaust* (Atlanta: Rodopi, 1998)
Miller, Lawrence, *Samuel Beckett: The Expressive Dilemma* (Basingstoke:
    Macmillan, 1992)
Miller, Tyrus, *Late Modernism: Politics, Fiction and the Arts Between the
    World Wars* (Berkeley and Los Angeles: University of California Press,
    1999)
Mills, Catherine, 'Linguistic Survival and Ethicality – Biopolitics,
    Subjectification, and Testimony in *Remnants of Auschwitz*', in *Politics,
    Metaphysics, Death – Essays on Giorgio Agamben's 'Homo Sacer'*,
    ed. by Andrew Norris (London: Duke University Press, 2005),
    pp. 198–221
Murphy, P. J., Huber, Werner, Breuer, Rolf, and Schoell, Konrad, *Critique
    of Beckett Criticism: A Guide to Research in English, French, and
    German* (Columbia, SC: Camden House, 1994)
Nealon, Jeffrey, 'Samuel Beckett and the Postmodern: Language Games,
    Play and *Waiting for Godot*', *Modern Drama*, 31.4 (1988), 520–28
Neumann, Boaz, 'The National Socialist Politics of Life', *New German
    Critique*, 85 (2002), 107–30
Ngai, Sianne, *Ugly Feelings* (Cambridge, MA: Harvard University Press,
    2005)
Nicholas, Matthew Brian '"Scrupulous Sympathy": James Joyce's
    "Ulysses" and the Ethics of Modern Sentimentality', Doctoral
    dissertation, May 2008, Washington University (Proquest, 2011).
Nietzsche, Friedrich, 'On the Uses and Disadvantages of History for Life',
    in *Untimely Meditations*, ed. by Daniel Breazeale (Cambridge:
    Cambridge University Press, 1997), pp. 57–124
Nixon, Mark, *Samuel Beckett's German Diaries 1936–37* (London:
    Continuum, 2011)
Obrdlik, Antonin J., 'Gallows Humor – A Sociological Phenomenon',
    American Journal of Sociology, 47.5 (1942), 709–16
O'Hara, James Donald, *Samuel Beckett's Hidden Drives: Structural Uses
    of Depth Psychology* (Gainesville: University Press of Florida, 1997)

Orr, John, *Tragicomedy and Contemporary Culture: Play and Performance from Beckett to Shepard* (Basingstoke: Macmillan, 1991)

Otto, G. G., *Der Jude als Weltparasit* (Munich: Eher Verlag, 1943)

Paley, William, *Natural Theology* (Oxford: Oxford University Press, [1802] 2006)

Parrott, Jeremy, 'The Gnostic Gospel of Sam: Watt as Modernist Apocryphon', *Samuel Beckett Today/Aujourd'hui*, Endlessness in the Year 2000, ed. by Angela Moorjani and Carola Veit (Amsterdam: Rodopi, 2001), 425–33

Parrott, Jeremy, '"Nothing Neatly Named": The Beckettian Aesthetic and Negative Theology', *Samuel Beckett, Today/Aujourd'hui, Three Dialogues Revisited*, ed. by Marius Buning et al. (Amsterdam: Rodopi, 2003) 91–101

Patterson, Charles, *Eternal Treblinka: Our Treatment of Animals and the Holocaust* (New York: Lantern, 2002)

Perloff, Marjorie, '"In Love with Hiding": Samuel Beckett's War', *Iowa Review*, 35.2 (2005), 76–103

Pfister, Manfred, 'Beckett, Barker, and Other Grim Laughter', in *A History of English Laughter – Laughter from Beowulf to Beckett and Beyond*, ed. by Manfred Pfister (New York: Rodopi, 2002), pp. 175–89

Pick, Anat, *Creaturely Poetics: Animality and Vulnerability in Literature and Film* (New York: Columbia University Press, 2011)

Pilling, John, *A Samuel Beckett Chronology* (Basingstoke: Palgrave Macmillan, 2006)

Pound, Ezra, *The Selected Letters of Ezra Pound, 1907–1941* (New York: New Directions, 1971)

Provine, Robert, *Curious Behaviour: Yawning, Laughing, Hiccupping, and Beyond* (Cambridge, MA: Harvard University Press, 2012)

Rabaté, Jean-Michel, 'Philosophizing with Beckett: Adorno and Badiou' in *A Companion to Samuel Beckett*, ed. by S. E. Gontarski (Chichester: Wiley-Blackwell, 2010), pp. 97–111.

Ratcliffe, Sophie, *On Sympathy* (Oxford: Oxford University Press, 2008)

Rees, Lawrence, *Auschwitz: The Nazis and the 'Final Solution'* (London: BBC, 2005)

Rilke, Rainer Maria, *Duino Elegies*, trans. by J. B. Leishman and Stephen Spender (London: Hogarth, 1963)

Rosenzweig, Franz, *The Star of Redemption*, trans. by William W. Hallo (New York: Holt, Rinehart and Winston, 1971)

Salisbury, Laura, *Samuel Beckett: Laughing Matters, Comic Timing* (Edinburgh: Edinburgh University Press, 2012)

Santner, Eric L., *On Creaturely Life* (Chicago: University of Chicago Press, 2006)

Santner, Eric L., *The Royal Remains – The People's Two Bodies and the Endgames of Sovereignty* (Chicago: University of Chicago Press, 2011)

Sartre, Jean-Paul, *What is Literature?*, trans. by Bernard Frechtman (London: Methuen, 1950)

Sax, Boria, *Animals in the Third Reich – Pets, Scapegoats, and the Holocaust* (New York: Continuum, 2000)

Schopenhauer, Arthur, *The World as Will and Representation*, Vol. 1, trans. by E. F. J. Payne (New York: Dover, [1818] 1969)

Shainberg, Lawrence, 'Exorcising Beckett', *The Paris Review*, 29.104 (1987), 100–36

Sheehan, Paul, *Modernism, Narrative and Humanism* (Cambridge: Cambridge University Press, 2002)

Shelley, Mary, *Frankenstein* (London: Penguin, 2003)

Shenker, Israel, 'An Interview with Beckett', in *Samuel Beckett: The Critical Heritage*, ed. by Raymond Federman and Lawrence Graver (London: Routledge, 1979), pp. 160–3

Simmons, Laurence, 'Shame, Levinas's Dog and Derrida's Cat (and Some Fish)', in *Knowing Animals*, ed. by Laurence Simmons and Phillip Armstrong (Boston: Brill, 2007), pp. 27–43

Simon, J. C., *Why We Laugh: A New Understanding* (Carmel, IN: Starbrook Publishing, 2008)

Singer, Peter, *Animal Liberation* (London: Pimlico, 1995)

Slade, Andrew, *Lyotard, Beckett, Duras and the Postmodern Sublime* (New York: Peter Lang, 2007)

Smith, Richard Carter, 'Beckett and the Animal: Writing from "No-Man's-Land"' *ELH* 79.1 (2012), 211–35

Spencer, Herbert, *Essays on Education* (London: J. M. Dent & Sons, [1860] 1911)

Stein, Gertrude, *The Geographical History of America, or The Relation of Human Nature to the Human Mind* (New York: Vintage, 1973)

Szafraniec, Asja, *Beckett, Derrida and the Event of Literature* (Stanford, CA: Stanford University Press, 2007)

Tenenbaum, Joseph, *Race and Reich – The Story of an Epoch* (New York: Twayne, 1956)

Topsfield, Valerie, *The Humour of Samuel Beckett* (New York: St. Martin, 1988)

Uhlmann, Anthony, *Beckett and Poststructuralism* (Cambridge: Cambridge University Press, 1999)

Uhlmann, Anthony, ed., *Samuel Beckett in Context* (Cambridge: Cambridge University Press, 2013)

Van Hulle, Dirk, '"Accursed Creator": Beckett, Romanticism, Modern Prometheus', *Samuel Beckett Today/Aujourd'hui*, All Sturm and No

Drang, Beckett and Romanticism, ed. by Dirk Van Hulle and Mark Nixon (Amsterdam: Rodopi, 2007), 115–29

Vermeulen, Pieter, 'Abandoned Creatures: Creaturely Life and the Novel Form in J. M. Coetzee's *Slow Man*', *Studies in the Novel*, 45.4, Winter 2013, 655–74

Weber-Caflisch, Antoinette, *Chacun son dépeupleur sur Samuel Beckett* (Paris: Les Éditions de Minuit, 1994)

Weil, Kari, 'A Report on the Animal Turn', *Differences*, 21.2 (2010), 1–23

Weisberg, David, *Chronicles of Disorder: Samuel Beckett and the Cultural Politics of the Modern Novel* (New York: State University of New York, 2006)

Weller, Shane, *Beckett, Literature, and the Ethics of Alterity* (Basingstoke: Palgrave Macmillan, 2006a)

Weller, Shane, 'Not Rightly Human', *Samuel Beckett Today/Aujourd'hui*, Borderless Beckett, 19 (Amsterdam: Rodopi, 2006b), 211–21

Weller, Shane, 'Forms of Weakness: Animalisation in Kafka and Beckett', *Beckett and Animals*, ed. by Mary Bryden (Cambridge: Cambridge University Press, 2013), pp. 13–27

Wheatley, David 'Quite Exceptionally Anthropoid': Species Anxiety and Metamorphosis in Beckett's Humans and Other Animals' *Beckett and Animals*, ed. by Mary Bryden (Cambridge: Cambridge University Press, 2013), pp. 59–70

Wiesel, Elie, 'Liberation of Auschwitz', First Person Singular: Elie Wiesel. Available at: http://www.pbs.org/eliewiesel/life/auschwitz.html (accessed 4 April 2015)

Wolfe, Cary, *Before The Law: Humans and Other Animals in a Biopolitical Frame* (Chicago: University of Chicago Press, 2013)

Wood, David, 'Thinking with Cats', in *Animal Philosophy – Ethics and Identity*, ed. by P. Atterton and M. Calarco (London: Continuum, 2004), pp. 129–44

Woolf, Virginia, *Mr. Bennett and Mrs. Brown* (London: Hogarth Press, 1924)

Yusin, Jennifer, 'Writing the Disaster: Testimony and *The Instant of My Death*', *Colloquy*, Text Theory Critique, 10 (Victoria: Monash University Press, 2005), 134–49

INDEX

Printed in Great Britain
by Amazon

35229260R00151